This book is dedicated to my dad, Fred H. Pollak. Thanks, Dad, for everything.

Contents at a Glance

Contents

▮CHAPTER 7   Traits and Types and Gnarly Stuff for Architects 171

Foreword

A curious attribute of the Scala programming language is that it expends a lot of expressive power in order to make the life of casual programmers simpler. For instance, Scala provides sophisticated type parametrization and traits so that more advanced programmers can design libraries which are at the same time general and easy to use.

Casual users can profit from these libraries long before they discover the full power of Scala's abstraction constructs. The language design avoids the temptation of simply defining some handy primitives in the syntax, even if these primitives would be useful many times to many users. Instead of fixed primitives, the language design tries very hard to provide general construction principles, with which users can then define their own fundamental constructs, at no loss in syntactic convenience. This idea ranges from simple things, such as being able to define your own numeric data types, to full-blown domain-specific APIs such as Scala's support for concurrent actors.

There is hardly a better example of this approach than David Pollak's Lift Web Framework for Scala. It leverages the full expressive power of Scala to provide a framework that's at the same time simple to use, powerful, and secure. David has been one of the earliest adopters of Scala. He has become a crystallization point for many important developments in the Scala community. He fostered the vibrant Lift community, organized the first Scala Lift Off conference in 2008, and promoted the adoption of Scala in many important industrial applications.

His experience puts him in a unique position to explain the language thoroughly and competently. At the same time, David is a great communicator, and he has always the needs of beginners to the language in mind. This book shows these two traits of his very well.

Written by an expert user of the language, it puts the focus on what's important for a beginner.

It moves you swiftly from simple examples to more complete applications, explaining both language and core libraries. It manages to show that Scala is, fundamentally, a pretty simple language to pick up, and at the same time a language with few limits if you want to progress.

I hope you'll enjoy reading it as much as I did.

Martin Odersky
EPFL
Designer of Scala

About the Author

 **DAVID POLLAK** has been writing commercial software since 1977. He wrote the first real-time spreadsheet, Mesa, and the world's highest-performance spreadsheet engine, Integer. Since 1996, David has been using and devising web development tools. As CTO of CMP Media, David oversaw the first large-scale deployment of WebLogic. David was CTO and VPE at Cenzic, a web application security company. David has also developed numerous commercial projects in Ruby on Rails.

In 2007, David founded the Lift Web Framework open source project. Lift is an expressive and elegant framework for writing web applications. Lift stresses the importance of security, maintainability, scalability, and performance, while allowing for high levels of developer productivity. Lift open source software is licensed under an Apache 2.0 license.

David is a consultant in San Francisco and works on Lift-based projects including Innovation Games Online and ESME.

About the Technical Reviewer

PAUL SNIVELY is a 30-year veteran of the software industry with a passion for programming languages. Studying computer science at Indiana University hooked him on Scheme and functional programming. The launch of the Macintosh in 1984 introduced him to objects via Smalltalk, Object Pascal, and MacApp. He later discovered object-functional programming in OCaml, and is thrilled to find a language as powerful as Scala for the JVM. Paul is a former contributing editor for *MacTutor Magazine*, served as a technical reviewer for *Paradigms of Artificial Intelligence Programming: Case Studies in Common Lisp* by Peter Norvig (Morgan Kaufmann, 1991) and is an editor for http://lambda-the-ultimate.org, the programming languages weblog.

Acknowledgments

I'd like to thank a lot of people for the opportunity to write *Beginning Scala*. My dad gave me the encouragement to seek and share knowledge. My wife, Annette, and my kids have been great through the process, cheering me on and hugging me when I needed it. Paul Snively has been a wicked-awesome, over-the-top-great technical reviewer. Martin Odersky's amazing balance between theory and reality make Scala possible, and the people he has attracted into the community are brilliant. Luke Hohmann has fed my Scala and Lift habits. Dan O'Leary has asked great questions about Scala. The Lift committers and community make me smile and make me think and make me code. Gary Cornell had faith in me as an author, although he mistimed it by eight years. Finally, Steve Anglin and the Apress team have been a total pleasure to work with, and they carry on Gary's vision of Apress as the author's publisher.

Introduction

Ouch! That hurts my brain! Stop making me think differently. Oh, wait . . . it hurts less now. I get it. This different way of solving the problem has some benefits. I felt that way after my first year of law school. I felt that way for a while when I began coding Scala. What's this `Option` thingy? Give me back my null! How do you get the fifth element from a `Seq`? On and on it went. Day after day of head-splitting paradigm changing and breaking 30 years of coding habits, I am somewhat at peace with the Scala way of coding. Yes, my coding habits were borne out of 6800 machine code coding. Talk about imperative coding. That's all you've got when you've got an accumulator, a program counter, and an index register. I grew up through BASIC, Pascal, C, C++, Objective-C, and Java. And along comes this Scala stuff, this functional-objective way of thinking, these compositional design patterns. Who thought this wacky stuff up?

After more than two years of coding Scala, I've come to understand that the Scala idioms are really better. My brain has finally stopped hurting. I've finally stopped fighting for flow of control statements. I see that it's more important for me to take small elements and compose them together into complex systems. I understand that if a method always returns the same output given the same input, I can safely glue that function together with other functions into a very complex structure. I understand that explicit looping in my code is a distraction from the business logic that is buried in the code. My path was hard, and I hope yours will be easier.

The first step in writing Scala is not being afraid of the fact that Scala's going to warp your brain. The next step in writing Scala is accepting that your code is going to look like Java, Ruby, Python, whatever code for a while. It will take you time and effort and more time to code Scala using the idioms in this book. It will take you time to design code that fits into Scala paradigms and to discover and devise paradigms of your own. It will take time but hopefully less time than it took me.

This book is for you. It's my attempt to show you a different way of thinking about and writing code. I hope that you'll enjoy our journey through Scala together. I hope that by the end of this book you'll have a new perspective on coding. I hope that you'll be writing better code and fewer lines of code yet be happier about the code that you're writing. So, come along. Stick that little toe in the Scala waters and see if they feel as good for you as they have for me.

Who This Book Is For

This book is for folks with some programming background who want to dip their little toe into Scala, check the temperature, and perhaps wade in some more.

How This Book Is Structured

Chapters 1–3 are meant to give you a basic grounding in Scala syntax and Scala idioms. Chapters 4–6 tour key Scala features: functions, pattern matching, and Actors. Chapter 7 is a deep dive into Scala's type system. Chapter 8 rolls the pieces together with an exploration of Scala's parser combinator library. Chapter 9 discusses bringing Scala into your organization and building teams around Scala coding.

Prerequisites

You should have the Java JDK 1.5 or higher installed on your machine as well as Scala 2.7.3 or higher.

Downloading the Code

The source code for this book is available to readers at www.apress.com in the Source Code section of this book's home page. Please feel free to visit the Apress web site and download all the code there. You can also check for errata and find related titles from Apress.

Contacting the Author

David blogs Scala at http://scala-blogs.org and rants about things on his personal blog at http://blog.lostlake.org. But David can most often be found on the Lift user group, http://groups.google.com/group/liftweb/.

CHAPTER 1

About Scala and How to Install It

Scala is a programming language that provides a best-of-all-worlds experience for developers. Java™ programmers will find that their libraries are fully interoperable with Scala code.[1] Dynamic-language users will find Scala's concise syntax and type inferencing a way to reduce the boilerplate needed when writing programs in Java and C#. Functional programmers will find Scala's powerful type system a great way to reason about code. Scala bridges a lot of the divides in programming languages.

In this chapter, I'll discuss my journey learning Scala as well as where Scala comes from, how to install it, and the Scala community.

Scala: A Great Language for the Java Virtual Machine

I've been writing computer programs for a long time. I've written commercial code in 6502 assembler, BASIC, Pascal, C, C++, Objective-C, Java, C#, Visual Basic, Smalltalk, Ruby, JavaScript, and Scala. Over the years, I've had a couple of "Oh my!" reactions to computer languages.

In 1996, when I first found Java, it was a revelation. I no longer had to worry about freeing memory, and Java had a sane and normal exception-handling mechanism. Overnight, 70 percent of the defects in my programs went away. For many years, I used and loved Java.

---

1. Scala can call any Java code, subclass any Java class, and implement any Java interface. Java code can call into Scala code if the Scala code subclasses a Java class or implements a Java interface. There are features of Scala that cannot be accessed from Java, including traits with defined methods, classes and methods that have names illegal in Java, and Scala's advanced types.

In the Java 1.0 and 1.1 days, the Java Virtual Machine (JVM) was slow, and garbage collection was a costly operation. Over the years, the JVM matured. The JVM's overall performance improved with HotSpot, and by JDK 1.3, Java application code was as fast as C++ application code. Java programs could run for weeks, months, and in some cases, years without restarting.[2]

NOTE While there is a lot of discussion of this issue, my experience is that well-tuned Java code runs as fast or faster than well-tuned C and C++ code. Integer, a pure Java spreadsheet that I wrote, performed as well as Excel in Sun benchmarks on a single-processor machine. Integer outperformed Excel by significant margins on symmetric multiprocessing (SMP) machines. Sam Pullara benchmarked Java's String classes against Objective-C's NSString classes and found that Java outperformed native code by a wide margin. See http://www.theserverside.com/news/thread.tss?thread_id=25743 (the original citation is gone). I agree that a hyper-tuned C or C++ program can outperform a Java program and that Java programs require 100 percent more RAM to perform as well as their C or C++ counterparts, but for any moderately complex project that is not at the operating system kernel level, a JVM program will outperform a C or C++ program.

Over the years, Java, the language, failed to mature. Java stagnated in syntax, and web frameworks built on Java became increasingly top-heavy. It took more and more lines of Java, XML, and other pieces of glue to express simple concepts such as fields and to generate HTML forms from those fields. I used Java on most projects but became increasingly disillusioned with it.

Java 5 brought enumerations and generics. I found these to be welcome additions at the conceptual level, but at the coding level I could no longer use a simple text editor to write Java; I had to use an IDE (integrated development environment). The nasty declaration syntax for `HashMap<String, ArrayList<Integer>> = new HashMap<String, ArrayList<Integer>>();` meant that I really needed a tool that did code completion in order to write the simplest of programs.

Beyond Java

I started searching for a way to express the code in my brain in a simpler, more direct way. I found Ruby and Rails. I felt liberated. Ruby allowed me to express concepts in far fewer lines of code. Rails was so much easier to use than Spring MVC, Hibernate, and the other "streamlined" Java web frameworks. With Ruby and Rails, I got to express a lot more of

---

2. The web site http://dogscape.com ran for 13 months between restarts. I had to restart the Java process when I needed to upgrade the OS.

what was in my head in a shorter period of time. It was similar to the liberation I felt when I moved from C++ to Java.

But I found the ugly underbelly of Ruby and Rails. Ruby's runtime was so slow and flakey that I was embarrassed to deliver Ruby-based projects to my clients. I had to do my prototypes in Ruby and then port the code over to Java.

As my Ruby and Rails projects grew beyond a few thousand lines of code and as I added team members to my projects, the challenges of dynamic languages became apparent. We were spending more than half our coding time writing tests, and much of the productivity gains we saw were lost in test writing. Most of the tests would have been unnecessary in Java because most of them were geared toward making sure that we'd updated the callers when we refactored code by changing method names or parameter counts. Also, I found that working on teams where there were mind melds between two to four team members, things went well in Ruby, but as we tried to bring new members onto the team, the mental connections were hard to transmit to new team members.

I went looking for a new language and development environment. I was looking for a language that was as expressive as Ruby but as safe and high-performance as Java. In November 2006, I found this combination and a whole lot more in Scala.

Finding Scala

The same person, Martin Odersky, who wrote the Java compiler and Java Generics, designed Scala. Wow. Martin has a team dedicated to maintaining Scala as well as researching ways to mature the language. Beyond being an academic project, Scala is fast and concise, and it has even more type-safety features than does Java. Scala compiles down to Java bytecode, runs fast on the JVM, and is interoperable with Java code.

When I first found Scala, I couldn't believe its claims of performance and Java compatibility. But as I pushed on Scala, I found that it was stable. As I pushed on Scala, I found that it was fast. As I pushed on Scala, I found that it worked perfectly with all the Java libraries that I threw at it.

But most importantly, Scala taught me to program and reason about programming differently. I stopped thinking in terms of allocating buffers, structs, and objects, and of changing those pieces of memory. Instead, I learned to think about most of my programs as transforming input to output. This change in thinking has lead to lower defect rates, more modular code, and more testable code. Scala has also given me the tools to write smaller, more modular units of code and assemble them together into a whole that is maintainable, yet far more complex than anything that I could write in Java or Ruby for that matter.

After more than two years of writing and loving Scala, the only regrets that I have are that I didn't learn Lisp in college or take any programming language theory courses in grad school.[3] Each morning that I sit down at the keyboard and start coding Scala, I get a feeling of calm, peace, and power. I know that I'm going to have another day of taking the ideas in my head and reducing them to a running computer program that will be fast and low in defects.

So, please join me in exploring the Scala programming language. Most of the book will be oriented to writing simple code. I find that most of my work is done in this mode. We'll do a little exploration of Scala's type system and component architecture, but I find that I use those Scala features rarely, when I'm in "library writer" mode.

■**NOTE** Scala is the first language that has let me think and code differently depending on whether I'm a library consumer or a library producer. Scala provides tools for me as an architect that allow me to specify complex relationships between types and classes and ultimately lets me reason about my code. Working with these tools requires a lot of thinking on my part, and often when I'm working in this mode, I will produce seven lines of code in a day and feel very proud of it. In this mode, I worry about view bounds, covariance and contravariance, implicit conversions, and so on. However, most of my coding time is spent in library consumer mode. In this mode, my code looks a whole lot like Ruby or Python code. I spit out hundreds of lines of code a day, and I know the type system is there to back me up so my tests focus on the logic, not the mechanics, of my code. This book is mostly geared toward simple code—library consumption. Chapter 7 will touch on some of the library-producer coding features of Scala.

A quick diversion: Warren Henning (http://metacircular.wordpress.com/) showed me this Scala code sample:

```
def fact(n: Int) = 1 to n reduceLeft (_*_)
```

It calculates the factorial of the input. It's simple, clean, functional, and very readable. I'll be writing a lot of code like this (although perhaps a bit more practical) throughout this book. Let's go and have some fun.

---

3. See http://www.joelonsoftware.com/articles/ThePerilsofJavaSchools.html. I never learned the functional way of thinking. While I've been programming professionally for 30 years or more, it's only in the last two years that I've come to appreciate recursion and the other things that were part of Lisp from the beginning.

Scala's History

Martin Odersky (http://lampwww.epfl.ch/~odersky/) evolved Scala over many years. He is an ACM Fellow and runs the Programming Methods Laboratory (LAMP) group at Swiss Federal Institute of Technology in Lausanne (EPFL). Odersky and his team balance between working with Scala as research into how to make programming languages better for all programmers and working with Scala as a tool for commercial software development.[4] They deliver timely updates to Scala along with rapid bug fixes and excellent support. Scala is open source software available under a BSD-like license.

In 1995, Martin Odersky and Philip Wadler (http://homepages.inf.ed.ac.uk/wadler/) discovered the JVM. They began doing computer science research and programming language development targeted to the JVM. In 1997, Sun approached Odersky to write the Java 1.1 compiler; he was the lead developer of javac from Java 1.1 through Java 1.4.

Odersky and Wadler conspired on a language called Pizza that compiled to Java bytecode and had generics, first-class functions, and pattern matching. Along with some folks at Sun, they evolved Pizza into Generic Java (GJ), a generics layer on top of Java. GJ became JSR-014 and ultimately, in 2004, Java Generics.

In 2001, Odersky started work on Scala and released the first version in 2003. He and his team started using Scala as a teaching language at EPFL. In 2006, they released Scala 2.0.

Martin Odersky is the core of the Scala group, but he's attracted some extremely talented individuals[5] who have contributed significantly to Scala over the years. These folks include

- Lex Spoon (http://www.lexspoon.org/), who has written much of the Scala internals. Lex has been seen in the Squeak Smalltalk community.

- Burak Emir (http://burak.emir.googlepages.com/), who built Scala's XML support and has done a lot of work on Scala's pattern matching. Further, Burak has served as my guide and mentor in learning Scala.

- Adriaan Moors (http://www.cs.kuleuven.be/~adriaan/), who visited Martin's group for a number of months and provided enhancements to Scala's type system and Scala's parser combinator.

---

4. http://dsc.sun.com/learning/javaoneonline/2007/pdf/TS-2844.pdf
5. Personally, I think they're extremely, awesomely, wickedly cool and talented folks, but I tend to be over the top, so after you spend significant time in the Scala community, please find accolades of your own.

- Philipp Haller (`http://lamp.epfl.ch/~phaller/`), who wrote Scala's Actor support and has always been eager and excellent at adding features to Actors necessary for my work.

- Many other folks, including Don Syme, designer of F# (`http://blogs.msdn.com/dsyme/archive/2007/03/23/f-and-scala-in-lovely-lausanne.aspx`), who have influenced and shaped Scala over the years.

Martin provides the gravity to draw in some excellent brains into the building of Scala, but Martin is committed to Scala as a commercial language while satisfying the research needs of his team.

As of this writing, Scala is at version 2.7.3 and has matured significantly. More than half a dozen people have earned PhDs based on their Scala-based research. Scala is in production at some of the largest and best-known companies in the world, including SAP and Twitter.

Installing Scala

In order to run Scala, you must have Java 1.5 or greater installed on your computer. If you are running Mac OS X, you already have the Java Development Kit (JDK) on your machine. If you're running Windows, please download Java from `http://java.sun.com`. If you're running Linux or Solaris, please consult with your distribution's Java installation instructions.

You can download Scala from `http://www.scala-lang.org/downloads`.

Installing on Windows

First, you must set the `JAVA_HOME` environment variable and add the JDK's `bin` directory to your `PATH` variable. In Windows XP, right-click on My Computer and select the Properties menu item. In Vista, right-click Computer and select Change settings. In both, now select the Advanced tab and click the Environment Variables button. In the System variables area, click the New button. Set the Variable Name to `JAVA_HOME` and the Variable Value to the place that you installed the JDK. On my machine, that's `C:\Program Files\Java\jdk1.6.0_11`.

Next, select the `PATH` variable and click the Edit button. Move the cursor to the beginning of the Variable Value and type **%JAVA_HOME%\bin;** before the rest of the line. Click the OK buttons in the Edit System Variable dialog, in the Environment Variables dialog, and in the System Properties dialog.

Test that you can access the JDK. Click the Start button and select Run…; in the dialog, type **cmd** and click the OK button. A DOS window should appear with a prompt that looks like the following:

```
C:\Documents and Settings\dpp>
```

At this prompt, type **java -version** and press Enter. You should see something like the following:

```
java version "1.6.0_11"
Java(TM) SE Runtime Environment (build 1.6.0_11-b03)
Java HotSpot(TM) Client VM (build 11.0-b16, mixed mode, sharing)
```

Next, test to see that the Java compiler is installed. Type **javac -version**. You should see something like the following:

```
javac 1.6.0_11
```

Next, let's install Scala. Download the Scala lzPack installer from http://scala-tools.org/downloads. This download is typically the first on the page. Save this file to the Desktop or some other place that you can find it. Double-click on the scala-2.7.3.final-installer.jar file to start the install process. Once complete, you need to create the SCALA_HOME environment variable and add Scala to your PATH variable. Follow the same process that you used for creating JAVA_HOME, but name the variable SCALA_HOME and set the PATH to the place Scala was installed. Next, update the PATH variable to include **%SCALA_HOME%\bin;**.

Open a new command prompt and type **scala**. You should see the following:

```
Welcome to Scala version 2.7.3.final (Java HotSpot(TM) Client VM, Java 1.6.0_11).
Type in expressions to have them evaluated.
Type :help for more information.
```

Congratulations, you've installed Scala.

Installing on Mac OS X and Linux

Make sure you've got the Java JDK 1.5 or 1.6 installed. By default, the JDK is installed on Mac OS X 10.4 and greater. Download the Scala lzPack installer from http://scala-tools.org/downloads. Open a terminal window and change directories to the location where you downloaded the Scala installer. Type the following:

```
sudo java -jar scala-2.7.3.final-installer.jar
```

Now select /usr/local/share as the place to install Scala. Once Scala is installed, run the following commands:

```
cd /usr/local/share
sudo ln -s scala-2.7.3-final scala
cd /usr/local/bin
sudo ln -s ../share/scala/bin/scala scala
sudo ln -s ../share/scala/bin/fsc fsc
sudo ln -s ../share/scala/bin/scalac scalac
sudo ln -s ../share/scala/bin/scaladoc scaladoc
```

Change to your home directory and type **scala**. You should see the following:

```
Welcome to Scala version 2.7.3.final (Java HotSpot(TM) 64-Bit Server VM, Java
1.6.0_07).
Type in expressions to have them evaluated.

Type :help for more information.
scala>
```

Congratulations, you've installed Scala on your machine.

The Scala Community

The Scala community is a wide-ranging, rich, and vibrant group of people. It's a warm and welcoming place for newbies, but it also offers academically rigorous debate and lots of ideas from the cutting edge of computer science made practical.

There are lots of cool people from lots of different backgrounds in the Scala community.

- You'll find academics like Martin and his team. They actively participate in the community, answering questions from newbies and from seasoned folks about Scala basics, design choices, and more.

- There's a cohort of extremely skilled and experienced functional programming gurus, including David MacIver. They help drive Scala forward.

- James Iry is another highly skilled functional programming guru who has a magic touch when it comes to explaining complex Scala concepts to just about anyone.

- Jon Pretty and Jamie Webb of Sygneca provide consulting services and a ton of backbone for the Scala list and Scala community.

- You may hear from Jorge Ortiz who, like James, is great at explaining complex Scala topics to folks at all skill levels.

The list of Scala mailing lists managed by EPFL (Martin's group) can be found at `http://www.scala-lang.org/node/199`.

The main Scala list is available at `scala@listes.epfl.ch`, or you can access it on the Web via Nabble at `http://www.nabble.com/Scala-f14147.html`. This list is for discussing Scala, asking questions, and making observations. It's a great place for intermediate and advanced Scala developers to exchange ideas and information.

The Scala User list is oriented toward newbies, and it's a great place for folks to learn about Scala by seeing the kind of questions that other newbies have about the language. The e-mail for the list is `scala-user@listes.epfl.ch`, and it's available on Nabble via a web interface at `http://www.nabble.com/Scala---User-f30217.html`.

The Scala Debate list is a place for seasoned Scala folks to discuss the language, make suggestions, and conspire to move Scala forward. You can post to the list via e-mail at `scala-debate@listes.epfl.ch` or via Nabble at `http://www.nabble.com/Scala---Debate-f30218.html`. Note that this list is a hard-core, no-holds-barred discussion of Scala that sees some minor flame wars occasionally break out among the mathematically inclined. If you venture into this forum, keep in mind that it does, from time to time, devolve into discussion that is not kind and gentle and that often the discussion is indecipherable for those of us who do not have a PhD in mathematics. If this is the kind of discussion that is interesting to you, please check out Lambda the Ultimate at http://lambda-the-ultimate.org. LtU provides a forum for a broad spectrum of programming language theory (PLT) discussions.[6]

Lift is the leading web framework for Scala. The Lift community is hosted at Google. You can learn more at http://groups.google.com/group/liftweb/. While I'm the lead developer for Lift, we're not going to focus much on web development in this book, but if you're a web developer, I'd love it if you'd join the Lift community.

Those are the main mailing lists in the Scala community. As you explore with Scala, please join the online discussion and share your questions and thoughts.

Summary

You've learned a little about what attracted me to Scala, a little about where Scala comes from, and you've installed Scala. You've learned about, and hopefully joined, the Scala community. Now it's time to explore Scala and see whether it resonates with you the same way it resonates with me. Turn the page and write your first Scala program.

---

6. Paul Snively, the technical editor of this book, is an editor on LtU. It's a pleasure and an honor to have him participate in this project. If you dive deep into PLT, I hope you find Paul to be a compass and a beacon as I do.

■ ■ ■ ■

CHAPTER 2

Scala Syntax, Scripts, and Your First Scala Programs

We're going to get our hands dirty with Scala code in this chapter. We'll write some Scala code, starting with the ubiquitous "Hello World," and moving on to more complex Scala programs. This will give your eyes and brain an idea of what Scala code looks like. Next, we're going to take a long and boring tour of Scala's syntax. Finally, we're going to see some options for running (and compiling) Scala programs.

Scala at the Command Line and Scala Scripts

Scala offers different ways to run programs:

- You can run them interactively at a REPL (read-eval-print loop) command line.

- You can run single-file Scala scripts.

- You can compile your Scala programs into class files that can be combined into JAR files, just as in Java.

Scala's flexibility allows you to choose the environment that's best for you.

Interactive Scala

When I'm exploring a new construct or library, I want instant feedback. I want to type a couple of lines of code and see what happens. Scala's REPL gives me the immediacy and interactivity that I need when I'm exploring.

To start Scala's REPL, open a command prompt or terminal and type **scala**. You should see the following:

```
>scala
Welcome to Scala version 2.7.3.final (Java HotSpot(TM) Client VM, Java 1.6.0_11)
Type in expressions to have them evaluated.
Type :help for more information.

scala>
```

You can start typing things and see how they're evaluated in Scala, for example:

```
scala> 1 + 1
```

```
res0: Int = 2
```

```
scala> res0 * 8
```

```
res1: Int = 16
```

```
scala> val x = "Hello World"
```

```
x: java.lang.String = Hello World
```

```
scala> var xl = x.length
```

```
xl: Int = 11
```

You can even access Java libraries:

```
scala> import java.util._
```

```
import java.util._
```

```
scala> val d = new Date
```

```
d: java.util.Date = Wed Jan 14 22:03:31 PST 2009
```

Most of the examples in this book are done at the Scala REPL.

Scala Scripts

If your program grows beyond the few lines in the REPL, you can start building Scala scripts. Scala scripts are single files of Scala code. They do not have an explicit main method. In fact, when you run your script, Scala wraps the entire file into the main method of a class, compiles the code, and calls the generated main method. All you have to do is put valid Scala code in a file. To invoke the script, type

```
> scala MyFile.scala
```

You can access the command-line arguments in your script with the argv variable, which is an Array[String].

Compiling Scala Programs

You can compile Scala programs just as you compile Java programs, and the results are JVM class files that can be packaged into JAR files. The Scala compiler requires that source files contain one or more class, trait, or object definitions. To compile Scala source files into class files, type the following:

```
> scalac File1.scala File2.scala
```

However, startup time for the compiler is non-trivial. You can also compile using the fast Scala compiler, `fsc`:

```
> fsc File1.scala File2.scala
```

`fsc` is a separate compiler process that continues to run, waiting for new compilation jobs, even after the compilation process is finished. This results in much faster compilation times, but if you're on a machine with limited RAM, you might not want to keep the compilation process alive.

If you are working on medium-sized to large projects, you probably use some sort of build tool such as Ant or Maven. There are Scala plug-ins for both Ant and Maven, so you can integrate Scala code into existing Java projects with very little effort and no requirement of using new build tools.[1]

Your First Scala Programs

In this section, we're going to write a couple of basic Scala programs. These programs will give you a sense of Scala's flavor and get you acquainted with running Scala programs.

Hello World

Yep, it's the ubiquitous "Hello World" program. In Scala, it's short, simple, and to the point. Open up your favorite text editor: Emacs, vi, TextMate, whatever. Create a new file called `HelloWorld.scala` and place the following line in it:

```
println("Hello World!")
```

Save the file. Open a terminal window or command prompt and change into the directory where the file is and type **scala HelloWorld.scala**.

You should see

```
Hello World!
```

---

1. See `http://www.scala-lang.org/node/91` for an up-to-date list of IDE plug-ins and other tools for creating Scala programs. You can join the Scala tools mailing list at `http://www.scala-lang.org/node/199`.

In Scala, you can write simple programs that look and feel like scripts that you would write in Ruby or Python. In this case, you're calling the `println` method with the string constant `Hello World!`. It's a thin layer on top of `System.out.println()`. Because `println` is used so frequently, it's part of Scala's `Predef`, the predefined stuff that's automatically part of every program. This is like the `java.lang` package that is automatically imported in every Java program.

Printing Some Numbers

Let's write a program that will print the numbers from 1 to 10 in the `Print1.scala` file:

```
for {i <- 1 to 10}
  println(i)
```

You can run the code by typing **scala Print1.scala** in the terminal. The program assigns the numbers 1 to 10 to the variable i and then executes `println(i)`, which prints the numbers 1 to 10. `for` means much more in Scala than in Java. You can nest expressions in a `for` comprehension (the fancy Scala name for the `for` statement). In the `Print2.scala` file, put

```
for {i <- 1 to 10
     j <- 1 to 10}
  println(i * j)
```

In this program, we're iterating over 1 to 10 in an outer loop and assigning each number to i. In the inner loop, we're also iterating from 1 to 10 and assigning each number to j. The product of i * j is printed, so you'll see 100 lines output. There are many more uses of the `for` comprehension that we'll cover later in the book.

Adding Things Up

The next program will read all the lines from the input and sum each line that contains a valid integer. This program introduces you to a substantial number of Scala's concepts, including passing functions as parameters, Scala's type system, immutable data structures, and more. It's a bit of a dive into the deep end, so let's go. Create a file called `Sum.scala` containing the code in Listing 2-1.

Listing 2-1. *Sum.scala*

```scala
import scala.io._


def toInt(in: String): Option[Int] =
  try {
    Some(Integer.parseInt(in.trim))
  } catch {
    case e: NumberFormatException => None
  }

def sum(in: Seq[String]) = {
  val ints = in.flatMap(s => toInt(s))
  ints.foldLeft(0)((a, b) => a + b)
}

println("Enter some numbers and press ctrl-D (Unix/Mac) ctrl-C (Windows)")

val input = Source.fromInputStream(System.in)

val lines = input.getLines.collect

println("Sum "+sum(lines))
```

Let's go through this file in detail.

Importing Stuff

The import scala.io._ code imports all the classes from the scala.io package. This is the same as Java's import scala.io.*;. Scala uses the _ rather than the * as a wildcard. Coming from Javaland, it takes a little getting used to, but it'll soon make sense.

Parsing a String to an Int

Next, we define the toInt method, which takes a single parameter called in. That parameter has the type String:

```scala
def toInt(in: String): Option[Int] =
```

In Scala, method definitions begin with the def keyword. The method name follows, along with the method's parameter list. In this case, the toInt method takes one parameter: in, whose type declaration follows it rather than precedes it. In some cases, the Scala compiler can figure out or infer the type of a variable or the return type of a method. You need to declare the parameter types for a Scala method, but we may omit the return type if the return type can be inferred and the method is not recursive.[2] We declare the return type as Option[Int]. In general, if the return type is not immediately obvious, it's an act of kindness and good citizenship to your fellow programmers and your future self to declare the return type.

What's Option and what are those funky square brackets around Int? Option is a container that holds one or zero things. If it holds zero elements, it's None, which is a singleton, which means that only one instance of None. If the Option holds one element, it's Some(theElement).

The funky square brackets denote the type of thing that's held by the Option. In this case, the Option holds an Int.

In Scala, everything is an instance of a class, even Int, Char, Boolean, and the other JVM primitive types. The Scala compiler puts primitive types in instance boxes (boxing) only when necessary. The result is that you can treat all classes uniformly in Scala, but if your primitive data does not require boxing, you'll see the same program performance you see using primitives in Java. If your primitive does require boxing, the Scala compiler does all the boxing and unboxing for you, and it even does null testing when it unboxes—nice and polite.

So, Option[Int] is a container that holds zero or one Int value.[3] Using Option is one of the ways that Scala lets you avoid null pointer exceptions and explicit null testing. How? You can apply your business logic over all the elements in the Option. If the Option is None, then you apply your logic over zero elements. If the Option is Some, then you apply your business logic over one element. Option can be used and nested in the for comprehension. We'll explore Option in more depth in Chapter 3.

When I'm writing code, I return Option from any method that, based on business logic, might return some value or might return none. In this case, converting a String to an Int might succeed if the String can be parsed or might fail if the String cannot be parsed into an Int. If the String cannot be parsed, it is not something that's worthy of an exception because it's not an exceptional situation. It is merely a calculation that has no legal value, thus it makes sense to return None if the String cannot be parsed. This mechanism also avoids the Java patchwork of sometimes returning null when there's no legal value to return and sometimes throwing an exception.

Speaking of exceptions, that's exactly what Integer.parseInt does when it cannot parse the String into an Int. So, in our code, we wrap a try/catch around Some(Integer.parseInt(in.trim)). If the Integer.parseInt method succeeds, a new instance of Some will be created and returned from the toInt method. There's no explicit return statement as the last expression evaluated in the method is its return value.

---

2. A recursive method is a method that calls itself.
3. Option[Int] is a "variant type" or "sum type" with None as one variant and Some[Int] as the other. Neither None nor Some[Int] is the same as Int, but if you're working with an Option[Int] that happens to be of the variant Some[Int] then you can extract the actual Int from it by calling the get method.

If `Integer.parseInt` throws an exception, it will be caught by the `catch` block. The `catch` block looks different from Java's `catch`. In Scala, there's a single `catch` and a series of patterns to match the exception. Pattern matching is a language-level Scala construct, and it's uniformly applied across the language. In this code, we have

```
case e: NumberFormatException => None
```

This pattern matches the exception to `NumberFormatException` and returns the expression `None`, which is the last expression in the method. Thus `toInt` will return `None` if `parseInt` throws a `NumberFormatException`.

To summarize: `toInt` takes a `String` and attempts to convert it to an `Int`. If it succeeds, `toInt` returns `Some(convertedValue)`, otherwise it returns `None`.

Summing Things Up

Next, let's tackle the `sum` method. We define our method:

```
def sum(in: Seq[String]) = {
```

We don't declare the return type for `sum` because the compiler can figure it out and the method is short enough that a quick glance at the code shows us that the return type is an `Int`.

The in parameter is a `Seq[String]`. A `Seq` is a trait (which is like a Java interface) that is inherited by many different collections classes. A `Seq` is a supertrait to `Array`, `List`, and other sequential collections. As `Option[Int]` is an `Option` of `Int`, `Seq[String]` is a sequence of `String` elements.

A trait has all the features of the Java interface construct. But traits can have implemented methods on them. If you are familiar with Ruby, traits are similar to Ruby's mixins. You can mix many traits into a single class. Traits cannot take constructor parameters, but other than that they behave like classes. This gives you the ability to have something that approaches multiple inheritance without the diamond problem (http://en.wikipedia.org/wiki/Diamond_problem).

The first line of the `sum` method transforms the `Seq[String]` to `Seq[Int]` and assigns the result to a `val` named `ints`:

```
val ints = in.flatMap(s => toInt(s))
```

This maps and flattens each element by calling the `toInt` method for each `String` in the sequence. `toInt` returns a collection of zero or one `Int`. `flatMap` flattens the result such that each element of the collection, the `Option`, is appended to the resulting sequence. The result is that each `String` from the `Seq[String]` that can be converted to an `Int` is put in the `ints` collection.

In Scala, you can declare variables as assign-once or assign-many. Assign-once Scala variables are the same as Java's `final` variables. They are identified with the `val` keyword. Assign-multiple variables in Scala are the same as Java variables and are identified with the `var` keyword. Because I'm not changing the value of `ints` after I set it, I chose the `val` keyword. I use `val` in my programs unless there's a compelling reason to use `var`, because the fewer things that can change, the fewer defects that can creep into my code.

Another fancy thing that we've done is create a function that calls the `toInt` method and passes it to the `flatMap` method. `flatMap` calls the function for each member of the sequence, `in`. In our example, we defined a function that takes a single parameter, `s`, and calls `toInt` with that parameter. We pass this function as the parameter to `flatMap`, and the compiler infers that `s` is a `String`. Thus, an anonymous function is created, and an instance of that function is passed to the `flatMap` method. Additionally, Scala sees that the return type of `toInt` is an `Option[Int]`, so it infers that the `ints` variable has the type `Seq[Int]`. So, you've done your first bit of functional programming. Woo-hoo!

The next line sums up the `Seq[Int]`:

```
ints.foldLeft(0)((a, b) => a + b)
```

`foldLeft` takes a seed value, `0` in this case, and applies the function to the seed and the first element of the sequence, `ints`. It takes the result and applies the function to the result and the next value in the sequence repeatedly until there are no more elements in the sequence. `foldLeft` then returns the resulting accumulated value. `foldLeft` is useful for calculating any accumulated value. In math, sum, prod, min, max, and so on can be implemented easily with `foldLeft`. In this case, we defined a simple function that takes two parameters, `a` and `b`, and returns the sum of those parameters. We did not have to declare the types of `a` or `b`, because the Scala compiler infers that they are both `Int`s. The `foldLeft` line is the last expression in the method, and the `sum` method returns its results.

Program Body

The following defines the `input` variable:

```
val input = Source.fromInputStream(System.in)
```

Its type is `Source`, a source of input, which wraps the JVM's `System.in InputStream`. In this case, we didn't have to do anything fancy to access a Java class. We used it just as we might have from a Java program. This illustrates the awesome interoperability between Scala and Java.

The next line gets the lines from our source and collects them into a `Seq[String]`:

```
val lines = input.getLines.collect
```

Finally, we print a message on the console with the sum of the lines with parsible integers on them:

```
println("Sum "+sum(lines))
```

To run the program, type

```
> scala Sum.scala
```

When you're prompted, enter some lines with numbers. When you're done, press Ctrl-D (Unix/Linux/Mac OS X) or Ctrl-C (Windows), and the program will display the sum of the numbers.

Great, you've written a Scala program that makes use of many of Scala's features including function passing, immutable data structures, and type inference. Now, let's look more deeply into Scala's syntax.

Basic Scala Syntax

Scala, like Java, is a C-derivative language, and many familiar C syntactic constructs are visible in Scala. The biggest syntactic difference between Scala and Java is that the ; line end character is optional. There are other differences, but they should be pretty understandable and self-explanatory.

In this section, I'll review the parts of Scala's syntax that you'll need for the rest of the book. The complete Scala syntax and language definition can be found in the Scala Language Specification (`http://www.scala-lang.org/sites/default/files/linuxsoft_archives/docu/files/ScalaReference.pdf`).

Number, String, and XML Constants

Scala has all the same constants as Java, with the same memory footprint and precision.

- *Integer*: 1, 882, -1

- *Boolean*: true, false

- *Double*: 1.0, 1d, 1e3

- *Long*: 42L

- *Float*: 78.9f

- *Characters*: '4', '?', 'z'

- *Strings*: "Hello World"

Scala also supports multilined `Strings` that start and end with triple quotes:

```
"""Hello
 Multiline
 World"""
```

Scala supports XML constants, including embedded Scala code. We'll explore this more in Chapter 3.

```
<b>Foo</b>
<ul>{(1 to 3).map(i => <li>{i}</li>)}</ul>
```

package

A package is a named module of code. Java and Scala convention dictates that package names are the reversed domain name of the code owner. For example, the packages in the Lift Web Framework (`http://liftweb.net`) begin with `net.liftweb`. Typically, the package also contains a descriptive name for the module. For example, the Lift utility package is `net.liftweb.util`. The package declaration is the first non-comment line in the source file:

```
package com.liftcode.stuff
```

import

Scala packages can be imported so that they can be referenced in the current compilation scope. The following statement imports the contents of the `scala.xml` package:

```
import scala.xml._
```

Import statements are made in the scope of prior imports. The following statement imports the `scala.xml.transform` package:

```
import transform._
```

You can import a single class and object (more on objects very soon), for example, `HashMap` from the `scala.collection.mutable` package:

```
import scala.collection.mutable.HashMap
```

You can import more than one class or object from a single package, for example, `TreeMap` and `TreeSet` from the `scala.collection.immutable` package:

```
import scala.collection.immutable.{TreeMap, TreeSet}
```

Finally, you can import a class or object and rename it. For example, you can import the JSON class/object from the scala.util.parsing.json package and rename it to JsonParser:

```
import scala.util.parsing.json.{JSON => JsonParser}
```

Class, Trait, and Object Definition

Scala's object model allows you to model any Java class. Everything you can do with a Java class you can do with a Scala class. Scala's class declaration syntax and rules are different from and, in my opinion, more flexible than Java's. It's common to declare far more classes in a Scala program than in a Java program. Scala removes Java's constraint of one public class per file. You can put as many classes in a file as you want, and you can name the file whatever you want. Your IDE will help you navigate from class to file.[4]

In Scala, everything has public access level unless otherwise declared. You can define the public Foo class that has no methods:

```
class Foo
```

This declaration corresponds to the Java class declaration:

```
public class Foo {
}
```

If the constructor or method takes zero parameters, you can omit the parameter list. To create an instance of Foo, you can type the following:

```
new Foo
```

But, this works just as well:

```
new Foo()
```

To define the Bar class that takes a single constructor parameter, name, which is a String:

```
class Bar(name: String)
```

To create an instance of Bar:

```
new Bar("Working...")
```

---

4. The declaration of Scala classes is syntactically more lightweight than Java's declarations. Classes with constructors, properties, and so on can be declared in a single line of code. Classes in Scala are often used to enforce type safety. For example, you might return an instance of Name rather than String. As we explore more about Scala, you'll see why Scala programs often group many class definitions into a single source file.

To define Baz with a constructor that tests name and throws an exception if name is null:

```
class Baz(name: String) {
  // constructor code is inline
  if (name == null) throw new Exception("Name is null")
}
```

The Java interface defines a set of methods that must be implemented on all classes that implement the interface. Scala supports interfaces but calls them traits. Traits can do everything that interfaces can do, but they can also include method implementations. This comes in very handy because you don't have to create complex class hierarchies in order to avoid duplicating code. You just write the code in the trait, and every class that implements the trait gets those methods. Scala's traits correspond to Ruby's mixins.

Let's define the trait Dog:

```
trait Dog
```

To add the Dog trait to the Fizz2 class:

```
class Fizz2(name: String) extends Bar(name) with Dog
```

To define the Cat trait, which requires that any extending classes implement the meow method:

```
trait Cat {
  def meow(): String
}
```

To define the FuzzyCat trait that extends Cat and implements the meow method:

```
trait FuzzyCat extends Cat {
  override def meow(): String = "Meeeeeeow"
}
```

To define the OtherThing trait with the hello method:

```
trait OtherThing {
  def hello() = 4
}
```

And to define the Yep class that extends FuzzyCat and OtherThing:

```
class Yep extends FuzzyCat with OtherThing
```

Using the REPL, let's see what happens when we call the meow and hello methods on a Yep instance:

```
scala> (new Yep).meow()
```

```
res36: String = Meeeeeeow
```

```
scala> (new Yep).hello()
```

```
res79: Int = 4
```

Scala does not allow you to declare static methods or variables, but it does support an alternative model for singletons called objects. If you declare something as an object, only one instance of it exists in the scope in which it was declared. An object will be instantiated the first time it is accessed. A Scala object can exist at the package scope, and it replaces Java's static methods and variables. The advantage of Scala's object over Java's static mechanism is that a Scala object is an instance of a class and can be passed as a parameter to methods.

You declare a singleton object with the object keyword instead of the class or trait keyword:

```
object Simple
```

You can include methods in an object:

```
object OneMethod {
  def myMethod() = "Only One"
}
```

and extend classes and traits:

```
object Dude extends Yep
```

and override methods:

```
object Dude2 extends Yep {
  override def meow() = "Dude looks like a cat"
}
```

and add new methods:

```
object OtherDude extends Yep {
  def twoMeows(otherparam: Yep) = meow + ", " + param.meow
}
```

Let's access our objects and show how the Dude and Dude2 objects can be passed into a method that takes a Yep as a parameter:

```
scala> OtherDude.meow
```

```
res39: String = Meeeeeeow
```

```
scala> OtherDude.twoMeows(Dude)
```

```
res40: java.lang.String = Meeeeeeow, Meeeeeeow
```

```
scala> OtherDude.twoMeows(Dude2)
```

```
res80: java.lang.String = Meeeeeeow, Dude looks like a cat
```

The previous example demonstrates that the meow method is invoked on the Dude object and the Dude2 object. The objects were passed as a parameter into the twoMeows method just like any other instance.

You can embed an object in a class, trait, or object. One instance of the object is created for each instance of the enclosing scope. Thus, each HasYep instance will have a single myYep that will be created when it is accessed:

```
class HasYep {
  object myYep extends Yep {
    override def meow = "Moof"
  }
}
scala> (new HasYep).myYep.meow
```

```
res43: java.lang.String = Moof
```

Classes, objects, and traits can have inner classes, objects, and traits, which have special access to private methods, variables, and so on:

```
class HasClass {
  private class MyDude extends FuzzyCat
  def makeOne(): FuzzyCat = new MyDude
}
```

I need to take a brief digression back to the import statement. import can be used inside any code block, and the import will be active only in the scope of that code block. For example, we can import something inside a class body:

```
class Frog {
  import scala.xml._
  def n: NodeSeq = NodeSeq.Empty
}
```

Scala's import statement can also import the methods of an object so that those methods can be used without explicit reference to the object that owns them. This is much like Java's static import. Combining local scope import and importing objects allows you to fine-tune where the objects and their associated methods are imported.

```
scala> object Moose {
     def bark = "woof"
     }
defined module Moose

scala> import Moose._
import Moose._

scala> bark
```

```
res78: java.lang.String = woof
```

Scala's Class Hierarchy

In Scala, everything (except a method) is an instance of a class. This means that Java primitives such as int are treated as instances by the Scala compiler. This is done at the compilation level, but the bytecode is optimized so that adding two Ints in Scala results in the same bytecode and performance as adding two ints in Java. On the other hand, in Scala, Int has methods including hashCode and toString. The Scala compiler will put primitive types in a box when they are being passed to something that expects an Any, such as putting an Int in a HashMap.

In keeping with the naming convention that all classes have uppercase letters at the beginning of their name, Scala representations of JVM primitives are called Int, Long, Double, Float, Boolean, Char, Short, and Byte. They are all subclasses of AnyVal. Scala also has an object representation of Java's void called Unit, which is also a subclass of AnyVal. You can explicitly return Unit from a method with the () singleton (yep, you read that right, an open and a close parenthesis).

```
scala> val v = ()
```

```
v: Unit = ()
```

```
scala> List(v)
```

```
res1: List[Unit] = List(())
```

Nothing is cool. Any method that returns Nothing will never normally return. It *must* throw an exception. This makes the None singleton that we encountered in our sum.scala program possible. None is an Option[Nothing], which means its get method returns a Nothing. This sounds like word games, but it means that the compiler enforces that the get method in None throws an exception rather than returning some other bottom-of-the-hierarchy value such as null.

Any is the root of the Scala class hierarchy, like Object is the root of the Java class hierarchy. But, because of Nothing, primitives, and so on, Scala needed a root class that is underneath Object.

AnyVal is the root of Scala's objectification of the JVM's primitives.

AnyRef means the same thing as Java's Object but has a few extra compiler-managed methods, including the eq, ne, == and != methods. == is a call to the equals method rather than the Java meaning of reference comparison. If you want to do a reference comparison in Scala, use the eq method.

Method Declaration

Scala method declarations have the def keyword, the method name, parameters, optional return type, the = keyword, and the method body. myMethod takes no parameters and returns a String:

```
def myMethod(): String = "Moof"
```

myOtherMethod takes no parameters and returns a String, but we don't have to explicitly declare the return type because the compiler infers the return type. Type inferencing is powerful and useful, but please use it carefully. Any time that it's not immediately obvious what the return type is, declare it explicitly.

```
def myOtherMethod() = "Moof"
```

You declare the parameters inside the method declaration's parentheses. The parameter name must be followed by the parameter's type:

```
def foo(a: Int): String = a.toString
```

You can declare multiple parameters:

```
def f2(a: Int, b: Boolean): String = if (b) a.toString else "false"
```

You can pass the type of a parameter or the return type as a parameter. The following code takes a parameter p and a type parameter T and returns a List of T. Thus, if you pass an Int, you'll get a List[Int], and if you pass a String, you'll get a List[String]. For the most part, the type inferencer will calculate the type parameters so you don't have to explicitly pass them.

```
scala> def list[T](p: T): List[T] = p :: Nil
list: [T](T)List[T]

scala> list(1)
```

```
res2: List[Int] = List(1)
```

```
scala> list("Hello")
```

```
res3: List[java.lang.String] = List(Hello)
```

And the last parameter in the list may be repeated—a variable-length argument. If the last parameter is a variable-length argument, it is a Seq of the type of the variable-length argument, so in this case the as parameter is a Seq[Int]:

```
def largest(as: Int*): Int = as.reduceLeft((a, b) => a max b)
```

A variable-length argument method may be called as follows:

```
largest(1)
largest(2, 3, 99)
largest(33, 22, 33, 22)
```

You can mix type parameters with variable-length arguments:

```
def mkString[T](as: T*): String = as.foldLeft("")(_ + _.toString)
```

And you can put bounds on the type parameters. In this case, the types that are passed in must be Number or a subclass of Number:

```
def sum[T <: Number](as: T*): Double = as.foldLeft(0d)(_ + _.doubleValue)
```

Methods can be declared within any code scope, except at the top level, where classes, traits, and objects are declared. Methods can reference any variables in their scope:

```
def readLines(br: BufferedReader) = {
  var ret: List[String] = Nil

  def readAll(): Unit = br.readLine match {
    case null =>
    case s => ret ::= s ; readAll()
  }

  readAll()
  ret.reverse
}
```

In this example, the readAll method is defined inside the scope of the readLines method. Thus, the readAll method has access to the variables br and ret because these variables are within the scope of the readLines method. The readAll method calls a method on br, and it updates ret, even though these variables are not explicitly passed to readAll. As we go through more examples in subsequent chapters, we'll see how being able to use methods within methods and being able to access to all the variables in scope comes in very handy.

Note that we'll see the case construct in the "Basic Pattern Matching" section later in the chapter. Its basic functionality is like Java's switch statement.

Overriding methods in Scala is different than Java. Methods that override declared methods must include the override modifier. Methods that override abstract methods may include the override modifier.

```
abstract class Base {
  def thing: String
}
class One extends Base {
  def thing = "Moof"
}
```

Methods that take no parameters and variables can be accessed the same way, and a val can override a def in a superclass. This principle of uniform access turns out to be very useful.

```
class Two extends One {
  override val thing = (new java.util.Date).toString
}
class Three extends One {
  override lazy val thing = super.thing + (new java.util.Date).toString
}
```

Variable Declaration

Variables are declared like methods but start with the val, var, or lazy val keyword. var variables can be changed after they are set, like Java variables. val variables are assign-once, and the value is calculated when the code block containing the val is entered, like final variables in Java. lazy val variables are calculated once, the first time the variable is accessed. You would use a lazy val if the variable may not be used and the cost of calculating it is very long.

```
var y: String = "Moof"
val x: String = "Moof"
lazy val lz: String = someLongQuery()
```

As a matter of style, I write my code with val variables unless there is a compelling reason to use a var. Given that mutability leads to unexpected defects, minimizing mutability in code minimizes mutability-related defects.

Scala's type inferencer infers types for variables as well. In general, I don't declare variable types unless it's not obvious what the variable type is.

```
var y2 = "Moof"
val x2 = "Moof"
```

Scala supports multiple assignment. If a code block or method returns a Tuple, the Tuple can be assigned to a `val` variable.

```
val (i1: Int, s1: String) = Pair(33, "Moof")
```

And the type inferencer gets it right:

```
val (i2, s2) = Pair(43, "Woof")
```

Code Blocks

Method and variable definitions can be single lines:

```
def meth9() = "Hello World"
```

Or methods and variables can be defined in code blocks that are denoted by curly braces: { }. Code blocks may be nested. The result of a code block is the last line evaluated in the code block.

```
def meth3(): String = {"Moof"}
def meth4(): String = {
  val d = new java.util.Date()
  d.toString()
}
```

Variable definitions can be code blocks as well. This comes in handy when defining `val` variables, and the logic required to compute the value is non-trivial.

```
val x3: String = {
  val d = new java.util.Date()
  d.toString()
}
```

Call-by-Name

In Java, all method invocations are call-by-reference or call-by-value (for primitive types). What this means is that the parameter's value, or reference in the case of an `AnyRef`, is placed on the stack and passed to the callee. Scala gives you an additional mechanism for passing parameters to methods (and functions): call-by-name, which passes a code block to the callee. Each time the callee accesses the parameter, the code block is executed and the value is calculated. Call-by-name allows you to pass parameters that might take a long time to calculate but may not be used. For example, in a call to the logger you can use call-by-name, and the express to print is only calculated if it's going to be logged. Call-by-name also allows you to create flow of control structures such as while, doWhile, and so on.

We declare a nano method, which prints a message and returns the current time with nano-second resolution:

```
def nano() = {
  println("Getting nano")
  System.nanoTime
}
```

Next we declare the delayed method, which takes a call-by-name parameter by putting the => symbol between the variable name and the type. delayed prints a message demonstrating that the method has been entered. Next, delayed prints a message with t's value. Finally, delayed returns t.

```
def delayed(t: => Long) = {
  println("In delayed method")
  println("Param: "+t)
  t
}
```

Let's see what happens when we call delayed with nano as a parameter:

```
scala> delayed(nano())
```

```
In delayed method
Getting nano
Param: 4475258994017
Getting nano
res3: Long = 4475259694720
```

This indicates that delayed is entered before the call to nano and that nano is called twice. Let's compare this to call-by-reference:

```
def notDelayed(t: Long) = {
  println("In not delayed method")
  println("Param: "+t)
  t
}
```

Let's try calling notDelayed:

```
scala> notDelayed(nano())
```

```
Getting nano
In not delayed method
Param: 4513758999378
res4: Long = 4513758999378
```

nano is called before notDelayed is called because the parameter to notDelayed, nano(), is calculated before notDelayed is called. This is the way Java programmers expect code to work.

Method Invocation

Scala provides a number of syntactic variations for invoking methods. There's the standard Java dot notation:

```
instance.method()
```

But if a method does not take any parameters, the ending parentheses are optional:

```
instance.method
```

This allows methods without parameters methods to appear as properties or fields on the target instance. This results in more visually pleasing code.

Methods that take a single parameter can be invoked just as in Java:

```
instance.method(param)
```

But methods that take a single parameter can be invoked without dots or parentheses:

```
instance method param
```

Because Scala allows method names to contain symbols such as +, -, *, and ?, Scala's dotless method notation creates a syntactically neutral way of invoking methods that are hard-coded operators in Java.

```
scala> 2.1.*(4.3)
```

```
res5: Double = 9.03
```

```
scala> 2.1 * 4.3
```

```
res6: Double = 9.03
```

Finally, you invoke multiparameter methods in Scala just as in Java:

```
instance.method(p1, p2)
```

If a Scala method takes a type parameter, typically, the type parameter will be inferred by the compiler, but you can also explicitly pass the type parameter:

```
instance.method[TypeParam](p1, p2)
```

Functions, apply, update, and Compiler Magic

Scala is a functional language, which means that you can pass functions to methods and return them from methods and functions. A function is a block of code that takes parameters and returns a value. In Scala, functions are instances. Given that Scala is constrained by the Java Virtual Machine, it cannot pass a pointer to an arbitrary block of code, so Scala implements functions as anonymous inner classes that have a particular interface. When you pass a function, you're just passing an object with a certain trait (interface).

The trait that defines functions that take one parameter and return a value is

```
Function1[A, B]
```

where A is the parameter type and B is the return type.

All functions have an apply method, which is the method that applies, or invokes, the function.

```
Function1.apply(p: A): B
```

Thus, you can define a method that takes a function and invokes the function with the parameter 42:

```
def answer(f: Function1[Int, String]) = f.apply(42)
```

If an object has an apply method, you can invoke that method without explicitly calling apply by putting the parameter list just after the object:

```
def answer(f: Function1[Int, String]) = f(42)
```

The Scala compiler desugars f(42) to f.apply(42) so that syntactically, it looks like you're calling a function or method, but in reality, the apply method is being invoked. This makes your code look good, and it makes it look like a function is being passed and invoked.

The Scala compiler has lots more syntactic sugar related to functions and other common constructs. Scala has a shorthand for describing functions, so the following two descriptions are the same:

```
Function1[Int, String]
Int => String
```

The latter conveys a lot more directly that the parameter is a function that takes an Int and returns a String:

```
def answer(f: Int => String) = f(42)
```

The syntactic sugar for the apply method works on any class that has an apply method:

```
class Ap {
  def apply(in: Int) = in.toString
}
scala> val a = new Ap
scala> a(44)
```

```
res67: java.lang.String = 44
```

If a class has an update method, Scala also adds sugar to the update method. An update method that takes two parameters will be called when the compiler parses an assignment:

```
class Up {
  def update(k: Int, v: String) = println("Hey: "+k+" "+v)
}
scala> val u = new Up
scala> u(33) = "Hello"
```

```
Hey: 33 Hello
```

Scala's Array and HashMap classes use update for setting values. This mechanism provides a way for your classes to have the same features as Scala library classes. The update mechanism works with different parameter counts from one on up:

```scala
scala> class Update {
  def update(what: String) = println("Singler: "+what)
  def update(a: Int, b: Int, what:String) = println("2d update")
}
defined class Update

scala> val u = new Update
```

```
u: Update = Update@17d6c1
```

```scala
scala> u() = "Foo"
```

```
Singler: Foo
```

```scala
scala> u(3, 4) = "Howdy"
```

```
2d update
```

Scala's syntactic sugar makes writing understandable code much easier. And it helps deliver on the interoperability promise with Java: knowing what the sugar translates to can help in developing Java code that plays nicely with Scala and in adapting Java libraries that may lack source code.

Case Classes

Scala has a mechanism for creating classes that have the common stuff filled in. Most of the time, when I define a class, I have to write the toString, hashCode, and equals methods.[5]

---

5. These methods are defined in Java's Object class. According to Joshua Bloch in *Effective Java* (Prentice Hall, 2008), it's best practice to define these methods so the instances can be used in hash tables and printed.

These methods are boilerplate. Scala provides the case class mechanism for filling in these blanks as well as support for pattern matching. A case class provides the same facilities as a normal class, but the compiler generates toString, hashCode, and equals methods (which you can override). Case classes can be instantiated without the use of the new statement. By default, all the parameters in the case class's constructor become properties on the case class. Here's how to create a case class:

```
case class Stuff(name: String, age: Int)
```

You can create an instance of Stuff without a new (you can use new if you want):

```
scala> val s = Stuff("David", 45)
```

```
s: Stuff = Stuff(David,45)
```

The case class's toString method does the right thing:

```
scala> s.toString
```

```
res70: String = Stuff(David,45)
```

Stuff's equals method does a deep comparison:

```
scala> s == Stuff("David", 45)
```

```
res72: Boolean = true
```

```
scala> s == Stuff("David", 43)
```

```
res73: Boolean = false
```

And the instance has properties:

```
scala> s.name
```

```
res74: String = David
```

```
scala> s.age
```

```
res75: Int = 45
```

If you want to write your own class that does the same thing as a case class, it would look like the following:

```scala
class Stuff(val name: String, val age: Int) {
  override def toString = "Stuff("+name+","+age+")"
  override def hashCode = name.hashCode + age
  override def equals(other: AnyRef) = other match {
    case s: Stuff => this.name == s.name && this.age == s.age
    case _ => false
  }
}

object Stuff {
  def apply(name: String, age: Int) = new Stuff(name, age)
  def unapply(s: Stuff) = Some((s.name, s.age))
}
```

Case classes also come in handy for pattern matching, a topic we'll explore in the next subsection.

Basic Pattern Matching

Scala's pattern matching allows you to construct very complex tests in very little code. Pattern matching is like Java's switch statement, but you can test against almost anything, and you can even assign pieces of the matched value to variables. Like everything in Scala, pattern matching is an expression, so it results in a value that may be assigned or returned. The most basic pattern matching is like Java's switch, except there is no break in each case as the cases do not fall through to each other. This example matches the number against a constant, but with a default:

```
44 match {
  case 44 => true // if we match 44, the result is true
  case _ => false // otherwise the result is false
}
```

Like C#, you can match against a String:

```
"David" match {
  case "David" => 45 // the result is 45 if we match "David"
  case "Elwood" => 77
  case _ => 0
}
```

You can pattern match against case classes. Case classes provide a particularly good set of pattern-matching semantics. In this case, we are matching against a Stuff instance with name == David and age == 45 in a declarative form:

```
Stuff("David", 45) match {
  case Stuff("David", 45) => true
  case _ => false
}
```

We can test the name but accept any age:

```
Stuff("David", 45) match {
  case Stuff("David", _) => "David"
  case _ => "Other"
}
```

And we can extract the age field into the howOld variable:

```
Stuff("David", 45) match {
  case Stuff("David", howOld) => "David, age: "+howOld
  case _ => "Other"
}
```

We can place a guard between the pattern and the => that adds further testing that cannot be described declaratively. In this case, we'll extract the age, and if it's less than 30, the result will be "young David", otherwise the result will be "old David":

```
Stuff("David", 45) match {
  case Stuff("David", age) if age < 30 => "young David"
  case Stuff("David", _) => "old David"
  case _ => "Other"
}
```

Pattern matching can also test whether the input is an instance of a given class and do the casting if it is:

```
x match {
  case d: java.util.Date => "The date in milliseconds is "+d.getTime
  case u: java.net.URL => "The URL path: "+u.getPath
  case s: String => "String: "+s
  case _ => "Something else"
}
```

The previous code replaces the following Java code:

```
if (x instanceOf Date) return "The date in milliseconds is "+((Date) x).getTime();
if (x instanceOf URL) return "The URL path: "+((URL) x).getPath();
if (x instanceOf String) return "String "+((String) x);
return "Something else";
```

if/else and while

It may seem strange that we're covering simple flow of control statements late in this section. It turns out that while is used very rarely in Scala code. if/else is used more frequently, a bit more frequently than the ternary operator is used in Java. The result of if and while expressions is always Unit. The result of if/else is based on the type of each part of the expression.

This will print "yes" if exp is true:

```
if (exp) println("yes")
```

Like Java, an if expression may have a multiline code block:

```
if (exp) {
  println("Line one")
  println("Line two")
}
```

if/else behaves like the ternary operator in Java:

```
val i: Int = if (exp) 1 else 3
```

and either (or both) parts of the expression may have multiline code blocks:

```
val i: Int = if (exp) 1
else {
  val j = System.currentTimeMillis
  (j % 100L).toInt
}
```

while executes its code block as long as its expression evaluates to true, just like Java. In practice, using recursion, a method calling itself, provides more readable code and enforces the concept of transforming input to output rather than changing, mutating, variables. Recursive methods can be as efficient as a while loop.[6]

```
while (exp) println("Working...")
while (exp) {
  println("Working...")
}
```

The for comprehension

At first blush, Scala's for comprehension looks a lot like Java's for loop. However, they are significantly different. The basic form implements flow of control, executing the body one time for each value:

```
scala> for {i <- 1 to 3} println(i)
```

```
1
2
3
```

Scala's for comprehension allows for nesting of expressions. You don't have multiple for comprehensions nested in order to have nested expressions, thus there's an entire iteration of the inner variable, j, for each value of the outer variable, i.

```
scala> for {i <- 1 to 3
            j <- 1 to 3} println(i * j)
```

```
1
2
...
9
```

---

6. See http://en.wikipedia.org/wiki/Tail_recursion.

The for comprehension also supports guards:

```
scala> def isOdd(in: Int) = in % 2 == 1
isOdd: (Int)Boolean
scala> for {i <- 1 to 5 if isOdd(i)} println(i)
```

```
1
3
5
```

And the guards can be part of the expression nesting:

```
scala> for {i <- 1 to 5
            j <- 1 to 5 if isOdd(i * j)} println(i * j)
```

```
1
3
5
3
9
15
5
15
25
```

I primarily use the for comprehension to transform a collection or set of collections into a new collection. Let's define some data:

```
scala> val lst = (1 to 18 by 3).toList
```

```
lst: List[Int] = List(1, 4, 7, 10, 13, 16)
```

If the yield keyword introduces the for comprehension's body, the for comprehension returns a collection rather than simply calling the code block. Thus:

```
scala> for {i <- lst if isOdd(i)} yield i
```

```
res11: List[Int] = List(1, 7, 13)
```

And the nesting rules and guards work the same way:

```
scala> for {i <- lst; j <- lst if isOdd(i * j)} yield i * j
```

```
res12: List[Int] = List(1, 7, 13, 7, 49, 91, 13, 91, 169)
```

We've explored a little bit of the syntax of the for comprehension. In Chapter 3, we'll see how it can be used with a variety of collections to provide powerful, syntactically pleasing, concise data transformations.

throw, try/catch/finally, and synchronized

Throwing exceptions is the same in Scala and Java:

```
throw new Exception("Working...")
```

The try/finally construct is the same:

```
try {
  throw new Exception("Working...")
} finally {
  println("This will always be printed")
}
```

The try/catch construct is different. First, it's an expression that results in a value. This makes it possible to wrap a call in a try/catch and assign a default value if the call fails. Second, the exception is pattern matched in the catch block rather than having separate catch clauses for each different exception. Guards are legal in the patterns as well. Here's a basic try/catch expression:

```
try {
  file.write(stuff)
} catch {
  case e: java.io.IOException => // handle IO Exception
  case n: NullPointerException => // handle null pointer
}
```

Here's an example of calling Integer.parseInt and defaulting to 0 if an exception is thrown:

```
scala> try{Integer.parseInt("dog")} catch {case _ => 0}
```

```
res16: Int = 0
```

```
scala> try{Integer.parseInt("44")} catch {case _ => 0}
```

```
res17: Int = 44
```

To synchronize based on an instance, call the instance's synchronized method with a code block:

```
obj.synchronized {
  // do something that needs to be serialized
}
```

There's no synchronized modifier for methods. Synchronize a method this way:

```
def foo(): Int = synchronized {
  42
}
```

Comments

Scala comments are much like Java and C++ comments. Multiline comments are started with /* and ended with */.

```
/*
This is a multi-line comment
*/
```

A single-line comment is started with // and continues to the end of the line:

```
// This is a single line comment
```

In Scala, you can nest multiline comments:

```
/*
  This is an outer comment
  /* And this comment
     is nested
  */
  Outer comment
*/
```

We've gone through an overview of Scala's syntax. Now, let's contrast Scala with Java and Ruby.

Scala vs. Java vs. Ruby

Scala, Java, and Ruby are object-oriented languages. They share many similarities and some differences. In this section, we'll compare and contrast these popular languages.

Classes and Instances

Scala and Ruby are pure object-oriented languages. Everything in each language is an instance of a class. In Java, there are primitives and statics that are outside of the OO model. In Scala and Ruby, all operations on entities are via method calls. In Java, operators are treated differently and are not method calls. The uniformity of instances in Scala means that the developer does not have to perform special tests or to have different code paths to deal with primitive data types (int, char, long, and so on) The following is legal in Scala:

```
scala> 1.hashCode
```

```
res0: Int = 1
```

```
scala> 2.toString
```

```
res1: java.lang.String = 2
```

You can define a method that takes a function that transforms an Int to an Int:

```
scala> def with42(in: Int => Int) = in(42)
```

and pass a function that is applying the + method to 33:

```
scala> with42(33 +)
```

```
res4: Int = 75
```

At the language level, it's very convenient and easy on the brain and the design to have everything be uniform. Scala and Ruby's pure OO approach achieves this goal. As a side note, you may worry about performance. The Scala compiler optimizes operations on JVM primitives such that the performance of Scala code is nearly identical to the performance of Java code.

Traits, Interfaces, and Mixins

Every Java class, except Object, has a single superclass. Java classes may implement one or more interfaces. An interface is a contract that specifies the methods an implementing class must have. Java has interfaces. Interfaces define a contract for a given class. A class has zero or more interfaces. Interfaces define the methods that the class must implement. Parameters to a method call may be specifically defined as classes or interfaces. Interfaces provide a powerful mechanism for defining the contract that a given class must implement, requiring that a parameter to a method implement particular methods without specifying the concrete class of the parameter. This is the basis for dependency injection, using mocks in testing, and other abstraction patterns.

Scala has traits. Traits provide all the features of Java interfaces. However, Scala traits can contain method implementations and variables. Traits are a great way of implementing methods once and mixing those methods into all the classes that extend the trait.

Ruby has mixins, which are collections of methods that can be mixed into any class. Because Ruby does not have static typing and there is no way to declare the types of method parameters, there's no reason way to use mixins to define a contract like interfaces. Ruby mixins provide a mechanism for composing code into classes but not a mechanism for defining or enforcing parameter types.

Object, Static, and Singletons

In Java, a class can have static methods and data. In this way, there is a single point of access to the method, and there's no need to instantiate a class in order to access static methods. Static variables provide global access to the data across the JVM.

Scala provides a similar mechanism in the form of objects. Objects are implementations of the singleton pattern. There is one object instance per class loader. In this way, it's possible to have globally shared state. However, objects adhere to Scala's uniform OO model, and objects are instances of classes rather than some class-level constant. This allows objects to be passed as parameters.

Ruby has a singleton mixin that provides the singleton pattern in Ruby programs. In addition, Ruby also has class-level methods. In Ruby, you can add methods to the class. There is one instance of a class object per class in Ruby. You can add methods and properties to class objects, and those become globally available without instantiating an instance of the class. This provides another mechanism for sharing global state.

Functions, Anonymous Inner Classes, and Lambdas/Procs

The Java construct to pass units of computation as parameters to methods is anonymous inner classes. The use of anonymous inner classes was popularized with the Swing UI libraries. In Swing, most UI events are handled by interfaces that have one or two methods on them. The programmer passes the handlers by instantiating an anonymous inner class that has access to the private data of the enclosing class.

Scala's functions are anonymous inner classes. Scala functions implement a uniform API with the `apply` method being the thing that's invoked. The syntax for creating functions in Scala is much more economical than the three or four lines of boilerplate for creating anonymous inner classes in Java. Additionally, the rules for accessing variables in the local scope are more flexible in Scala. In Java, an anonymous inner class can only access final variables. In Scala, a function can access and mutate `vars`.

Ruby has a collection of overlapping features that allow passing blocks, Procs, and lambdas as parameters to methods. These constructs have subtle differences in Ruby, but at their core, they are chunks of code that reference variables in the scope that they were created. Ruby also parses blocks such that block of code that are passed as parameters in method calls are syntactically identical to code blocks in `while` and `if` statements.

Scala has much in common with Ruby in terms of an object model and function passing. Scala has much in common with Java in terms of uniform access to the same code libraries and static typing. It's my opinion that Scala has taken the best of both Java and Ruby and blended these things together in a very cohesive whole.

Summary

We've covered a lot of ground in this chapter. We looked at how to build and run Scala programs. We walked through a bunch of Scala programs that demonstrated various aspects of Scala. We did an overview of Scala's syntax and basic constructs. In the next chapter, we're going to explore a bunch of Scala's data types that allow you to write powerful programs in very few lines of code with very few bugs.

CHAPTER 3

■■■

Collections and the Joy of Immutability

In this chapter, we're going to explore Scala's collections classes and how to use them. Most Scala collection classes are immutable, meaning that once they are instantiated, the instances cannot be changed. You're used to immutability, as Java `Strings` are immutable. The conjunction of collections being immutable and providing powerful iteration features leads to more concise, higher-performance code that does extremely well in multicore, multithreaded concurrency situations.

Thinking Immutably

In Java, the most commonly used types are immutable. Once an instance is created, it cannot be changed. In Java, `String`, `int`, `long`, `double`, and `boolean` are all immutable data types. Of these, `String` is a subclass of `Object`. Once a `String` is created, it cannot be changed. This has lots of benefits. You don't have to synchronize access to a `String`, even if it is shared by many threads, because there's no chance that it will be modified while another thread is accessing it. You don't have to keep a private copy of a `String` in case another method modifies it out from under you. When you pass `String` and other immutable types around in a Java program, you don't have to be defensive about using the instance. You can store it without fear that another method or thread will `toLowerCase` it.

Using immutable data structures means less defensive programming, fewer defects, and, in most cases, better performance. So, you ask, why doesn't Java have a lot more immutable data structures?

There are two ends of the programming spectrum: the how end and the what end. Assembly language is at the far end of the how part of the spectrum. When you program in assembly language, you direct the CPU to move bytes around memory, perform arithmetic operations and tests, and change the program counter. These directions—imperatives if you will—direct the computer's operation (in other words, we tell it how to do its tasks). C is a thin layer on top of assembly language and continues to be a language oriented toward directing the steps that the CPU will take.

Spreadsheets are far at the what end of the spectrum. Spreadsheets contain formulas that define the relationship between cells (so we tell the computer what we want to do). The order of evaluating the cells, the cells that are calculated based on changes in other cells, and so on, are not specified by the user but are inferred by the spreadsheet engine based on the relationships among the cells (the computer does the how part for us). In a C program, one always thinks about changing memory. In a spreadsheet (which is a program; Excel is the most popular programming language in the world), one thinks about altering input (changing nonformula cells) and seeing the output (what is recalculated).

Java evolved from imperative roots and spouted mostly mutable data structures in its standard libraries. The number of mutable classes in `java.util.*` far outnumber the immutable classes. By default, variables in Java are mutable, and you have to explicitly declare them as `final` if you want them to be assign-once. Despite that I've written a couple of commercial spreadsheets,[1] and should have understood the benefits of the functional "what" approach, until I spent a lot of time with Scala, I did not think about immutable data structures. I thought about flow of control. It took over a year of practicing immutability and avoiding flow-of-control imperatives in my code before I really grokked immutability and what-oriented coding. So, why doesn't Java have more immutable data structures? Because it's not obvious that Java needs them until you code with them for a while, and very few Java developers I know spent a lot of time with Lisp, ML, or Haskell. But immutability is better.

With a good garbage collector like the one in the JVM, immutable data structures tend to perform better than mutable data structures. For example, Scala's `List`, which is an immutable linked list, tends to perform better than Java's `ArrayList` using real-world data. This advantage exists for a couple of reasons. `ArrayList` pre-allocates an internal array of 10 slots to put items in. If you store only two or three items in the `ArrayList`, seven or eight slots are wasted. If you exceed the default 10 slots, there's an O(n) copy operation to move the references from the old array to the new array. Contrast this with Scala's `List`, which is a linked list. Adding elements is a constant-time, O(1), operation. The only memory consumed for storing items is the number of items being stored. If you have hundreds of items or if you're going to do random access on the collection, an `Array` is a better way to store data. But, most real-world applications are moving two to five items around in a collection and accessing them in order. In this case, a linked list is better.

Immutable data structures are part of the formula for more stable applications. As you start thinking about immutable data structures, you also start reducing the amount of state that is floating around in your application. There will be less and less global state. There will be fewer things that can be changed or mutated. Your methods will rely less and less on setting global state or changing the state of parameters, and your methods will become more and more transformative. In other words, your methods will transform the

---

1. Mesa for NextStep, which is still available for Mac OS X (http://www.plsys.co.uk/mesa), and Mesa 2 for OS/2 and the Integer multiuser spreadsheet engine for the JVM.

input values to output values without referring to or modifying external state. These methods are much easier to test using automated test tools such as ScalaCheck. Additionally, they fail less frequently.

One common failure mode for mutable state programs is that a new team member changes program state in an unpredictable way. There may be some setters that create state for an object. It's implied (and probably quite logically) that once the object is handed off to the "do work" method and goes beyond a certain barrier, its setters are not to be called. But along comes a developer who doesn't know about the implied barrier and uses a setter that causes some program logic to fail.

At this point, you may be resisting and saying, "Ten million Java, C++, C, and C# developers can't be wrong." I thought that way when I first started coding in Scala. But I set some goals for myself to learn and understand immutability. Over time, I came to appreciate that many of the defects that I was used to dealing with in Javaland and Rubyland went away as I used more and more immutable data structures and worked to isolate the state in my application from the logic of my application.

Scala List, Tuple, Option, and Map Classes

Scala has a wide variety of collections classes. Collections are containers of things. Those containers can be sequenced, linear sets of items (e.g., List):

```
scala> val x = List(1,2,3,4)
```

```
x: List[Int] = List(1, 2, 3, 4)
```

```
scala> x.filter(a => a % 2 == 0)
```

```
res14: List[Int] = List(2, 4)
```

```
scala> x
```

```
res15: List[Int] = List(1, 2, 3, 4)
```

They may be indexed items where the index is a zero-based Int (e.g., Array) or any other type (e.g., Map).

```
scala> val a = Array(1,2,3)
```

```
a: Array[Int] = Array(1, 2, 3)
```

```
scala> a(1)
```

```
res16: Int = 2
```

```
scala> val m = Map("one" -> 1, "two" -> 2, "three" -> 3)
```

```
m: … Map[java.lang.String,Int] = Map(one -> 1, two -> 2, three -> 3)
```

```
scala> m("two")
```

```
res17: Int = 2
```

The collections may have an arbitrary number of elements or be bounded to zero or one element (e.g., Option). Collections may be strict or lazy.

Lazy collections have elements that may not consume memory until they are accessed (e.g., Range). Let's create a Range:

```
scala> 0 to 10
```

```
res0: Range.Inclusive = Range(0, 1, 2, 3, 4, 5, 6, 7, 8, 9, 10)
```

The nifty thing about Ranges is that the actual elements in the Range are not instantiated until they are accessed. So we can create a Range for all positive Integers but take only the first five elements. This code runs without consuming many gigabytes of RAM because only the elements that are needed are created.

```scala
scala> (1 to Integer.MAX_VALUE - 1).take(5)
```

```
res18: RandomAccessSeq[Int] = RandomAccessSeq(1, 2, 3, 4, 5)
```

Collections may be mutable (the contents of the reference can change) or immutable (the thing that a reference refers to is never changed). Note that immutable collections may contain mutable items.

In this chapter, we'll be focusing on List, Option, and Map. These immutable data structures form the backbone of most of the programs I write.

List[T]

Scala's List[T] is a linked list of type T. That means it's a sequential list of any type, including Java's primitives (Int, Float, Double, Boolean, Char) because Scala takes care of boxing (turning primitives into objects) for you. Internally, List is made up of a "cons" cell (the scala.:: class [yes, that's two colons]) with a tail that refers to another cons cell or the Nil object. It's easy to create a List:

```scala
scala> 1 :: 2 :: 3 :: Nil
```

```
res20: List[Int] = List(1, 2, 3)
```

The previous code creates three cons cells, each with an Int in it. Anything that looks like an operator with a : (colon) as the first character is evaluated right to left. Thus, the previous code is evaluated just like the following:

```scala
scala> new ::(1, new ::(2, new ::(3, Nil)))
```

```
res21: ::[Int] = List(1, 2, 3)
```

:: takes a "head" which is a single element and a "tail" which is another List. The expression on the left of the :: is the head, and the expression on the right is the tail. To create a List using ::, we must always put a List on the right side. That means that the right-most element has to be a List, and in this case, we're using an empty List, Nil.

We can also create a List using the List object's apply method (which is defined as def apply[T](param: T*): List[T], which translates to "the apply method of type T takes zero or more parameters of type T and returns a List of type T"):

```scala
scala> List(1,2,3)
```

```
res22: List[Int] = List(1, 2, 3)
```

The type inferencer is pretty good at figuring out the type of the List, but sometimes you need to help it along:

```scala
scala> List(1, 44.5, 8d)
```

```
res27: List[AnyVal] = List(1, 44.5, 8.0)
```

```scala
scala> List[Number](1, 44.5, 8d)
```

```
res28: List[java.lang.Number] = List(1, 44.5, 8.0)
```

If you want to prepend an item to the head of the List, you can use ::, which actually creates a new cons cell with the old list as the tail:

```scala
scala> val x = List(1,2,3)
scala> 99 :: x
```

```
res0: List[Int] = List(99, 1, 2, 3)
```

Note that the list referred to by the variable x is unchanged, but a new List is created with a new head and the old tail. This is a very fast, constant-time, O(1), operation.

You can also merge two lists to form a new List. This operation is O(n) where n is the number of elements in the first List:

```
scala> val x = List(1,2,3)
scala> val y = List(99, 98, 97)
scala> x ::: y
```

```
res3: List[Int] = List(1, 2, 3, 99, 98, 97)
```

Getting Functional

The power of List and other collections in Scala come when you mix functions with the collection operators. Let's say we want to find all the odd numbers in a List. It's easy:

```
scala> List(1,2,3).filter(x => x % 2 == 1)
```

```
res4: List[Int] = List(1, 3)
```

The filter method iterates over the collection and applies the function, in this case, an anonymous function, to each of the elements. If the function returns true, the element is included in the resulting collection. If the function returns false, the element is not included in the resulting collection. The resulting collection is the same type of collection that filter was invoked on. If you invoke filter on a List[Int], you get a List[Int]. If you invoke filter on an Array[String], you get an Array[String] back. In this case, we've written a function that performs mod 2 on the parameter and tests to see whether the result is 1, which indicates that the parameter is odd. There's a corresponding remove method, which removes elements that match the test function:

```
scala> List(1,2,3).remove(x => x % 2 == 1)
```

```
res5: List[Int] = List(2)
```

We can also write a method called isOdd and pass the isOdd method as a parameter (Scala will promote the method to a function):

```
scala> def isOdd(x: Int) = x % 2 == 1
```

```
isOdd: (Int)Boolean
```

```
scala> List(1,2,3,4,5).filter(isOdd)
```

```
res6: List[Int] = List(1, 3, 5)
```

`filter` works with any collections that contain any type. For example:

```
scala> "99 Red Balloons".toList.filter(Character.isDigit)
```

```
res9: List[Char] = List(9, 9)
```

In this case, we're converting a String to a List[Char] using the toList method and filtering the numbers. The Scala compiler promotes the isDigit static method on Character to a function, thus demonstrating interoperability with Java and that Scala methods are not magic.

Another useful method for picking the right elements out of a List is takeWhile, which returns all the elements until it encounters an element that causes the function to return false. For example, let's get all the characters up to the first space in a String:

```
scala> "Elwood eats mice".takeWhile(c => c != ' ')
```

```
res12: Seq[Char] = ArrayBuffer(E, l, w, o, o, d)
```

Contrast with Java

I grew up writing machine code and later assembly language. When I wrote this code, I was telling the machine exactly what to do: load this register with this value, test the value, branch if some condition was met, and so on. I directed the steps that the CPU took in order to perform my task. Contrast this with writing formula functions in Excel. In Excel, we describe how to solve some problem using the formula functions and cell addresses, and it's up to Excel to determine what cells need to be recalculated and the order for the recalculation.

Directing the machine's steps is termed imperative coding. Imperative coding describes, as we saw earlier, the "how." Writing functions describing the "what"—the goal to be achieved—and allowing the computer to figure out the "how" is termed functional programming. Scala allows you to express code in a way that's further toward the functional end of the coding spectrum. Let's do a little exploring of the differences between the two.

Let's compare `filter` in Scala to the Java implementation shown in Listing 3-1.

Listing 3-1. *Java Implementation of Odd Filtering*

```
int[] x = {1,2,3,4,5};
ArrayList<Integer> res = new ArrayList<Integer>();
for (int v : x) {
  if (v % 2 == 1) res.add(new Integer(v));
}
```

In this code, the logic gets lost in the boilerplate. There are two pieces of logic that we are concerned with: what operation is being performed and the formula for that logic. When you first write the previous code, you know what the intent is. If you didn't comment your code with `// filtering the odd array elements`, you, or someone who picks up the code in a year or two, will have to puzzle about the meaning of the loop. The filter logic is buried in the middle of the code. Compare the Java code to the line of Scala code: `filter(v => v % 2 == 1)`, where the very essence of the operation appears in the code and nothing else.

As the complexity of your code increases and the time between writing and maintaining a particular module increases, removing boilerplate while maintaining visible business logic makes code easier to maintain and decreases defects. Let's look at the `takeWhile` Java translation in Listing 3-2.

Listing 3-2. *Java Implementation of Take Until First Space*

```
char[] x = "Elwood Eats Mice".toCharArray();
ArrayList<Character> res = new ArrayList<Character>();
for (char c : x) {
  if (c != ' ') res.add(new Character(c));
  else break;
}
```

Once again, one line in Scala expresses what takes many lines in Java. This example also demonstrates the mental shift that is common in imperative code. In one line in the loop, we mutate or change the `res` variable. In the next line, in the `else`, we have the `break` flow of control statement. Your brain has to think about two distinct concepts: "what variable is being mutated" and "what's the next statement the program is going to execute" all rolled into two lines.

When I was programming in Java, I never gave constructs like this a second thought. After programming in Ruby and Scala, I find that thinking about "what's happening to my data" and "what's the flow of control in my program" at the same time is very challenging. My brain has morphed into thinking about "what is business logic for transforming input to output?" I find this focuses me on the business logic task at hand. As we continue to explore transformations, let's look at other ways to transform a List.

Transformation

The map method on List (and Seq), transforms each element of a collection based on a function. For example, if we have a List[String] and want to convert it to all lowercase:

```scala
scala> List("A", "Cat").map(s => s.toLowerCase)
```

```
res29: List[java.lang.String] = List(a, cat)
```

We can shorten the function so the code reads:

```scala
scala> List("A", "Cat").map(_.toLowerCase)
```

```
res30: List[java.lang.String] = List(a, cat)
```

The number of elements in the returned collection is the same as the number of elements in the original collection, but the types may be different. If the function passed into map returns a different type, then the resulting collection is a collection of the type returned from the function. For example, we can take a List[String] and calculate the length of each String, which will result in a List[Int]:

```scala
scala> List("A", "Cat").map(_.length)
```

```
res31: List[Int] = List(1, 3)
```

map provides a very powerful and uniform way to transform data from one type to another. We can transform our Strings to lowercase, to a List of their length, and we can extract data from a collection of complex objects. For example, if we have a database query that returns records of type `Person` defined as having a `first` method that returns a `String` containing the person's first name, we can create a `List` of the first names of the people in the `List`:

```scala
scala> trait Person {def first: String }
```

```
defined trait Person
```

```scala
scala> val d = new Person {def first = "David" }
scala> val e = new Person {def first = "Elwood"}
scala> val a = new Person {def first = "Archer"}
scala> List(a, d, e).map(_.first)
```

```
res35: List[String] = List(Archer, David, Elwood)
```

Or, if we're writing a web app, we can create an `<li>` (an HTML list element) containing the first name of each `Person` in our `List`:

```scala
scala> List(a,d,e).map(n => <li>{n.first}</li>)
```

```
List(<li>Archer</li>, <li>David</li>, <li>Elwood</li>)
```

`List` also has a `sort` method, which takes a function that compares the two parameters. We can sort a `List[Int]`:

```scala
scala> List(99, 2, 1, 45).sort(_ < _)
```

```
res47: List[Int] = List(1, 2, 45, 99)
```

We can sort a List[String]:

```scala
scala> List("b", "a", "elwood", "archer").sort(_ < _)
```

```
res48: List[java.lang.String] = List(a, archer, b, elwood)
```

And we can sort longest to shortest:

```scala
scala> List("b", "a", "elwood", "archer").
       sort(_.length > _.length)
```

```
res49: List(archer, elwood, a, b)
```

We can combine the operations. Let's update our Person trait:

```scala
trait Person {
    def age: Int
    def first: String
    def valid: Boolean
}
```

Now we can write the code shown in Listing 3-3 to find all the valid Person records, sort by age, and return the first names.

Listing 3-3. *First Name of Valid Persons, Sorted by Age*

```scala
def validByAge(in: List[Person]) =
  in.filter(_.valid).
  sort(_.age < _.age).
  map(_.first)
```

Transformation vs. Mutation

While sometimes you may do complex logic like this in the database, other times you may have a collection of records in memory and you need to perform different transformations on those records. Let's, once again, compare the Scala code in Listing 3-3 to the Java implementation in Listing 3-4.

Listing 3-4. *Java Implementation of First Name of Valid Persons, Sorted by Age*

```java
public ArrayList<String> validByAge(ArrayList<Person> in) {
  ArrayList<Person> valid = new ArrayList<Person>();
  for (Person p: in) {
    if (p.valid()) valid.add(p);
  }

  Person[] people = valid.toArray(new Person[0]);

 Arrays.sort(people, new Comparator<Person>() {
    public int compare(Person a, Person b) {
      return a.age() - b.age();
    } } );

  ArrayList<String> ret = new ArrayList<String>();

  for (Person p: people) {
    ret.add(p.first());
  }

  return ret;
}
```

Our code expanded from 4 lines to 16 lines (not including blank lines). While we can still discern the intent of the Java code, it requires mentally filtering out the boilerplate loops and looking inside them. You have to look past the how in order to understand the what. On the other hand, even the Scala beginner should be able to read the lines in the Scala code to understand the meaning. We even see a hint of functional programming in the Java code with the construction of Comparator, which consumes four lines of code rather than Scala's one line of code.

Interestingly, under the covers, Scala is creating anonymous inner classes for each of the functions and passing them to filter, map, and sort. Just as it makes sense in Java not to have lots of sorting routines floating around code, so there's a set of sort methods (and other helper methods) on Arrays, Scala puts the looping constructs into map, filter, and so on as well so that your code contains more logic and less boilerplate.

Reduxio

Scala has other abstractions for common collections operations. reduceLeft allows you to perform an operation on adjacent elements of the collection where the result of the first operation is fed into the next operation. For example, if we want to find the biggest number in a List[Int]:

```scala
scala> List(8, 6, 22, 2).reduceLeft(_ max _)
```

```
res50: Int = 22
```

In this case, reduceLeft takes 8 and 6 and feeds them into our function, which returns the maximum value of the two numbers: 8. Next, reduceLeft feeds 8 (the output of the last iteration) and 22 into the function, resulting in 22. Next, reduceLeft feeds 22 and 2 into the function, resulting in 22. Because there are no more elements, reduceLeft returns 22.

We can use reduceLeft to find the longest word:

```scala
scala> List("moose", "cow", "A", "Cat").
       reduceLeft((a, b) => if (a.length > b.length) a else b)
```

```
res41: java.lang.String = moose
```

Because Scala's if expression works like Java's ternary operator, the if in the previous code returns a if it's longer than b. We can also find the shortest word:

```scala
scala> List("moose", "cow", "A", "Cat").
       reduceLeft((a, b) => if (a.length < b.length) a else b)
```

```
res42: java.lang.String = A
```

reduceLeft will throw an exception on an Nil (empty) List. This is correct behavior as there is no way to apply the function on the members of the List as a Nil List has no elements.

foldLeft is similar to reduceLeft, but it starts with a seed value. The return type of the function and the return type of foldLeft must be the same type as the seed. The first example is summing up List[Int]:

```scala
scala> List(1,2,3,4).foldLeft(0) (_ + _)
```

```
res43: Int = 10
```

In this case, the seed value is 0. Its type is Int. foldLeft feeds the seed and the first element of the List, 1, into the function, which returns 1. Next, foldLeft feeds 1 (the result of the previous iteration) and 2 (the next element) into the function, resulting in 3. The process continues, and the sum of the List[Int] is generated: 10. We can generate the product of the List the same way:

```scala
scala> List(1,2,3,4).foldLeft(1) (_ * _)
```

```
res44: Int = 24
```

But because the return type of foldLeft is the type of the seed, not the type of the List, we can figure out the total length of a List[String]:

```scala
scala> List("b", "a", "elwood", "archer").foldLeft(0)(_ + _.length)
```

```
res51: Int = 14
```

I find that sometimes I need to work with more than one collection at a time. For example, if we want to generate the List of products of the numbers from 1 to 3:

```scala
scala> val n = (1 to 3).toList
```

```
n: List[Int] = List(1, 2, 3)
```

```
scala> n.map(i => n.map(j => i * j))
```

```
res53: List[List[Int]] = List(List(1, 2, 3), List(2, 4, 6), List(3, 6, 9))
```

We have nested map invocations, and that results in a List[List[Int]]. In some cases, this may be what we want. In other cases, we want the results in a single List[Int]. In order to nest the map operations but flatten the results of nested operations, we use the flatMap method:

```
scala> n.flatMap(i => n.map(j => i * j))
```

```
res58: List[Int] = List(1, 2, 3, 2, 4, 6, 3, 6, 9)
```

Look Ma, No Loops

So far, we've written a bunch of code that manipulates collections without explicit looping. By passing functions, that is, logic, to methods that control the looping, we let the library writers define the looping, and we define the logic in our app. However, syntactically, nested map, flatMap, and filter can get ugly. For example, if we want to find the product of the odd numbers from 1 to 10 times the even numbers from 1 to 10, we could write the following:

```
scala> def isOdd(in: Int) = in % 2 == 1
scala> def isEven(in: Int) = !isOdd(in)
scala> val n = (1 to 10).toList
scala> n.filter(isEven).flatMap(i => n.filter(isOdd).map(j => i * j))
```

```
res60: List[Int] = List(2, 6, 10, 14, 18, … 10, 30, 50, 70, 90)
```

Scala provides the `for` comprehension, which provides syntactically pleasing nesting of `map`, `flatMap`, and `filter`. We can convert the nested statements from the previous example into a syntactically pleasing statement:

```
scala> for {i <- n if isEven(i); j <- n if isOdd(j)} yield i * j
```

```
res59: List[Int] = List(2, 6, 10, 14, 18, … 10, 30, 50, 70, 90)
```

The `for` comprehension is not a looping construct but is a syntactic construct that the compiler reduces to `map`, `flatMap`, and `filter`. In fact, the two lines

```
n.filter(isEven).flatMap(i => n.filter(isOdd).map(j => i * j))
```

and

```
for {i <- n if isEven(i); j <- n if isOdd(j)} yield i * j
```

result in the same bytecode. The `for` comprehension can be used with any class, including user-generated classes, that implement `map`, `flatMap`, `filter`, and `foreach`. This means you can create your own classes that work with the `for` comprehension.

`Lists` also work well with Scala's pattern matching and recursive programming. We'll be exploring pattern matching in depth in Chapter 5. For this example, pattern matching is a lot like Java's `switch` statement, but it can be used to compare things that are more complex than `Ints`, and Scala's pattern matching allows you to match some elements and extract, or capture, others into variables.

The pattern-matching syntax is the same as `List` construction syntax. For example, if we are matching against `List[Int]`, `case 1 :: Nil =>` will match `List(1)`. `case 1 :: 2 :: Nil =>` will match `List(1,2)`. `case 1 :: rest =>` will match any `List` that starts with 1 and will put the tail of the `List` into the variable `rest`.

Our example will convert a `List[Char]` of Roman numerals to their Arabic numeral equivalent. The code matches the `List` to a series of patterns. Based on the matched pattern, a value is returned. The patterns are matched in order of appearance. However, the compiler may optimize the patterns by eliminating duplicate tests.[2] The code to convert from Roman numerals to `Int` is in Listing 3-5.

---

2. You can see exactly how Scala turns patterns into code by typing **scalac -print FileName.scala**. This will cause the Scala compiler to emit desugared code that looks strangely like Java code.

Listing 3-5. *Roman Numerals*

```
def roman(in: List[Char]): Int = in match {
    case 'I' :: 'V' :: rest => 4 + roman(rest)
    case 'I' :: 'X' :: rest => 9 + roman(rest)
    case 'I' :: rest => 1 + roman(rest)
    case 'V' :: rest => 5 + roman(rest)
    case 'X' :: 'L' :: rest => 40 + roman(rest)
    case 'X' :: 'C' :: rest => 90 + roman(rest)
    case 'X' :: rest => 10 + roman(rest)
    case 'L' :: rest => 50 + roman(rest)
    case 'C' :: 'D' :: rest => 400 + roman(rest)
    case 'C' :: 'M' :: rest => 900 + roman(rest)
    case 'C' :: rest => 100 + roman(rest)
    case 'D' :: rest => 500 + roman(rest)
    case 'M' :: rest => 1000 + roman(rest)
    case _ => 0
}
```

case 'I' :: 'V' :: rest => 4 + roman(rest) tests the first two characters, and if they are IV, the method returns 4 plus the Roman numeral conversion of the rest of the List[Char]. If the test falls through to case _ => 0, there are no more Roman numerals, 0 is returned, and there's no more recursion—no more calls back into the roman() method. Without explicit looping or length testing or explicit branching logic, we've written a concise, readable method.

Scala's List and other sequential collections provide powerful ways to define business logic in a concise, maintainable way. In the next section, we're going to explore Tuples, which are fixed-length collections where each element can be a different type.

Tuples

Have you ever written a method that returns two or three values? Let's write a method that takes a List[Double] and returns the count, the sum, and the sum of squares returned in a three-element Tuple, a Tuple3[Int, Double, Double]:

```
def sumSq(in: List[Double]): (Int, Double, Double) =
    in.foldLeft((0, 0d, 0d))((t, v) =>  (t._1 + 1, t._2 + v, t._3 + v * v))
```

The sumSq method takes a List[Double] as input and returns a Tuple3[Int, Double, Double]. The compiler desugars (Int, Double, Double) into Tuple3[Int, Double, Double]. The compiler will treat a collection of elements in parenthesis as a Tuple. We seed the foldLeft with (0, 0d, 0d), which the compiler translates to a Tuple3[Int, Double, Double]. The function takes two parameters: t and v. t is a Tuple3, and v is a Double. The function returns a new Tuple3 by adding 1 to the first element of the Tuple, adding v to the second element of the Tuple, and adding the square of v to the third element of the Tuple. Using Scala's pattern matching, we can make the code a little more readable:

```
def sumSq(in: List[Double]) : (Int, Double, Double) =
   in.foldLeft((0, 0d, 0d)){
   case ((cnt, sum, sq), v) =>  (cnt + 1, sum + v, sq + v * v)}
```

You can create Tuples using a variety of syntax:

```
scala> Tuple2(1,2) == Pair(1,2)
scala> Pair(1,2) == (1,2)
scala> (1,2) == 1 -> 2
```

The last example, 1 -> 2, is a particularly helpful and syntactically pleasing way for passing pairs around. Pairs appear in code very frequently, including name/value pairs for creating Maps.

Map[K, V]

A Map is a collection of key/value pairs. Any value can be retrieved based on its key. Keys are unique in the Map, but values need not be unique. In Java, Hashtable and HashMap are common Map classes. The default Scala Map class is immutable. This means that you can pass an instance of Map to another thread, and that thread can access the Map without synchronizing. The performance of Scala's immutable Map is indistinguishable from the performance of Java's HashMap.

We can create a Map:

```
scala> var p = Map(1 -> "David", 9 -> "Elwood")
```

```
p: … Map[Int,String] = Map(1 -> David, 9 -> Elwood)
```

We create a new Map by passing a set of Pair[Int, String] to the Map object's apply method. Note that we created a var p rather than a val p. This is because the Map is immutable, so when we alter the contents on the Map, we have to assign the new Map back to p.

We can add an element to the Map:

```
scala>  p + 8 -> "Archer"
```

```
res4: … Map[Int,String] = Map(1 -> David, 9 -> Elwood, 8 -> Archer)
```

But we haven't changed the immutable Map:

```scala
scala> p
```

```
res5: … Map[Int,String] = Map(1 -> David, 9 -> Elwood)
```

In order to update p, we have to assign the new Map back to p:

```scala
scala> p = p + 8 -> "Archer"
```

or:

```scala
scala> p += 8 -> "Archer"
```

And we can see that p is updated:

```scala
scala> p
```

```
res7: Map[Int,String] = Map(1 -> David, 9 -> Elwood, 8 -> Archer)
```

We can get elements out of the Map:

```scala
scala> p(9)
```

```
res12: java.lang.String = Elwood
```

What happens when we ask for an element that doesn't exist?

```scala
scala> p(88)
```

```
java.util.NoSuchElementException: key not found: 88
```

This is mighty inconvenient. If you try to get an element that's not in the Map, you get an exception. That's kind of jarring. So far, we haven't seen much in Scala that results in exceptions being thrown, but it makes logical sense. If you request something that doesn't exist, that's an exceptional situation. Java's Map classes handle this situation by returning null, which has two drawbacks. First, you have to null-test the result of every Map access. Second, it means you can't store a null in a Map. Scala has a kinder and gentler mechanism for dealing with this situation. The get() method on Map returns an Option (Some or None) that contains the result:

```
scala> p.get(88)
```

```
res10: Option[java.lang.String] = None
```

```
scala> p.get(9)
```

```
res11: Option[java.lang.String] = Some(Elwood)
```

You can return a default value if the key is not found:

```
scala> p.getOrElse(99, "Nobody")
```

```
res55: java.lang.String = Nobody
```

```
scala> p.getOrElse(1, "Nobody")
```

```
res56: java.lang.String = David
```

We can also use flatMap with Options to find all the values with keys between 1 and 5:

```
scala> 1 to 5 flatMap(p.get)
```

```
res53: Seq.Projection[java.lang.String] = RangeG(David)
```

In this case, we create a range of numbers from 1 to 5. We `flatMap` this collection, passing in a function, `p.get`. Wait, you say, `p.get` isn't a function, it's a method, but you didn't include the parameter. Scala is very cool, because if it's expecting a function with parameters of a particular type and you pass a method that takes those parameters, Scala will promote the method with its missing parameters to a function. We'll explore `Options` in the next subsection.

Let's continue exploring `Map`. We can remove elements from our `Map`:

```scala
scala> p -= 9
scala> p
```

```
res20: Map[Int,String] = Map(1 -> David, 8 -> Archer)
```

We can test the `Map` to see whether it contains a particular key:

```scala
scala> p.contains(1)
```

```
res21: Boolean = true
```

We can operate on the collection of keys. We get a collection of keys from our `Map` and use `reduceLeft` to find the largest key:

```scala
scala> p.keys.reduceLeft(_ max _)
```

```
res22: Int = 8
```

And we can use `reduceLeft` on the collection of values to find the largest `String`:

```scala
scala> p.values.reduceLeft((a, b) => if (a > b) a else b)
```

```
res23: java.lang.String = David
```

We can test whether any of the values contains the letter "z":

```
scala> p.values.exists(_.contains("z"))
```

```
res28: Boolean = false
```

You can also add a bunch of elements to a Map using the ++ method:

```
scala> p ++= List(5 -> "Cat", 6 -> "Dog")
```

```
p: Map[Int,String] = Map(1 -> David, 8 -> Archer, 5 -> Cat, 6 -> Dog)
```

And you can remove a bunch of keys with the -- method:

```
scala> p --= List(8, 6)
```

```
res40: Map[Int, String] = Map(1 -> David, 5 -> Cat)
```

Maps are Scala collections and have collection manipulation methods. This means we can use methods including map, filter, and foldLeft. One of the tricky parts of using Java's immutable collections is iterating over the collection and simultaneously removing elements. In my code, I have to create an accumulator for the keys I'm going to remove, loop over the collection, find all the keys to remove, and then iterate over the collection of keys to remove and remove them from the collection. Not only that, but I frequently forget how brittle Hashtable is and inevitably forget this sequence and get some nasty runtime errors. In Scala, it's much easier. But there's a simpler way to remove unwanted elements from a Map:

```
def removeInvalid(in: Map[Int, Person]) = in.filter(kv => kv._2.valid)
```

Pretty cool, huh? Map has a filter method that works just like List's filter method. The kv variable is a Pair representing the key/value pair. The filter method tests each key/value pair by calling the function and constructs a new Map that contains only the elements that passed the filter test.

Let's finish up our exploration of some of Scala's immutable data types by examining Option.

Option[T]

Option[T] provides a container for zero or one element of a given type. Option provides a very powerful alternative to Java's null. An Option[T] can be either Some[T] or None. None is an object. There is a single instance of None in your Scala program, so it's kind of like null. But None has methods on it, so you can invoke map, flatMap, filter, foreach, and so on no matter whether you have Some or None.

Let's say we have a method that retrieves a record from the database based on a primary key:

```
def findPerson(key: Int): Option[Person]
```

The method will return Some[Person] if the record is found but None if the record is not found. We can then build a method that returns the age from the primary key:

```
def ageFromKey(key: Int): Option[Int] = findPerson(key).map(_.age)
```

If the record is found in the database, ageFromKey will return Some[Int], otherwise it will return None. We can cascade mapping/flatMapping of Option without explicitly testing for None. For example, let's say we have a Map that contains parameters passed as part of a web request and a couple of helper methods. Let's make a start implementing this:

```
scala> import java.lang.{Boolean => JBool}
```

This imports java.lang.Boolean but renames it locally to JBool so it doesn't conflict with Scala's Boolean class.

```
scala> def tryo[T](f: => T): Option[T] = try {Some(f)} catch {case _ => None}
```

We define a method that wraps an operation in a try/catch block. If the operation succeeds, we wrap the result in a Some instance, otherwise return None.

```
scala> def toInt(s: String): Option[Int] = tryo(s.toInt)
scala> def toBool(s: String) = tryo(JBool.parseBoolean(s))
```

We define methods that convert String to Int or Boolean. If the String can be converted, Some will be returned, otherwise None will be returned.

With these helpers, we can define our method that converts from the parameters to a Person instance. This is shown in Listing 3-6.

Listing 3-6. *Convert a Map to a Person*

```
def personFromParams(p: Map[String, String]): Option[Person] =
  for {name <- p.get("name")
       ageStr <- p.get("age")
       age <- toInt(ageStr)
       validStr <- p.get("valid")
       valid <- toBool(validStr)}
    yield new Person(name, age, valid)
```

In my code, any method that can logically fail (e.g., looking something up in a Map, converting a String to an Int) returns an Option. It is up to the calling code to determine what to do. Let's compare this to the Java implementation shown in Listing 3-7.

Listing 3-7. *Java Implementation of Convert a Map to a Person*

```
public Person personFromParams(Map<String, String> p) {
  try {
    if (!p.containsKey("name")) return null;
    String name = p.get("name");
    if (!p.containsKey("age")) return null;
    String ageStr = p.get("age");
    int age = Integer.parseInt(ageStr);
    if (!p.containsKey("valid")) return null;
    String validStr = p.get("valid");
    bool valid = Boolean.parseBoolean(validStr);
    return new Person(name, age, valid);
  } catch (Exception e) {
    return null;
  }
}
```

The Java code has to explicitly test each key. This increases the number of lines of code and reduces the readability. The Java code has multiple return paths. This makes it more difficult to understand under what conditions the code will continue to flow. At a glance, it's difficult to determine the conditions under which the method will return non-null.

Option has some methods to allow chaining. For example, if the parameter name that maps to "age" used to be called "years", we can express the code as ageStr <- p.get("age") orElse p.get("years"). If p.get("age") returns None, p.get("years") will be called. You can chain orElse just like chaining || in the if conditional. The right side of the orElse expression will be evaluated only if the left side is None.

You can retrieve the contents of an Option with the get method:

```
scala> Some(3).get
```

```
res57: Int = 3
```

But be careful, because if the Option is None, an exception will be raised:

```
scala> None.get
```

```
java.util.NoSuchElementException: None.get
```

Like Map, Option has a getOrElse method that returns a default value if the contents are undefined:

```
scala> Some(3).getOrElse(44)
```

```
res59: Int = 3
```

```
scala> None.getOrElse(44)
```

```
res60: Int = 44
```

Option is a very useful class for passing or returning values that may or may not be defined. Because Option has map, flatMap, filter, and foreach methods, it can be used in for comprehensions. Option provides a great way to avoid null problems and has methods that work conveniently with other Scala collections.

Wrapping Up List, Tuple, Map, and Option

We've covered a lot of ground in this section. We've seen some of Scala's foundation collection classes and the methods that allow for simple and powerful manipulation of these collections. These classes form the basis for much of my development. They also form the basis for other classes in Scala. For web development, XML is a very important mechanism for data exchange. Scala's immutable collections form the basis for Scala's XML support.

XML Creation and Manipulation

Scala has language-level support for defining XML constants. XML in Scala is immutable, just like `Strings` in Java. This means you can cache XML without worrying about copying it so it's not modified out from under you. In this section, we'll explore creating XML, parsing XML, and mutating XML. I'm covering XML in this chapter because it's an immutable data structure and because Scala treats XML as a collection on `Nodes`, so it gives us a chance to explore some more of the cool collections stuff we've been working on.

XML in Your Scala Code

Scala has XML literals built into the language syntax, just like Java has `String` literals built in. That means you can write

```
scala> <b>Hello World</b>
```

```
res0: scala.xml.Elem = <b>Hello World</b>
```

You can include attributes:

```
scala> <b id="greeting">Hello World</b>
```

```
res1: scala.xml.Elem = <b id="greeting">Hello World</b>
```

And the XML can span multiple lines:

```
scala> <b id="greeting">
       <span>Hello</span> World!
       </b>
```

```
res2: scala.xml.Elem =
<b id="greeting">
        <span>Hello</span> World!
        </b>
```

The XML elements can contain prefixes:

```
scala> <ns:b>Hello World from a namespace</ns:b>
```

```
res0: scala.xml.Elem = <ns:b>Hello World from a namespace</ns:b>
```

You can even have prefixes on the attributes:

```
scala> <b ns:hi='hello'>Hello</b>
```

```
res12: scala.xml.Elem = <b ns:hi="hello">Hello</b>
```

You can assign XML to a variable:

```
scala> val x = <b>Hello World!</b>
```

```
x: scala.xml.Elem = <b>Hello World!</b>
```

Scala represents XML as a Seq[Node], and Node is a superclass of NodeSeq, which is a subclass of Seq[Node]. That means all the collections methods that we've been exploring are available on XML collections including map, flatMap, filter, and foreach. This also means that XML can be used in for comprehensions. We'll explore that in the next subsection.

We can define a len method that takes a Seq of any type and returns the length:

```
scala> def len(seq: Seq[_]) = seq.length
```

```
len: (Seq[_])Int
```

and call it with an XML literal:

```
scala> len(<b>Hello</b>)
```

```
res1: Int = 1
```

Or we can call it with the XML variable x we defined previously:

```
scala> len(x)
```

```
res2: Int = 1
```

Or we can call it with a List[Int]:

```
scala> len(List(1,2,3))
```

```
res11: Int = 3
```

The ability to dynamically create XML in Scala is far more powerful than the ability to dynamically create Strings. Scala code can be embedded in any attribute or element body to dynamically render XML. For example, let's define a method that returns the current milliseconds as a String:

```
scala> def now = System.currentTimeMillis.toString
```

```
now: java.lang.String
```

We can call the now method from the attribute definition to add a time attribute:

```
scala> <b time={now}>Hello World</b>
```

```
res3: scala.xml.Elem = <b time="1230678511390">Hello World</b>
```

Attributes can be defined with Scala expressions of type String, NodeSeq, and Option[NodeSeq]. We did an example of String previously. Option[NodeSeq] in an attribute definition is very powerful. If the Option is None, the attribute will not be included in the resulting XML, but if the Option is Some, then the attribute will be included.

An example will help illustrate. Let's define a method that tests Long for being odd:

```
scala> def isOdd(in: Long) = in % 2L == 1L
```

```
isOdd: (Long)Boolean
```

Next we import Scala's XML package. XML literals are language-level, but the library that allows you to manipulate the literals must be imported.[3]

```
scala> import scala.xml._
import scala.xml._
```

We define the oddTime method, which will return Some[NodeSeq] if the time is odd and return None if it's even:

```
scala> def oddTime: Option[NodeSeq] = System.currentTimeMillis match {
       case t if isOdd(t) => Some(Text(t.toString))
       case _ => None
       }
```

```
oddTime: Option[scala.xml.NodeSeq]
```

And we can see that the time attribute is only included when the time is odd:

```
scala> <b time={oddTime}>Sometimes</b>
```

```
res6: scala.xml.Elem = <b time="1230679058437">Sometimes</b>
```

```
scala> <b time={oddTime}>Sometimes</b>
```

---

3. The Class class in Java is language-level, but we must explicitly import java.lang.reflect.* because Method is in that package rather than in java.lang.*.

```
res7: scala.xml.Elem = <b time="1230679061015">Sometimes</b>
```

```
scala> <b time={oddTime}>Sometimes</b>
```

```
res8: scala.xml.Elem = <b>Sometimes</b>
```

You can also generate tags, text, cdata, and so on from Scala code:

```
scala> <b>The time is {new java.util.Date}</b>
res4: scala.xml.Elem = <b>The time is Tue Dec 30 15:09:09 PST 2008</b>
```

If your embedded Scala code returns a NodeSeq, the NodeSeq will be embedded directly. If your Scala expression returns anything else, that thing will be converted to a scala.xml.Text node by calling toString on the thing.

Using map, we can convert from a given type to XML that's embedded:

```
scala> <stuff>
         {(1 to 3).map(i => <v id={i.toString}>#{i}</v>)}
         </stuff>
```

```
res0: scala.xml.Elem =
<stuff>
         <v id="1">#1</v><v id="2">#2</v><v id="3">#3</v>
         </stuff>
```

One thing to be careful about is making sure your if expressions have an else. The type of an if expression without an else is Unit, which converts to an empty String:

```
scala> <b>{if (true) "dogs"}</b>
```

```
res14: scala.xml.Elem = <b></b>
```

That's not what we expected, but this is:

```
scala> <b>{if (true) "dogs" else ""}</b>
```

```
res15: scala.xml.Elem = <b>dogs</b>
```

```
scala> <b>{if (false) "dogs" else ""}</b>
```

```
res16: scala.xml.Elem = <b></b>
```

Scala correctly escapes characters from your Scala expressions:

```
scala> <b>{"Hello & Goodbye"}</b>
```

```
res3: scala.xml.Elem = <b>Hello &amp; Goodbye</b>
```

```
scala> <b attr={"Hello < Zoo"}/>
```

```
res6: scala.xml.Elem = <b attr="Hello &lt; Zoo"></b>
```

So you don't have to worry about escaping XML characters. This is generally the right thing, but if you're trying to embed a script in your XML, it might not be the right thing:

```
scala> val info = """
       var x = "";
       if (true && false) alert('Woof');
       """
```

```
scala> <script>{info}</script>
```

```
res4: scala.xml.Elem =
<script>
       var x = &quot;&quot;;;
       if (true &amp;&amp; false) alert('Woof');
       </script>
```

You can use `PCData` to embed unescaped characters in your XML:

```
scala> <script>{PCData(info)}</script>
```

```
res5: scala.xml.Elem =
<script><![CDATA[
        var x = "";
        if (true && false) alert('Woof');
        ]]></script>
```

Scala's built-in XML support makes creating XML a breeze. Because the XML data structures are immutable, they can be shared and cached without concern that another thread or method may change the XML. As a side note, when I do browser-side HTML manipulation, I always have to be concerned about inserting some nodes into other nodes because the insertion causes parent node references to be changed. This means that if I had inserted the nodes elsewhere, they'll be unceremoniously removed from the old place to be inserted into the new place. This means I have to copy the entire node structure each time I do an insert, which is an $O(n)$ operation. With Scala's immutable XML data structures, I only have to change from the insertion point to the root node, an $O(\log n)$ operation.

Now that we've seen how to create XML in Scala, let's see how to parse and manipulate XML.

Parsing XML

Creating XML in Scala is done at the language level. The compiler needed to be changed to support XML literals. Parsing XML in Scala is all done at the library level. Let's explore XML parsing in combination with Scala's collection support. First, let's make sure the `scala.xml` package is imported:

```
scala> import scala.xml._
```

```
import scala.xml._
```

Next, let's grab some well-formed XML from the Web:

```
scala> val xml = XML.load("http://demo.liftweb.net/")
```

```
xml: scala.xml.Elem =
<html xmlns="http://www.w3.org/1999/xhtml"...
```

Next, let's find all the <a> tags in the document:

```
scala> xml \\ "a"
```

```
res6: scala.xml.NodeSeq = <a shape="rect" ...
```

The \\ (double backslash) operator finds all the tags with the given label in the document. The \ (single backslash) operator finds all the tags with the given label that are direct children of the current tag.

How many <a> tags on the page?

```
scala> (xml \\ "a").length
```

```
res7: Int = 25
```

OK, that's pretty cool. And note that the results of the using \ and \\ are Seq, so all the standard collection operations apply, including the for comprehension. Also, if the first character of the query String is an @, the query is performed against the attributes in the tag. Let's find all the <a> tags that refer to external resources:

```
scala> (xml \\ "a").map(_ \ "@href").map(_.text).filter(_ startsWith "http:")
```

```
res11: Seq[String] = ArrayBuffer(http://liftweb.net, http://scala-lang.org, ...
```

How many is that?

```
scala> (xml \\ "a").filter(n => (n \ "@href").text.startsWith("http:")).length
```

```
res9: Int = 8
```

Perhaps the code is easier to read in a `for` comprehension:

```scala
scala> val refs = for {a <- xml \\ "a"
      ext <- a \ "@href" if ext.text startsWith "http:"}
      yield ext.text
```

```
refs: Seq[String] = ArrayBufferRO(http://liftweb.net, ...)
```

How many?

```scala
scala> refs.length
```

```
res10: Int = 8
```

In combination with Scala's collection methods, we can do more fun stuff with XML. We can traverse the XML and sum the contents of particular tags. First, let's create some XML:

```scala
scala> val x2 = <x>{(1 to 3).map(i => <i>{i}</i>)}</x>
```

```
x2: scala.xml.Elem = <x><i>1</i><i>2</i><i>3</i></x>
```

Let's find all the `<i>` tags:

```scala
scala> x2 \ "i"
```

```
res26: scala.xml.NodeSeq = <i>1</i><i>2</i><i>3</i>
```

Now, get the text from each tag:

```scala
scala> (x2 \ "i").map(_.text)
```

```
res27: Seq[String] = ArrayBufferRO(1, 2, 3)
```

and convert to an `Int`:

```scala
scala> (x2 \ "i").map(_.text.toInt)
```

```
res28: Seq[Int] = ArrayBufferRO(1, 2, 3)
```

Finally, we sum up the collection:

```scala
scala> (x2 \ "i").map(_.text.toInt).foldLeft(0)(_ + _)
```

```
res29: Int = 6
```

Scala's XML parsing library provides a simple yet powerful way to traverse XML. Combined with XML's collection methods, it's very easy and concise to convert XML data to object representations. Next, let's see how to transform XML.

Modifying XML

Transforming flat data structures such as `List` or `Map` is pretty easy: you just take each element from the collection and return a transformed value. Transforming XML is more complex. XML contains many different types of elements. XML data is nested. A transformation may return many nodes for each transformed node.

In order to deal with these complexities, Scala provides a set of classes to help with XML transformation. These helpers can be found in the `scala.xml.transform` package. These helpers provide O(log n) cost for transformations. That means only the nodes that are changed and the direct path from the changed nodes to the root node are changed. This is far more efficient than the O(n) cost of copying an entire XML data structure if modifying the structure will cause unexpected results.

In order to transform XML, we need to create a rewrite rule. In this case, if the XML element contains the attribute `instruction` with the value `remove`, the node will be removed from the transformed XML. First, let's import the packages:

```scala
import scala.xml._
import scala.xml.transform._
```

Next, let's define a rule that removes the elements that have the remove instruction:

```
val removeIt = new RewriteRule {
    override def transform(n: Node): NodeSeq = n match {
      case e: Elem if (e \ "@instruction").text == "remove" => NodeSeq.Empty
      case n => n
    }
}
```

The RewriteRule overrides the transform method and pattern matches against an element that contains the remove instruction. If the pattern is matched, an empty node is returned. Otherwise the method returns the unmodified node. Let's create some test data:

```
val xmlBooks =
    <books instruction="update">
      <book instruction="remove" name="book1" status=""/>
      <book instruction="add" name="book2" status=""/>
    </books>
```

Next, let's transform xmlBooks using a RuleTransformer:

```
scala> new RuleTransformer(removeIt).transform(xmlBooks)
```

```
res0: Seq[scala.xml.Node] =
<books instruction="update">
<book instruction="add" status="" name="book2"></book>
</books>
```

The rule transformer applied our removeIt rule to the input and transformed this to the output. Let's create a RewriteRule to process the add instruction:

```
val addIt = new RewriteRule {
    override def transform(n: Node): NodeSeq = n match {
      case e: Elem if (e \ "@instruction").text == "add" =>
        new Elem(e.prefix, e.label,
          e.attributes.remove("instruction"),
          e.scope,
          transform(e.child) ++ <added>I added this</added> :_*)

      case n => n
    }
}
```

This `RewriteRule` matches nodes with the add `instruction` attribute. The method creates a new element with the same attributes, but removes the `instruction` attribute. It also transforms the child nodes and appends a child node.

Let's run this transformation:

```
scala> new RuleTransformer(addIt).transform(xmlBooks)
```

```
res2: Seq[scala.xml.Node] =
<books instruction="update">
  <book instruction="remove" status="" name="book1"></book>
  <book status="" name="book2"><added>I added this</added></book>
</books>
```

Note that the `book2` book has child nodes. We can run the transformation with both of the `RewriteRules`:

```
scala> new RuleTransformer(addIt, removeIt).transform(xmlBooks)
```

```
res3: Seq[scala.xml.Node] =
<books instruction="update">
  <book status="" name="book2"><added>I added this</added></book>
</books>
```

In this section, we've explored creating, parsing, and rewriting XML. Scala's awesome XML support makes it super-simple to write complex web-based applications. You can create Atom or RSS feeds in just a few lines that transform database records into the appropriate XML. You can parse incoming XML using the same constructs you use for other data sequences, which makes transformation from XML into data structures and objects easy and fast. Finally, Scala provides simple ways to transform XML.

In this chapter, we've explored Scala's immutable data types and the power and simplicity that they afford you. Next, let's see how we can use the immutable data structures in a highly concurrent situation. We're going to do concurrency without synchronization and see how immutability helps us out, big time.

Concurrency Without Synchronization

Writing multithreaded programs is a challenge. While simple data structures such as multithreaded queues or mailboxes are easy to write and relatively low in defects, most Java programs don't lend themselves to such simple abstractions. This is due in large part to passing around mutable data structures. Any data structure that can be changed without creating a new reference is a potential defect in a multithreaded application. The problem is exacerbated by the transitory nature of thread-related defects: it's hard to test for them.

There are many strategies for dealing with concurrency. One can synchronize everything, but this often leads to deadlocks because two threads are locking resources that depend on each other.

Another strategy is to copy everything that's passed to a thread. This strategy uses memory and CPU to work around the threading issue. Every time a resource is needed by a thread, the resource is copied for the thread's use. This means each Array, Hashtable, and so on that's requested by a given thread is copied. That way, the current thread does not have to synchronize the data.

Scala and immutable data structures offer another alternative. In this example, we're going to write a synchronize-free program (even the underlying data structures contain no synchronization) that has 2,000 threads each updating shared data every 100 milliseconds and a master thread that summarizes the shared data structure every second.

Create a file called Multics.scala and put the code from Listing 3-8 in it. We'll go through the code line by line after the listing.

Listing 3-8. *Multics.scala*

```scala
import java.util.concurrent.atomic.{AtomicReference => AtomR, AtomicLong}
import java.util.Random
import scala.collection.immutable.TreeHashMap

object Multics {
  type MT = Map[String, Int]

  val info: AtomR[MT] = new AtomR(TreeHashMap.empty)
  val clashCnt = new AtomicLong

  def main(argv: Array[String]) {
    runThread {
      repeatEvery(1000) {
        println("Clash Count: "+clashCnt+" Total: "+
                info.get.foldLeft(0)(_ + _._2))
    } }
```

```scala
  for (i <- 1 to 2000) runThread {
    var cnt = 0
    val ran = new Random
    val name = "K"+i

    doSet(info){old => old + (name -> 0)}
    repeatEvery(ran.nextInt(100)) {
      doSet(info){old => old + (name -> (old(name) + 1))}
      cnt = cnt + 1
      if (cnt != info.get()(name))
        throw new Exception("Thread: "+name+" failed")
    } }
  }

  def runThread(f: => Unit) =
  (new Thread(new Runnable {def run(): Unit = f})).start

  def doSet[T](atom: AtomR[T])(update: T => T) {
    val old = atom.get
    if (atom.compareAndSet(old, update(old))) ()
    else {
      clashCnt.incrementAndGet
      doSet(atom)(update)
    }
  }

  def repeatEvery(len: => Int)(body: => Unit): Unit = {
    try {
      while(true) {

        Thread.sleep(len)
        body
      }
    } catch {
      case e => e.printStackTrace; System.exit(1)
    }
  }
}
```

Let's go through the `Multics` code and see how it works.

```scala
import java.util.concurrent.atomic.{AtomicReference => AtomR, AtomicLong}
```

This imports Java's `AtomicReference` and renames it to `AtomR` and imports `AtomicLong`.

```
import java.util.Random
import scala.collection.immutable.TreeHashMap

object Multics {
```

This defines the object `Multics`.

```
  type MT = Map[String, Int]
```

Then we define a type, `MT`, that's a `Map[String, Int]`. Defining the type saves us some typing.

```
  val info: AtomR[MT] = new AtomR(TreeHashMap.empty)
```

`info` is the `AtomicReference` that holds the immutable `Map`. We can update the reference from any thread without synchronizing the `AtomicReference`. We use `TreeHashMap` as it has better characteristics for high write concurrency than Scala's default immutable `Map`.

```
  val clashCnt = new AtomicLong
```

`clashCnt` is an `AtomicLong` used the keep track of the number of times the threads clash when trying to write to `info`. `clashCnt` can be incremented without synchronization.

```
  def main(argv: Array[String]) {
    runThread {
     repeatEvery(1000) {
       println("Clash Count: "+clashCnt+" Total: "+
               info.get.foldLeft(0)(_ + _._2))
    } }
```

This code creates a new thread and starts it running the `repeatEvery` code. `repeatEvery(1000)` waits 1,000 milliseconds, then executes the body code. The body code prints the `clashCnt` and the sum of the values of all the `info` items. We can access the `Map` contained by `info` without synchronization because the `Map` is immutable, and we know it's not going to change out from under us. Next, we create 2,000 threads.

```
  for (i <- 1 to 2000) runThread {
    var cnt = 0
    val ran = new Random
    val name = "K"+i
```

This simply initializes the variables for this thread.

```
    doSet(info){old => old + (name -> 0)}
```

This initializes the count to zero for this thread. The doSet method takes a function that creates a new Map from the old Map.

```
repeatEvery(ran.nextInt(100)) {
```

This loops continuously, pausing a random amount between 0 and 100 milliseconds before each loop.

```
doSet(info){old => old + (name -> (old(name) + 1))}
```

This increments the count in info associated with this thread.

```
    cnt = cnt + 1
    if (cnt != info.get()(name))
      throw new Exception("Thread: "+name+" failed")
  } }
}
```

If the thread's local count doesn't match what's in info, there was a concurrency problem, so we throw an exception.

```
def runThread(f: => Unit) =
(new Thread(new Runnable {def run(): Unit = f})).start
```

This creates a new thread setting the run method to the function, f, and starts the thread. When the thread calls run, f will be invoked. This is an example of passing a block of code as a parameter.

```
def doSet[T](atom: AtomR[T])(update: T => T) {
  val old = atom.get
```

This does an atomic, synchronization-free update of atom. It reads the old value, passes it to the update function, and then tries to do an atomic set. If the atomic set succeeds (the old value has not changed during the update), then the set was successful because the mutation was done on the most recent version of the data. If compareAndSet fails, it increments the clashCnt and tries again.

```
    if (atom.compareAndSet(old, update(old))) ()
    else {
      clashCnt.incrementAndGet
      doSet(atom)(update)
    }
  }
```

The repeatEvery method creates a control structure. It takes two parameters, len and body. Both are call-by-name, which means that each time they're referenced in the body of repeatEvery, the code from the call site will be executed.

```
def repeatEvery(len: => Int)(body: => Unit): Unit = {
  try {
    while(true) {
```

This code repeats until an exception is thrown or the program terminates. It sleeps for len. Because len is call-by-name, the code that defines len will be executed each loop. Then the body is executed. If an exception is thrown, it will be caught and reported, and the program will terminate.

```
      Thread.sleep(len)
      body
    }
  } catch {
    case e => e.printStackTrace; System.exit(1)
  }
}
}
```

To run the code, save the file, type scalac Multics.scala to compile and scala Multics to run the program. You should see output like this:

>scala Multics

```
Clash Count: 50 Total: 13793
Clash Count: 283 Total: 41197
Clash Count: 351 Total: 78243
Clash Count: 389 Total: 115833
Clash Count: 434 Total: 153487
Clash Count: 483 Total: 191531
Clash Count: 524 Total: 229006
Clash Count: 561 Total: 266716
Clash Count: 1332 Total: 290839
Clash Count: 1387 Total: 327051
Clash Count: 1442 Total: 364706
Clash Count: 1486 Total: 402789
```

The Multics program demonstrates how to write synchronization-free code and the benefits of immutable data structures for multithreaded code.

Summary

In this chapter, we explored using Scala's immutable data structures to create powerful, flexible code that works well in multithreaded code. We saw how the methods of Scala's List class allow us to transform Lists and how the transformations highlight the business logic without the need for a lot of boilerplate. Scala's Tuples are syntactically pleasing and type-safe, and they make passing and returning things like name/value pairs super-simple and super-easy. Immutable Maps provide the same advanced ability to transform as Lists but in a convenient name/value form. The Option class is a great alternative to Java's overuse of null, and you can make very syntactically pleasing constructs with the for comprehension. We went on to see Scala's XML support, which is built on top of the immutability and manipulation constructs for Lists.

More important, we covered many of the basic constructs that you need to build Scala programs. We saw how functional, or transformation, code can be simultaneously more concise, more safe, and more performant than imperative code. We touched on passing functions and creating control structures. In the next chapter, we're going to dive deep into passing functions as parameters.

CHAPTER 4

Fun with Functions, and Never Having to Close That JDBC Connection

We saw Scala functions in action in the last chapter. Passing functions to `map` and `filter` allowed us to write code that was more readable and understandable. The looping was done in the method, allowing our application code to be cleaner and easier to maintain. In this chapter, we'll explore functions in more depth and learn about how functions allow us to encapsulate business logic and separate it from the imperative flow of control statements. We'll write our own control structures, including looping and automatic JDBC connection closers that will lead to cleaner, better code.

A Function Is an Instance

In Scala, functions are instances of classes. You can do anything to a function that you would do to an instance. We can create a function and assign it to a variable:

```
scala> val f: Int => String = x => "Dude: "+x
```

```
f: (Int) => String = <function>
```

We can call a method on the function:

```
scala> f.toString
```

```
res0: java.lang.String = <function>
```

We can compare the function:

```
scala> f == f
```

```
res2: Boolean = true
```

```
scala> f == 4
```

```
res7: Boolean = false
```

And we can apply the function to a parameter:

```
scala> f(55)
```

```
res9: String = Dude: 55
```

In this section, we're going to explore the basics of creating and managing function objects.

Passing Functions As Parameters

Functions are passed to methods and other functions just as with any other parameter. Let's define the w42 method that takes as a parameter a function that takes an Int and returns a String. The w42 method applies 42 to the function and returns the result:

```
scala> def w42(f: Int => String) = f(42)
```

```
w42: ((Int) => String)String
```

We can call the w42 method with the function variable that we declared in the last section:

```
scala> w42(f)
```

```
res10: String = Dude: 42
```

Let's define a method, fm, that takes an Int and returns a String and see the various ways to pass this method as a function to the w42 method.

```
scala> def fm(i: Int) = "fm "+i
```

```
fm: (Int)java.lang.String
```

We can create a function to pass to w42 by declaring the parameter i and its type, Int, and call fm with i:

```
scala> w42((i: Int) => fm(i))
```

```
res17: String = fm 42
```

But the Scala type inferencer can figure out that we're passing Int => String, so there's no reason to declare i's type:

```
scala> w42(i => fm(i))
```

```
res18: String = fm 42
```

We can further shorten things by passing fm and partially applying it. Partial application happens when we supply some but not all of the parameters required for the method or function.

```
scala> w42(fm _)
```

```
res19: String = fm 42
```

Or, we can just pass `fm` as if it were a variable, and the Scala compiler figures it out:

```
scala> w42(fm)
```

```
res20: String = fm 42
```

Despite the syntactic differences, the same function is being passed to `w42` in each of the last four examples. In fact, the desugared code looks just like passing an anonymous inner class to in Java:

```
scala> w42(new Function1[Int, String] {
        def apply(i: Int) = fm(i)
        })
```

```
res21: String = fm 42
```

You can pass functions that are multiline blocks of code. In this case, we're creating a range and then converting the range to a comma-separated `String` with `Seq`'s `mkString` method.

```
scala> w42 {
        i =>
        val range = 1 to i
        range.mkString(",")
        }
```

```
res11: String = 1,2,3,4,5,6,7, … ,40,41,42
```

Partial Application and Functions

Methods and functions are different things. In Scala, everything except a method is an instance; therefore methods are not instances. Methods are attached to instances and can be invoked on instances. Functions are instances that implement a FunctionNN trait, where NN is the number of parameters the function takes. There's nothing magic at runtime about functions. However, at compile time, there is plenty of syntactic sugar that makes the number of characters required to create a function very, very small.

Scala traces its roots to functional languages including ML and Haskell. In these languages, a function that takes two Ints and returns a String is the same as a function that takes an Int and returns a function that takes an Int and returns a String. Thus (Int, Int) => String and Int => Int => String are the same in Haskell but not in Scala. Haskell makes it easy to create a new function by applying the first parameter to a function that will return a new function that can then be passed around or applied. This is called partial application because some of the parameters are passed to the function rather than all the parameters being applied to the function. Scala requires a separate syntax to automatically generate partially applied functions.

In Scala, we can build partially applied functions out of methods:

```
scala> def plus(a: Int, b: Int) = "Result is: "+(a + b)
```

```
plus: (Int,Int)java.lang.String
```

```
scala> val p = (b: Int) => plus(42, b)
```

```
p: (Int) => java.lang.String = <function>
```

In the previous code, we've turned a method that takes two Int parameters into a function that supplies the first parameter, in this case 42, but that needs a second Int parameter to fulfill the requirements for the application of plus. In this case, p is a partial application of plus, and we can complete the application by supplying an Int to p.

It turns out that partial application of functions is a common thing. It allows you to build up functions based on values in a given scope and allows for better code reuse. Scala provides syntax to make it easier to build partially applied functions. Parameters can be specified in different parenthesis groups:

```scala
scala> def add(a: Int)(b: Int) = "Result is: "+(a + b)
```

```
add: (Int)(Int)java.lang.String
```

And we call methods defined this way with the following syntax:

```scala
scala> add(1)(2)
```

```
res27: java.lang.String = Result is: 3
```

At this point, you may be thinking that this syntax is not particularly pleasing. As they say in late-night TV ads, "But wait, there's more!" With this syntax, you can pass code blocks as parameters separately from other parameters. We'll see more of this when we create control structures.

```scala
scala> add(1){
        val r = new java.util.Random
        r.nextInt(100)
        }
```

```
res28: java.lang.String = Result is: 63
```

Ah, this might be useful after all. It also allows you to easily promote a method to a partially applied function very easily:

```scala
scala> w42(add(1))
```

```
res24: String = Result is: 43
```

You can also create a function by partially applying a method and converting this into a function:

```
scala> def f2 = add(1) _
```

```
f2: (Int) => java.lang.String
```

And that function can be passed to another method:

```
scala> w42(f2)
```

```
res25: String = Result is: 43
```

Functions and Type Parameters

Methods can have type parameters. Type parameters define the type of other parameters or of the method's return value. Note that functions cannot take type parameters. The parameter and return types of a function must be defined when the function is created.

We saw some type parameters in Chapter 2 when we saw how the return type of the function passed to map alters the type of the returned List. We can define a method, t42, which takes a type parameter, T, and a function that takes an Int and returns a T. The t42 method returns a T:

```
scala> def t42[T](f: Int => T): T = f(42)
```

```
t42: [T]((Int) => T)T
```

So, we can pass our f function, Int => String, and t42 returns a String:

```
scala> t42(f)
```

```
res29: String = Dude: 42
```

But, if we pass in a function that returns an Int, t42 returns an Int:

```
scala> t42(1 +)
```

```
res30: Int = 43
```

And we can pass in a function that returns a List[Int]:

```
scala> val intList: Int => List[Int] = i => (1 to i).toList
```

```
intList: (Int) => List[Int] = <function>
```

```
scala> t42(intList)
```

```
res31: List[Int] = List(1, 2, 3, 4, 5, … , 39, 40, 41, 42)
```

In the previous examples, we did not have to explicitly define the type parameter because the type inferencer figured it out for us. However, you could explicitly define it:

```
scala> t42[Int](1 +)
```

```
res30: Int = 43
```

Functions Bound to Variables in Scope

Functions are bound to the variables in the scope in which the function is created. This can come in very handy as it allows you to carry state around with them. For example, let's create a variable, foo, and assign it a value:

```
scala> val foo = "dog"
```

```
foo: java.lang.String = dog
```

Next, let's create a function that takes a function that references the variable:

```
scala> val whoTo = (s: String) => s+" "+foo
```

```
whoTo: (String) => java.lang.String = <function>
```

Let's call the function:

```
scala> whoTo("I love my")
```

```
res39: java.lang.String = I love my dog
```

```
scala> whoTo("I walk my")
```

```
res40: java.lang.String = I walk my dog
```

Functions can be bound to vars and vals. Functions can even modify vars. First, let's define the var strs which is a List[String]:

```
scala> var strs: List[String] = Nil
```

```
strs: List[String] = List()
```

Next, let's create a function that takes a String and returns a String but has the side effect of modifying the strs variable by prepending s to the list:

```
scala> val strF = (s: String) => {strs ::= s; s+" Registered"}
```

```
strF: (String) => java.lang.String = <function>
```

Let's call strF a couple of times:

```
scala> strF("a")
```

```
res0: java.lang.String = a Registered
```

```
scala> strF("b")
```

```
res1: java.lang.String = b Registered
```

Let's inspect strs:

```
scala> strs
```

```
res2: List[String] = List(b, a)
```

Cool. The side effect of calling strF is to update strs. Is this a local magical phenomenon or does it always work? Let's see:

```
scala> List("p", "q", "r").map(strF)
```

```
res3: List[java.lang.String] = List(p Registered, q Registered, r Registered)
```

Let's test strs:

```
scala> strs
```

```
res4: List[String] = List(r, q, p, b, a)
```

Yes, the strF function is still updating strs.

Putting Functions in Containers

Functions are instances, which means that whatever you can do with an instance, you can do with a function. Let's create a function, bf, which takes an Int and returns a function:

```
scala> def bf: Int => Int => Int = i => v => i + v
```

```
bf: (Int) => (Int) => Int
```

Next, let's create a sequence of 1 to 100 and map bf over the sequence:

```
scala> val fs = (1 to 100).map(bf).toArray
```

```
fs: Array[(Int) => Int] = Array(<function>, ...
```

We've got an Array[Int => Int], otherwise known as an array of functions that will convert an Int to an Int. Let's get the first element in the array and apply it to 1:

```
scala> fs(0)(1)
```

```
res34: Int = 2
```

The first element of the array was the 1 applied to the bf function. We applied 1 to this new function, and discover that 1 + 1 does equal 2. Does it work with other members of the array?

```
scala> fs(44)(3)
```

```
res35: Int = 48
```

It's theoretically cool that functions are instances that can be manipulated like any other instance. There are practical uses of putting functions in Maps and Lists. Functions represent blocks of code—instructions on how to do something that is within a particular context and that is bound to variables in a particular scope. The ability to bind functions to events, such as the user clicking a button on a screen, which may occur in the future, provides a powerful way to build interactive, event-based applications.

Functions and Interactive Applications

Callbacks are very common in interactive applications. For example, if a button is clicked, perform a particular action. Creating a callback in web applications is a particularly difficult task unless you've got powerful tools like the ones Scala gives you. Let's create a method that generates a random String that will serve as a globally unique identifier (GUID):

```
scala> def randomName = "I"+Math.abs((new java.util.Random).nextLong)
```

```
randomName: java.lang.String
```

Next, let's define a generic JavaScript trait. We need not flesh it out, but we can assume that it contains JavaScript commands that can be run in the browser:

```
scala> trait JavaScript
```

```
defined trait JavaScript
```

Next, let's create a Map to associate the GUID with a function that will generate some JavaScript:

```
scala> var callbacks: Map[String, () => JavaScript] = Map()
```

```
callbacks: Map[String,() => JavaScript] = Map()
```

Finally, we can create a method that registers the function and generates an HTML <button/>. When the button is clicked in the browser, an Ajax call will be made to the server, the function will be invoked, and the resulting JavaScript will be returned to the browser.

```
scala> def register(f: () => JavaScript) = {
       val name = randomName
       callbacks += name -> f
       <button onclick={"invokeSeverCall('"+name+"')"}>ClickMe</button>
       }
```

```
register: (() => JavaScript)scala.xml.Elem
```

When the user clicks the button, an Ajax HTTP request is generated with the GUID. The servlet looks up the GUID in the Map, and if the GUID is found, the function is invoked, and the resulting JavaScript is returned to the browser. The code looks like the following:

```
def handleAjax(guid: String): HttpResponse =
  functionMap.get(guid).map(f => f()) match {
    case Some(javaScript) => JavaScriptResponse(javaScript)
    case _ => Http404Response()
}
```

This code is a simplified version of what is done in the Lift Web Framework (http://liftweb.net). This code demonstrates a practical way that Scala and Lift abstract away the HTTP request/response cycle by associating a function with a client-side event. The developer writing code using this style gets to spend more brain cycles on the business logic of what to do when the user clicks the button and far fewer cycles worrying about the plumbing of servicing an HTTP request.

Building New Functions

So far, we've created simple functions and manipulated the function instances. However, we can also build functions from other functions. Functional composition provides the basis for a lot of cool things in Scala including the parser combinator, which we will explore in Chapter 8. But for now, let's see the difference between interpreting a series of commands and "compiling" a function that interprets them.

First, let's define a grammar. In our grammar, we have expressions, which can be constant values or named variables. Expressions can also be addition or multiplication of other expressions. Here's a collection of case classes that describes our grammar (recall that we covered case classes in Chapter 2):

```
sealed trait Expr
case class Add(left: Expr, right: Expr) extends Expr
case class Mul(left: Expr, right: Expr) extends Expr
case class Val(value: Int) extends Expr
case class Var(name: String) extends Expr
```

We can build expressions like 1 + 1, Add(Val(1), Val(1)), 3 * (1 + 1), Mul(Val(3), Add(Val(1), Val(1)), and a * 11, Mul(Var("a"), Val(11)). We can evaluate an expression by interpreting the expression:

```
def calc(expr: Expr, vars: Map[String, Int]): Int = expr match {
  case Add(left, right) => calc(left, vars) + calc(right, vars)
  case Mul(left, right) => calc(left, vars) * calc(right, vars)
  case Val(v) => v
  case Var(name) => vars(name)
}
```

Let's look at how this method works. expr is the expression to evaluate, and vars is a Map that contains our variables. We use pattern matching to determine what to do based on the case class. If expr is an Add, we extract the left and right parameters, which are themselves Exprs. We call calc to calculate the value of the left and right parameters and add the results. If expr is Mul, we do the same thing (except we multiply things rather than adding them). If expr is Val, we simply extract the value and return it. If expr is Var, we extract the name and return the lookup of the name in the vars Map.

We can turn this from a method call into a function. Having a function allows us to pass around the logic that the expression represents. It also means that we don't have to interpret the tree of Exprs each time. Let's see how we can compose a function based on the Expr.

```
def buildCalc(expr: Expr): Map[String, Int] => Int = expr match {
  case Add(left, right) =>
    val lf = buildCalc(left)
    val rf = buildCalc(right)
    m => lf(m) + rf(m)

case Mul(left, right) =>
    val lf = buildCalc(left)
    val rf = buildCalc(right)
    m => lf(m) * rf(m)

  case Val(v) => m => v

  case Var(name) => m => m(name)
}
```

The buildCalc method returns a function that can be passed to other functions. Also, the JVM can optimize the composed functions so that they perform better than the interpreted version. The performance of the composed function is better because there is no overhead associated with pattern matching each element. The function is evaluated by repeatedly calling the function's apply method. Thus, the cost of each node is one or two method dispatches rather than the cost of the pattern matching.

Let's turn to other ways that functions can help us improve performance and readability.

Call-by-Name, Call-by-Value, and General Laziness

In Java programs, when you call a method with parameters, the value of the parameters are all calculated before the method is called. Thus, in

```
foo(1 + 1, "A String".length());
```

the expressions 1 + 1 and "A String".length() are both evaluated before the call to foo is made. This is usually what we want. However, there are some cases when we want to parameters to be optionally evaluated or repeatedly evaluated. In these cases, Scala provides the call-by-name mechanism. There's no syntactic difference to the caller for call-by-name parameters.

The first example for call-by-name is the logging example. It's very computationally costly to calculate log messages simply to discard them if the message is not going to be logged. This is very common in Java code:

```
if (logger.level().intValue() >= INFO.intValue()) {
  logger.log(INFO, "The value is "+value);
}
```

In this code, we have to push the decision to evaluate logger.log(INFO, "The value is "+value); into the place where we call logger. This means we need to wrap the call to logger in an if statement. It would be much better from a coding perspective if the cost of evaluating the String to be logged were incurred only if the String is going to be logged *and* if the current log level is known to and tested by the code inside logger rather than in the call to logger. Call-by-name gives us the ability to delay the evaluation of the String to log only if that String will actually be logged.

In Scala, we can define a log method that takes the thing to log as call-by-name:

```
def log(level: Level, msg: => String) =
  if (logger.level.intValue >= level.intValue) logger.log(level, msg)
```

And you would call this code:

```
log(INFO, "The value is "+value)
```

The Scala version passes "The value is "+value as a function that is evaluated each time it is accessed in the log method. The log method will access it only if the log message is going to be printed. Your code is cleaner because you don't have to repeatedly test the log level, but it performs as well as the previous Java code that has the inline test.

In order to make something call-by-name, just put => before the type. So, foo(s: String) is call-by-reference, and foo(s: => String) is call-by-name.

You may be wondering how the code could possibly perform as well if a function object is being created and handed off to the log method. In the JVM, the cost of creating an object that never escapes the current thread and is very short-lived is zero or very near zero. The JVM may also inline the log method such that the test is performed without an actual method call. The result is that your code will run as quickly with the Scala code as it will with the Java code that has the repeated test for log level.

The first use of call-by-name is passing an expression that takes a long time to evaluate that may not be evaluated. The second use for call-by-name is the situation where we want to evaluate the expression many times in the target method, for example, if we want to evaluate an expression until some condition is met. That condition could be until the expression returns false or until the expression returns null. For example, we could collect all the Strings returned from an expression until we encounter a null:

```
def allStrings(expr: => String): List[String] = expr match {
  case null => Nil
  case s => s :: allStrings(expr)
}
```

We can test this method:

```
scala> import java.io._
```

```
import java.io._
```

```
scala> val br = new BufferedReader(new FileReader("foo.txt"))
```

```
br: java.io.BufferedReader = java.io.BufferedReader@2bfa91
```

```
scala> allStrings(br.readLine)
```

```
res0: List[String] = List(import scala.xml._, , object Morg {,…)
```

Each time the call-by-name parameter, expr, is accessed, it is applied. If it is passed as a parameter that is also call-by-name, it will be passed without evaluation. In the previous code, we pattern match against the application of expr. If it's null, we return an empty List, a Nil. If it's not null, we return a List that is the current String and the result of allStrings(expr).

Call-by-name is a very useful construct. In the next section, we'll use it to build complex control structures.

Build Your Own Control Structures

In this section, we'll use call-by-name variables and functions to create our own control structures. Scala has very limited control structures: try/catch/finally, if/else, and while. Most languages have a plethora of control structures including for, foreach, and so on. C# even has the using control structure. using provides an auto-close feature where the parameter passed to using will be closed when using's code block is exited. For example:

```
using (TextReader textReader = new StreamReader(filename))
{
  return textReader.ReadLine();
}
```

This provides a convenient mechanism to make sure that files, database connections, TCP/IP connections, and so on are closed without having to write a try/finally block for each thing you want to close.

Scala does not have a using statement, but we can write one. I'll show you all the code and then step through the pieces:

```
object Control {
  def using[A <: {def close(): Unit}, B](param: A)(f: A => B): B =
  try {
    f(param)
  } finally {
    param.close()
  }

  import scala.collection.mutable.ListBuffer
```

```
  def bmap[T](test: => Boolean)(block: => T): List[T] = {
    val ret = new ListBuffer[T]
    while(test) ret += block
    ret.toList
  }
}
```

Let's step through the code. First, we define the `Control` singleton object:

```
object Control {
```

Next, we define the `using` method. It takes two type parameters: `A` and `B`. The `B` type parameter is much like what we've seen in the past: it can be any type. We have put a structural type bound on `A`. `A` can be an instance of any class as long as that class has a `close` method on it. This is called structural typing. Scala allows you to define types based on their structure rather than their class. This is familiar to ECMAScript developers. It's also closer to the duck typing of Ruby and Python, but in the case of Scala, you have to declare the methods of the duck as part of the parameter. The `param` parameter is one of these `A` ducks that has a `close` method. The `f` parameter is something that takes the `A` and transforms it to a `B`.

```
  def using[A <: {def close(): Unit}, B](param: A)(f: A => B): B =
  try {
    f(param)
  } finally {
    param.close()
  }
```

The code is pretty simple. It wraps the function application in a `try`/`finally` block and makes sure that `param` is closed before the method returns. We could call the code like

```
using(new BufferedReader(otherReader)) {
  reader =>
  reader.readLine()
}
```

The next control statement we'll build is something that loops as long as a test is true. In each iteration, the method will collect the output of a pass-by-name value and append it to the list accumulator. First, let's import `ListBuffer` so we can accumulate the results:

```
import scala.collection.mutable.ListBuffer
```

Now we declare the Boolean Map, `bmap`, method. It takes `test` as a call-by-name parameter and `block`, the code block, as a call-by-name parameter. As long as the `test` results is `true`, the result of `block` will be appended to the `ret` accumulator. Finally, the accumulator is converted to a `List` and returned.

```scala
  def bmap[T](test: => Boolean)(block: => T): List[T] = {
    val ret = new ListBuffer[T]
    while(test) ret += block
    ret.toList
  }
}
```

We've built a couple of control structures. Now let's see how they work in real-world code.

JDBC Looping

In this section we'll apply the new control structures, using and bmap, to the real-world problem of performing a JDBC query, collecting the results, and closing the Statement and ResultSet. First, we'll write the code in Java and then see how it gets cleaner and more maintainable in Scala. Here's the Java code:

```java
import java.sql.*;
import java.util.ArrayList;

public class Person {
  private String name;
  private int age;
  private boolean valid;

  public Person(String n, int a, boolean v) {
    name = n;
    age = a;
    valid = v;
  }

  public static ArrayList<Person> findPeople(Connection conn)
    throws SQLException {
    Statement st = conn.createStatement();
    try {
      ResultSet rs = st.executeQuery("SELECT * FROM person");
      try {
        ArrayList<Person> ret = new ArrayList<Person>();
        while (rs.next()) {
          ret.add(new Person(rs.getString("name"),
                             rs.getInt("age"),
                             rs.getBoolean("valid")));
        }
```

```
      return ret;
    } finally {
      rs.close();
    }
  } finally {
    st.close();
  }
 }
}
```

The previous code is pretty straightforward. We define a Person class with a constructor. The class has a static method that queries the database for all of the person records. Let's see how the code looks in Scala.

First, let's define a Person class. In a single line, we define the class, its constructor, and its fields. It even gets toString, hashCode, and equals methods:

```
case class Person(name: String, age: Int, valid: Boolean)
```

Next, let's define a method, findPeople, that will take a JDBC connection and return a List[Person]. The code creates a Statement, executes a query on that Statement, and as long as there are more rows available on the ResultSet, a Person will be created. The method will close the ResultSet and Statement, and it will return the List[Person].

```
object Person {
  import Control._
  import java.sql._

  def findPeople(conn: Connection): List[Person] =
  using(conn.createStatement){st =>
    using (st.executeQuery("SELECT * FROM person")){rs =>
      bmap(rs.next){
        new Person(rs.getString("name"), rs.getInt("age"), rs.getBoolean("valid"))
      }
    }
  }
}
```

With all the boilerplate of try/finally, and so on, the Java code is much longer and more difficult to read. More important, if the developer forgets to write the try/finally block, the ResultSet or Statement may not be closed correctly, causing a hard-to-diagnose issue where the database runs out of resources. While this is something that can be caught in a code review, it's easier to have it built into the control structures.

In this example, we've used the generic control structures, using and bmap, to work with JDBC. We can use the same methods for file IO. In any case, Scala gives you the tools to make your code more concise, more understandable, and easier to maintain.

Summary

In this chapter, we explored creating and manipulating functions in Scala. In Chapter 3, we saw how passing functions to Scala library methods such as `List.map` and `List.filter` provided mechanisms for writing clear, understandable code with far less boilerplate than is required in Java code. We explored how to write the same kind of code so that you can abstract away the boilerplate of closing resources and collecting the calculations in loops.

In the next chapter, we're going to explore pattern matching, another cornerstone of the functional style of programming. We'll learn how to construct complex logic in a declarative format and how patterns are functions.

CHAPTER 5

■■■

Pattern Matching

So far, we've explored some of the basic functional cornerstones of Scala: immutable data types and the passing of functions as parameters. The third cornerstone of functional programming is pattern matching. At first glance, pattern matching looks like Java's switch statement. However, pattern matching provides a powerful tool for declaring business logic in a concise and maintainable way. Scala blends traditional functional programming pattern matching with object-oriented concepts to provide a very powerful mechanism for writing programs.

In this chapter, we're going to explore the basics of pattern matching. Then we're going to see how Scala's case classes bridge between object-oriented data encapsulation and function decomposition. Next, we'll see how Scala's pattern-matching constructs become functions that can be passed around and composed. Finally, we'll see how pattern matching provides a flexible alternative to the visitor pattern.

Basic Pattern Matching

Pattern matching, at its core, is a very complex set of if/else expressions and looks a lot like Java's switch statement. Let's start with a very simple example: calculating Fibonacci numbers:

```
def fibonacci(in: Int): Int = in match {
  case 0 => 0
  case 1 => 1
  case n => fibonacci(n - 1) + fibonacci(n - 2)
}
```

Let's write the same code in Java:

```
public int fibonacci(int in) {
  switch (in) {
    case 0:
      return 0;
```

```
    case 1:
      return 1;
    default:
      return fibonacci(in - 1) + fibonacci(in - 2);
  }
}
```

There is little difference between the Scala and Java versions. Note that there's no break statement between cases in Scala, where you need break or return at the end of the case in Java. Note also that the last case in Scala assigns the default value to the variable n. Pattern matching in Scala is also an expression that returns a value.

In Scala, we can have multiple tests on a single line:

```
case 0 | -1 | -2 => 0
```

That code corresponds to the following in Java:

```
case 0:
case -1:
case -2:
  return 0;
```

However, Scala allows guards to be placed in patterns to test for particular conditions that cannot be tested in the pattern declaration itself. Thus, we can write our Fibonacci calculator to return 0 if a negative number is passed in:

```
def fib2(in: Int): Int = in match {
  case n if n <= 0 => 0
  case 1 => 1
  case n => fib2(n - 1) + fib2(n - 2)
}
```

case n if n <= 0 => 0 is the first test in the pattern. The test extracts the value into the variable n and tests n to see whether it's zero or negative and returns 0 in that case. Guards are very helpful as the amount of logic gets more complex. Note that the case statements are evaluated in the order that they appear in the code. Thus, case n if n <= 0 => is tested before case n =>. Under the hood, the compiler may optimize the pattern[1] and minimize the number of tests, cache test results, and even cache guard results.

---

1. A huge thanks to David MacIver for improving Scala's pattern-matching code.

Matching Any Type

Like C#, Scala can pattern match against any type. Let's see how Scala pattern matching works with `Strings`:

```scala
def myMules(name: String) = name match {
  case "Elwood" | "Madeline" => Some("Cat")
  case "Archer" => Some("Dog")
  case "Pumpkin" | "Firetruck" => Some("Fish")
  case _ => None
}
```

The corresponding code in Java looks like the following:

```java
public String myMules(String name) {
  if (name.equals("Elwood") || name.equals("Madline")) {
    return "Cat";
  } else if (name.equals("Archer")) {
    return "Dog";
  } else if (name.equals("Pumpkin") || name.equals("Firetruck")) {
    return "Fish";
  } else {
    return null;
  }
}
```

If you're curious about how the Scala compiler expands a pattern into code, you can use the `-print` option in the Scala compiler. Create the `MyMules.scala` program:

```scala
object MyMules {
  def myMules(name: String) = name match {
    case "Elwood" | "Madeline" => Some("Cat")
    case "Archer" => Some("Dog")
    case "Pumpkin" | "Firetruck" => Some("Fish")
    case _ => None
  }
}
```

Compile it with the following line:

```
scalac -print MyMules.scala
```

The result follows:

```
package <empty> {
  final class MyMules extends java.lang.Object with ScalaObject {
    @remote def $tag(): Int = scala.ScalaObject$class.$tag(MyMules.this);
    def myMules(name: java.lang.String): Option = {
      <synthetic> val temp1: java.lang.String = name;
      if (temp1.==("Elwood"))
        body%0(){
          new Some("Cat")
        }
      else
        if (temp1.==("Madeline"))
          body%0()
        else
          if (temp1.==("Archer"))
            body%1(){
              new Some("Dog")
            }
          else
            if (temp1.==("Pumpkin"))
              body%2(){
                new Some("Fish")
              }
            else
              if (temp1.==("Firetruck"))
                body%2()
              else
                body%3(){
                  scala.None
                }
    };
    def this(): object MyMules = {
      MyMules.super.this();
      ()
    }
  }
}
```

More Pattern Matching

Patterns can match across different types in the same statement:

```scala
def test1(in: Any): String = in match {
  case 1 => "One"
  case "David" | "Archer" | Some("Dog") => "Walk"
  case _ => "No Clue"
}
```

The previous code introduces the _ as a wildcard pattern. This is consistent with Scala's use of the underscore as a wildcard in other contexts.

Testing Data Types

Pattern matching is a very powerful way to avoid explicit casting. In Java, there is a separation between the instanceof test and the casting operation. This often results in bugs when a block of test/cast code is copied and pasted. There's no compiler check that the instanceof test matches the cast, and it's not uncommon to have a mismatch between the test and the cast in Java code that's been copied and pasted. Let's write a method that tests an incoming Object to see whether it's a String, an Integer, or something else. Depending on what type it is, different actions will be performed.

```java
public String test2(Object in) {
  if (in == null) {
    return "null";
  }
  if (in instanceof String) {
    String s = (String) in;
    return "String, length " + s.length();
  }
  if (in instanceof Integer) {
    int i = ((Integer) in).intValue();
    if (i > 0) {
      return "Natural Int";
    }
    return "Another Int";
  }

  return in.getClass().getName();
}
```

The same code in Scala is shorter, and there's no explicit casting.

```
def test2(in: Any) = in match {
  case s: String => "String, length "+s.length
  case i: Int if i > 0 => "Natural Int"
  case i: Int => "Another Int"
  case a: AnyRef => a.getClass.getName
  case _ => "null"
}
```

The first line tests for a String. If it is a String, the parameter is cast into a String and assigned to the s variable, and the expression on the right of the => is returned. Note that if the parameter is null, it will not match any pattern that compares to a type. On the next line, the parameter is tested as an Int. If it is an Int, the parameter is cast to an Int, assigned to i, and the guard is tested. If the Int is a natural number (greater than zero), "Natural Int" will be returned. In this way, Scala pattern matching replaces Java's test/cast paradigm. I find that it's very, very rare that I do explicit testing and casting in Scala.

Case Classes

We saw case classes earlier in the book. They are classes that get toString, hashCode, and equals methods automatically. It turns out that they also get properties and extractors. Case classes also have properties and can be constructed without using new.

Let's define a case class:

```
case class Person(name: String, age: Int, valid: Boolean)
```

Let's create an instance of one:

```
scala> val p = Person("David", 45, true)
```

```
p: Person = Person(David,45,true)
```

You may use new to create a person as well:

```
scala> val m = new Person("Martin", 44, true)
```

```
m: Person = Person(Martin,44,true)
```

Each of the `Person` instances has properties that correspond to the constructor parameters:

```scala
scala> p.name
```

```
res0: String = David
```

```scala
scala> p.age
```

```
res1: Int = 45
```

```scala
scala> p.valid
```

```
res2: Boolean = true
```

By default, the properties are read-only, and the case class is immutable.

```scala
scala> p.name = "Fred"
```

```
<console>:7: error: reassignment to val
        p.name = "Fred"
```

You can also make properties mutable:

```scala
scala> case class MPerson(var name: String, var age: Int)
```

```
defined class MPerson
```

```
scala> val mp = MPerson("Jorge", 24)
```

```
mp: MPerson = MPerson(Jorge,24)
```

```
scala> mp.age = 25
scala> mp
```

```
res3: MPerson = MPerson(Jorge,25)
```

So far, this is just some syntactic sugar. How, you ask, does it work with pattern matching?

Pattern matching against case classes is syntactically pleasing and very powerful. We can match against our Person class, and we get the extractors for free:

```
def older(p: Person): Option[String] = p match {
  case Person(name, age, true) if age > 35 => Some(name)
  case _ => None
}
```

Our method matches against instances of Person. If the valid field is true, the age is extracted and compared against a guard. If the guard succeeds, the Person's name is returned, otherwise None is returned. Let's try it out:

```
scala> older(p)
```

```
res4: Option[String] = Some(David)
```

```
scala> older(Person("Fred", 73, false))
```

```
res5: Option[String] = None
```

```
scala> older(Person("Jorge", 24, true))
```

```
res6: Option[String] = None
```

Pattern Matching in Lists

As we saw in Chapter 3's Roman numeral example (Listing 3-5), Scala's pattern matching can also be applied to `List`s. Scala's `List` collection is implemented as a linked list where the head of the list is called a cons cell.[2] It contains a reference to its contents and another reference to the tail of the list, which may be another cons cell or the `Nil` object. `List`s are immutable, so the same tail can be shared by many different heads. In Scala, the cons cell is represented by the `::` case class. Perhaps you have just said, "Ah hah!" Creating a `List` is Scala is as simple as this:

```
1 :: Nil
```

`::` is the name of the method and the name of a case class. By keeping the creation method, `::`, and the case class name the same, we can construct and pattern match `List`s in a syntactically pleasing way. And as we've just seen, case classes can be used in pattern matching to either compare or extract values. This holds for `List`s as well and leads to some very pleasing syntax.

We construct a `List` with

```
scala> val x = 1
```

```
x: Int = 1
```

```
scala> val rest = List(2,3,4)
```

```
rest: List[Int] = List(2, 3, 4)
```

```
scala> x :: rest
```

```
res1: List[Int] = List(1, 2, 3, 4)
```

---

2. The naming of the cons cell traces its roots back to Lisp and came from the act of **cons**tructing a list. One **cons**tructs a list by linking a cons cell to the head of the list.

```
scala> (x :: rest) match { // note the symmetry between creation and matching
     case xprime :: restprime => println(xprime); println(restprime)
     }
```

```
1
List(2, 3, 4)
```

Then we can extract the head (x) and tail (rest) of the List in pattern matching.

Pattern Matching and Lists

Pattern matching and Lists go hand in hand. We can start off using pattern matching to sum up all the odd Ints in a List[Int].

```
def sumOdd(in: List[Int]): Int = in match {
  case Nil => 0
  case x :: rest if x % 2 == 1 => x + sumOdd(rest)
  case _ :: rest => sumOdd(rest)
}
```

If the list is empty, Nil, then we return 0. The next case extracts the first element from the list and tests it to see whether it's odd. If it is, we add it to the sum of the rest of the odd numbers in the list. The default case is to ignore the first element of the list (a match with the _ wildcard) and return the sum of the odd numbers in the rest of the list.

Extracting the head of a list is useful, but when pattern matching against List, we can match against any number of elements in the List. In this example, we will replace any number of contiguous identical items with just one instance of that item:

```
def noPairs[T](in: List[T]): List[T] = in match {
  case Nil => Nil
  case a :: b :: rest if a == b => noPairs(a :: rest)
    // the first two elements in the list are the same, so we'll
    // call noPairs with a List that excludes the duplicate element
  case a :: rest => a :: noPairs(rest)
    // return a List of the first element followed by noPairs
    // run on the rest of the List
}
```

Let's run the code and see that it does what we expect:

```
scala> noPairs(List(1,2,3,3,3,4,1,1))
```

```
res6: List[Int] = List(1, 2, 3, 4, 1)
```

Pattern matching can match against constants as well as extract information. Say we have a List[String] and we want to implement a rule that says that we discard the element preceding the "ignore" String. In this case, we'll use pattern matching to test as well as extract:

```
def ignore(in: List[String]): List[String] = in match {
  case Nil => Nil
  case _ :: "ignore" :: rest => ignore(rest)
    // If the second element in the List is "ignore" then return the ignore
    // method run on the balance of the List
  case x :: rest => x :: ignore(rest)
    // return a List created with the first element of the List plus the
    // value of applying the ignore method to the rest of the List
}
```

Let's compare this code to Java code that does the same thing. In the Scala code, the pattern matching takes care of length testing and other plumbing. Additionally, because the Scala code is recursive, there's no need for explicit looping or for setting up the accumulator. Looking at the Java code, there's a lot of boilerplate. The logic of incrementing the loop counter exists in different places, and the test (x < len - 1) is not intuitive. In fact, when I wrote the example, I got this test wrong; it wasn't until I ran the code that I discovered the problem.

```
public ArrayList<String> ignore(ArrayList<String> in) {
  ArrayList<String> ret = new ArrayList<String>();
  int len = in.size();
```

```
  for (int x = 0; x < len;) {
    if (x < len - 1 && in.get(x + 1).equals("ignore")) {
      x += 2;
    } else {
      ret.add(in.get(x));
      x++;
    }
  }

  return ret;
}
```

We've seen how to use pattern matching and Lists with extraction and equality testing. We can also use the class test/cast mechanism to find all the Strings in a List[Any]:

```
def getStrings(in: List[Any]): List[String] = in match {
  case Nil => Nil
  case (s: String) :: rest => s :: getStrings(rest)
  case _ :: rest => getStrings(rest)
}
```

However, the paradigmatic way of filtering a List[Any] into a List of a particular type is by using a pattern as a function. We'll see this in the "Pattern Matching As Functions" section.

In this section, we've explored how to do pattern matching. We've seen extraction and pattern matching with Lists. It may seem that List is a special construct in Scala, but there's nothing special about List in Scala. Let's look a little more at case classes.

Nested Pattern Matching in Case Classes

Case classes can contain other case classes, and the pattern matching can be nested. Further, case classes can subclass other case classes. For example, let's create the MarriedPerson subclass of Person:

```
case class MarriedPerson(override val name: String,
  override val age: Int,
  override val valid: Boolean,
  spouse: Person) extends Person(name, age, valid)
```

We've defined the class. Note that the override val syntax is ugly. It's one of the ugliest bits in Scala.

And let's create a new instance of MarriedPerson:

```
scala> val sally = MarriedPerson("Sally", 24, true, p)
```

```
sally: MarriedPerson = MarriedPerson(Sally,24,true,Person(David,45,true))
```

Let's create a method that returns the name of someone who is older or has a spouse who is older:

```
def mOlder(p: Person): Option[String] = p match {
  case Person(name, age, true) if age > 35 => Some(name)
  case MarriedPerson(name, _, _, Person(_, age, true))
    if age > 35 => Some(name)
  case _ => None
}
```

Let's see the new method in action:

```
scala> mOlder(p)
```

```
res7: Option[String] = Some(David)
```

```
scala> mOlder(sally)
```

```
res8: Option[String] = Some(Sally)
```

Scala's case classes give you a lot of flexibility for pattern matching, extracting values, nesting patterns, and so on. You can express a lot of logic in pattern declarations. Further, patterns are easy for people to read and understand, which makes code maintenance easier. And because Scala is statically typed, the compiler will help detect some code problems.

Examining the Internals of Pattern Matching

The next couple of paragraphs get into some gnarly parts of Scala. Let's write our own class that is nearly as syntactically pleasing as Scala's List. We will rely on a couple of syntactic features in Scala. The first is that Scala methods and classes can have operator characters as class names. The following are all valid method and class names: Foo, Foo_?, foo32, ?, ?:. The second is that methods that have a colon as their last character are evaluated right to left, rather than left to right. That means 3 :: Nil is desugared to Nil.::(3). Using these two features of Scala, let's define our own MList class that has the same pattern-matching beauty as Scala's List class. The code in this section must be compiled because there are circular class references. You cannot type this code at the REPL. Here's the whole listing:

```scala
class MList[+T] {
  def ?:[B >: T](x: B): MList[B] = new ?:(x, this)
}


case object MNil extends MList[Nothing]


case class ?:[T](hd: T, tail: MList[T]) extends MList[T]
```

First, let's define MList. It has a type of +T, which is part of Scala's type system, and it means that subclasses of MList have a covariant type.[3] Covariant means that T in subclasses of MList can be the same class or a superclass of T.

```scala
class MList[+T] {
  def ?:[B >: T](x: B): MList[B] = new ?:(x, this)
}
```

MList contains a single method, ?:, which is also the class name of the linked list cons cell. This allows chaining of constructing lists. Also, note that B, which is the type of the parameter, relates to T using the >: type relationship operator. This means that B must be the same class or a superclass of T. So, if you've got an MList[String] and you add an Int cell, the MList's type becomes the class that's the superclass of both: Any. If you have an MList[Number] and you add an Int, the list is still MList[Number].

Next, let's define the MNil singleton. This is an MList[Nothing]. Nothing is the subclass of every other class.[4] Because MList is covariant, MList[Nothing] can serve as a member of every MList. If we've got MNil and we call the ?: method with a String, because the superclass of the two is String, we add a String cell to MNil resulting in an MList[String].

```scala
case object MNil extends MList[Nothing]
```

---

3. Covariance and contravariance are scary terms and big concepts. We'll dive into them in Chapter 7.
4. It works best if you say it out loud.

Finally, let's define our cons cell. The cons cell holds the node and links to the tail of the list. The class name of the cons cell is ?:, which is the method name on MList that adds a new cell at the head of the list. The case class name ?: is the same as the method name ?: to unify the syntax of creating and pattern matching against the MList.

```
case class ?:[T](hd: T, tail: MList[T]) extends MList[T]
```

Finally, let's see how our new MList class looks in pattern matching:

```
def tryMList(in: MList[Any]) = in match {
  case 1 ?: MNil => "foo"
  case 1 ?: _ => "bar"
  case _ => "baz"
}
```

So, this demonstrates that there's no internal magic to support Scala's List class in pattern matching. You can write your own classes that are as syntactically pleasing as Scala's libraries.

Pattern Matching As Functions

Scala patterns are syntactic elements of the language when used with the match operator. However, you can also pass pattern matching as a parameter to other methods. Scala compiles a pattern match down to a PartialFunction[A,B], which is a subclass of Function1[A,B]. So a pattern can be passed to any method that takes a single parameter function. This allows us to reduce

```
list.filter(a => a match {
    case s: String => true
    case _ => false
})
```

to

```
list.filter {
  case s: String => true
  case _ => false
}
```

Because patterns are functions and functions are instances, patterns are instances. In addition to passing them as parameters, they can also be stored for later use.

In addition to Function1's apply method, PartialFunction has an isDefinedAt method so that you can test to see whether a pattern matches a given value. If you try to apply a PartialFunction that's not defined for the value, a MatchError will be raised. How is this useful?

If you're building a web application, you might have particular URLs that need special handling while others get handled in the default manner. The URL can be expressed as a List[String]. We can do the following:

```
def handleRequest(req: List[String])(
  exceptions: PartialFunction[List[String], String]): String =
  if (exceptions.isDefinedAt(req)) exceptions(req) else
  "Handling URL "+req+" in the normal way"
```

So, if the partial function exceptions (the pattern) matches the request req according to the isDefinedAt method, then we allow the request to be handled by the exceptions function. Otherwise, we do default handling. We can call handleRequest and handle any "api" requests by a separate handler:

```
handleRequest("foo" :: Nil) {
  case "api" :: call :: params => doApi(call, params)
}


def doApi(call: String, params: List[String]): String =
"Doing API call "+call
```

Partial functions can be composed into a single function using the orElse method.[5] So, we can define a couple of partial functions:

```
val f1: PartialFunction[List[String], String] = {
  case "stuff" :: Nil => "Got some stuff"
}


val f2: PartialFunction[List[String], String] = {
  case "other" :: params => "Other: "+params
}
```

And we can compose them:

```
val f3 = f1 orElse f2
```

And we can pass them into the handleRequest method:

```
handleRequest("a" :: "b" :: Nil)(f3)
```

---

5. Technically, combining multiple partial functions using orElse is not functional composition. A roomful of wicked smart functional developers at LShift (http://lshift.com) were unable to come up with a good name other than "functional smooshing."

In this way, Scala gives you a very nice, declarative way of handling complex filtering tasks. Partial functions can match on data and can be passed around like any other instances in Scala. Partial functions replace a lot of the XML configuration files in Java because pattern matching gives you the same declarative facilities as a configuration file, but they are type-safe, high-performance, and they can have guards and generally take advantage of any method in your code. Here's an example of using pattern matching to dispatch REST request in the ESME[6] code:[7]

```scala
def dispatch: LiftRules.DispatchPF = {
  case Req("api" :: "status" :: Nil, "", GetRequest) => status
  case Req("api" :: "messages" :: Nil, "", GetRequest) => getMsgs
  case Req("api" :: "messages" :: "long_poll" :: Nil, "", GetRequest) =>
    waitForMsgs
  case Req("api" :: "messages" :: Nil, "", PostRequest) =>
    () => sendMsg(User.currentUser.map(_.id.is), S)

case Req("api" :: "follow" :: Nil, _, GetRequest) =>
    following(calcUser)
  case Req("api" :: "followers" :: Nil, _, GetRequest) =>
    followers(calcUser)
  case Req("api" :: "follow" :: Nil, _, PostRequest) =>
    performFollow(S.param("user"))
}
```

Object-Oriented and Functional Tensions

At this point, the hard-core object-oriented designer folks may be somewhat unhappy about Scala case class's exposure of lots of internal information. Data hiding is an important part of OOP's abstraction. But in fact, most of the Java classes we define have getters and setters, so there is data exposed in OOP. But there is a tension between the amount of internal state that's exposed in our program and the amount of state that's hidden. In this section, we'll explore OOP and functional programming (FP) patterns for data hiding and exposure.

Another tension in OOP is how to define methods on class and interface hierarchies. Where does a method definition belong? What happens when a library is deployed but it's necessary to add new functionality to subclasses? How do we retrofit the defined-in-stone

---

6. ESME is the Enterprise Social Messaging Experiment (http://blog.esme.us).
7. This code will not compile without the rest of the ESME code, but it serves as an illustration of using pattern matching as an alternative to XML configuration files or annotations.

library classes to add this functionality? Put more concretely, if we have a library of shapes—circle, square, rectangle—that each have an area method but hide all their other data, how do we add a perimeter method to the shapes? Let's explore the tension and the tools Scala and FP give us to address the tension.

Shape Abstractions

If we have a collection of shapes that derive from the common trait OShape that has an area method on it, our object definitions would look something like the following if we used a traditional OOP approach:

```scala
trait OShape {
  def area: Double
}

class OCircle(radius: Double) extends OShape {
  def area = radius * radius * Math.Pi
}
class OSquare(length: Double) extends OShape {
  def area = length * length
}
class ORectangle(h: Double, w: Double) extends OShape {
  def area = h * w
}
```

Let's compare this with the pattern-matching implementation:

```scala
trait Shape

  case class Circle(radius: Double) extends Shape
  case class Square(length: Double) extends Shape
  case class Rectangle(h: Double, w: Double) extends Shape

object Shape {
  def area(shape: Shape): Double = shape match {
    case Circle(r) => r * r * Math.Pi
    case Square(l) => l * l
    case Rectangle(h, w) => h * w
  }
}
```

In the pattern-matching example, all of the logic for calculating area is located in the same method, but the fact that the method exists is not obvious from looking at the Shape trait. So far, the OOP methodology seems to be the right answer because it makes obvious what shapes can do.

However, if we have a shape library and we want to calculate the perimeter of each of the shapes, there's a benefit to pattern matching:

```
def perimeter(shape: Shape) = shape match {
  case Circle(r) => 2 * Math.Pi * r
  case Square(l) => 4 * l
  case Rectangle(h, w) => h * 2 + w * 2
}
```

In this case, the open data makes implementing the perimeter method possible. With the OOP implementation, we would have to expose data to make the perimeter method possible to implement. So our OOP implementation would look like

```
trait OShape {
  def area: Double
}

class OCircle(radius: Double) extends OShape {
  def area = radius * radius * Math.Pi
  def getRadius = radius
}
class OSquare(length: Double) extends OShape {
  def area = length * length
  def getLength = length
}
class ORectangle(h: Double, w: Double) extends OShape {
  def area = h * w
  def getHeight = h
  def getWidth = w
}
```

More broadly, it's rare that the designer of an object hierarchy implements all the methods that a library consumer is going to need.

The visitor pattern is a design pattern that allows you to add functionality to a class hierarchy after the hierarchy is already defined. Let's look at a typical visitor pattern implementation. Following is the interface that defines the visitor. The code contains circular class references and will not work at the REPL. So, first the code, and then a walk-through of the code:

```
trait OCarVisitor {
  def visit(wheel: OWheel): Unit
  def visit(engine: OEngine): Unit
  def visit(body: OBody): Unit
  def visit(car: OCar): Unit
}

trait OCarElement {
  def accept(visitor: OCarVisitor): Unit
}

class OWheel(val name: String) extends OCarElement {
  def accept(visitor: OCarVisitor) = visitor.visit(this)
}

class OEngine extends OCarElement {
  def accept(visitor: OCarVisitor) = visitor.visit(this)
}

class OBody extends OCarElement {
  def accept(visitor: OCarVisitor) = visitor.visit(this)
}

class OCar extends OCarElement {
  val elements = List(new OEngine, new OBody, new OWheel("FR"),
                      new OWheel("FL"), new OWheel("RR"), new OWheel("RL"))

  def accept(visitor: OCarVisitor) =
  (this :: elements).foreach(_.accept(visitor))
}
```

The library author has to think about extensibility and implement the visitor pattern. Note also that the class hierarchy is fixed in the visitor because the visitor has to implement an interface that defines all the possible classes that the visitor can handle:

```
trait OCarVisitor {
  def visit(wheel: OWheel): Unit
  def visit(engine: OEngine): Unit
  def visit(body: OBody): Unit
  def visit(car: OCar): Unit
}
```

Each element derives from a trait that creates a contract, which requires that the class implement the accept method:

```scala
trait OCarElement {
  def accept(visitor: OCarVisitor): Unit
}
```

We implement each subclass and implement the accept method:

```scala
class OWheel(val name: String) extends OCarElement {
  def accept(visitor: OCarVisitor) = visitor.visit(this)
}


class OEngine extends OCarElement {
  def accept(visitor: OCarVisitor) = visitor.visit(this)
}


class OBody extends OCarElement {
  def accept(visitor: OCarVisitor) = visitor.visit(this)
}


class OCar extends OCarElement {
  val elements = List(new OEngine, new OBody, new OWheel("FR"),
                      new OWheel("FL"), new OWheel("RR"), new OWheel("RL"))

  def accept(visitor: OCarVisitor) =
  (this :: elements).foreach(_.accept(visitor))
}
```

That's a lot of boilerplate.[8] Additionally, it violates the data-hiding principles of OOP because the visitor has to access some of the data in each element that it visits. Let's compare the pattern-matching version:

```scala
trait CarElement
case class Wheel(name: String) extends CarElement
case class Engine() extends CarElement
case class Body() extends CarElement
case class Car(elements: List[CarElement]) extends CarElement
```

---

8. Here is where a unityped language such as Ruby or Python has a material advantage over a static language such as Java. In Ruby, you don't need all the boilerplate, and the class hierarchy is not fixed at the time the OCarVisitor interface is defined.

The code is cleaner because there's no boilerplate `accept` method. Let's see what we do when we want to traverse the object hierarchy:

```
def doSomething(in: CarElement): Unit = in match {
  case Wheel(name) =>
  case Engine() =>
  case Body() =>
  case Car(e) => e.foreach(doSomething)
}
```

More generally, Burak Emir, one of Scala's authors, wrote an excellent paper on the intersection of pattern matching and object-oriented design. See `http://library.epfl.ch/theses/?nr=3899`.

Summary

In this chapter, we explored pattern matching and saw how pattern matching provides powerful declarative syntax for expressing complex logic. Pattern matching provides an excellent and type-safe alternative to Java's test/cast paradigm. Pattern matching used with case classes and extraction provides a powerful way to traverse object hierarchies and is an excellent alternative to the visitor pattern. And because patterns are functions and objects, they can be passed as parameters and used wherever functions are used.

In the next chapter, we'll explore Actors. Actors provide a great paradigm for concurrency without locks. Actors in Scala are entirely library-based. They take advantage of Scala's flexible syntax, interoperability with Java libraries, and pattern matching to provide awesome power and flexibility for building multicore-friendly applications.

CHAPTER 6

■■■

Actors and Concurrency

Java introduced the `synchronized` keyword, which provided language-level concurrency management. Coming from C++, built-in language-level concurrency had the benefits of a unified model, so each project or module had the same concurrency mechanism and there was no need to roll your own. Java's synchronization semantics are very simple. You lock an object for exclusive use on a given thread, and the JVM assures you that the object will not be locked by another thread. Furthermore, because the JVM assures you that you can enter the lock multiple times on the same thread and at the bytecode level, you know that the lock will be released no matter how your application unwinds the stack.[1]

In practical use, Java's synchronized mechanism is fraught with peril. The granularity at which you lock objects is a very tough call. If you lock too coarsely, then you wind up with a single-threaded application, because in practical terms the global lock will be asserted by the first thread that needs the given high-level object. If your granularity is too fine, there's a high likelihood of deadlocks, as locks are asserted by different threads on mutually interdependent objects.

As a practical matter, when you code Java, you never know when something is going to be synchronized. Even if your team defines a set of concurrency and synchronization patterns that work, enforcing the model is non-trivial, and often the only time the defects will be detected is during high-load production situations. There has to be a better way, and in fact there is. The Actor model of concurrency offers a different and generally superior mechanism for doing multithreaded and multicore coding.

A Different Approach to Concurrency: Look Ma, No Locks

The Actor model provides an alternative mechanism for dealing with concurrency and more generally, the listener pattern, event handling, and many of the other things we associate with object-oriented programming.

---

1. Except if you use `Thread.stop()`.

Actors are threadless, stackless units of execution that process messages (events) serially. Actors were originally developed by Carl Hewitt[2] and some other folks in 1973.[3] Actors process incoming messages and encapsulate their state. At this point, Actors sound a lot like OOP message sending and encapsulation, and it turns out this is the case. The Actor message-passing semantics grew out of Hewitt's review of Smalltalk. Scheme had an early implementation of Actors.[4] Today, the best-known Actor implementation is Erlang, which provides a very powerful distributed Actor mechanism.

Smalltalk, Objective-C, Ruby, JavaScript, and Python are unityped or duck-typed languages.[5] Instances in each of those languages is of the same type. You can send any message or invoke any method on any instance. The ability for an instance to process a method or message is determined at runtime. Scala, on the other hand, is a statically typed language where the class of every instance is known at compile time and the availability of a method on a given instance can be verified at compile time.

Like instances in duck-typed languages, Actors process messages at runtime, and there's no compile-time checking to see whether the Actor can process a particular message. The key differences between Actors and duck-typed instances are that Actors always process messages asynchronously and may not process messages in the order that they were delivered. Messages are delivered to an Actor's mailbox, and the Actor processes the mailbox by removing the first message from the mailbox that the Actor can currently process. If the Actor cannot process any messages currently in the mailbox, the Actor is suspended until the state of the mailbox changes. The Actor will only process one message at a time. Multiple messages can show up in the Actor's mailbox while the Actor is processing a message.

Because the Actor does not expose state and can only be modified or queried via messages, and because messages are processed serially, there's no reason to assert locks on internal Actor state. Thus, Actors are lockless at the application level, yet thread-safe.

Defining an Actor

To send a message to an Actor, you use the ! (bang) method. Thus `actor ! msg` is the syntax for sending a message to an Actor. Actors are implemented as a library, and there's no specific support for Actors in the Scala compiler. As we wrote our own `List` class, you could write your own Actor library.

Actors are defined in two parts. First, you define the messages that an Actor can receive, and second you define the Actor itself. Actors can receive any message that can be pattern matched in Scala. The following are legal messages, but we haven't defined the Actor's message handling, so we don't know what, if anything, these messages do.

---

2. http://carlhewitt.info/
3. http://en.wikipedia.org/wiki/Actor_model
4. http://www.brics.dk/~hosc/local/HOSC-11-4-pp399-404.pdf
5. The term "duck-typed" comes from the phrase "If it walks like a duck and quacks like a duck, it must be a duck." If an instance can process the walk and quack messages, it must be a duck.

```
a ! "Hello"
a ! 42
a ! ("Add", 1)
a ! List(1,2,3)
```

I find that except for the most trivial Actor code, I like to use case classes to define messages to an Actor. This allows me to change the parameters that a particular message accepts, and the compiler will flag places in the code where the messages is used. Thus

```
case class Add(i: Int)
a ! Add(1)
```

is better than

```
a ! ("Add", 1)
```

because we can change the message to

```
case class Add(i: Double)
```

and all references will be updated on recompile. This means that the messages themselves are type-safe, even if the Actor itself is unityped.[6]

Defining an Actor

To define an Actor, you subclass from Actor and implement the act method. The act method defines how your Actor processes messages. Most of my Actors place the react method inside the loop method:

```
class BasicActor extends Actor {
  def act = loop {
    react {
      case s => println("Got a message: "+s)
    }
  }
}
```

This Actor will accept any message and print the message on the console. The loop method loops on its content, the react method. The react method defines how the Actor will process an incoming message.

---

6. Philip Wadler refers to duck-typed languages as "unityped," which seems to me to be very descriptive. See http://jjinux.blogspot.com/2008/01/haskell-well-typed-programs-cant-be.html.

If you choose not to use the `loop` method, you have to explicitly loop at the end of each message. For example:

```
class LoopActor extends Actor {
  def act =
  react {
    case s: String =>
      println("Got a string: "+s)
      act

    case x =>
      println("Got a message: "+x)
      act
  }
}
```

Note the requirement to call `act` at the end of each handler. If you forget to call `act`, your Actor stops handling messages. In my experience, 40 percent of my Actor-related defects came from forgetting to call `act` at the end of my handler. So, you may ask, why isn't `loop` the default construct?

Would You Like State With That?

Scala's Actors are derived from Erlang Actors. Erlang does not support objects or any concept of mutable private fields, so Erlang Actors must carry all state on the stack and must explicitly and recursively call the handler with the current state. First, let's look at an Actor that counts the number of messages it has received.

```
class SomeState extends Actor {
  private var cnt = 0

  def act = loop {
    react {
      case _ => cnt += 1
        println("Received "+cnt+" messages")
    }
  }
}
```

The private `cnt` variable holds state. But if we want to write the Actor with no mutable state, it would look like the following:

```
class NoState extends Actor {
  def act = run(0)
```

```
private def run(cnt: Int): Unit =
react {
  case _ =>
    val newCnt = cnt + 1
    println("Received "+newCnt+" messages")
    run(newCnt)
  }
}
```

In this code, the NoState class has no explicitly mutable state, but the state is kept on the stack and passed back into run for each message processed. Personally, I prefer to keep state in private instance variables in my Actor. I find that it reduces bugs and allows for more flexible composition of traits into an Actor. I'll have more on composition as we travel through this chapter.

Instantiating an Actor

To create an Actor, we have to instantiate it and then start it:

```
val actor = new SomeState
actor.start
actor ! "Hello"
```

Actors will not process messages until they are started. Forgetting to start an Actor is one of the other common Actor-related defect patterns in my code. An Actor can be an object. This is very helpful if you have a singleton in your application that does something, like being a central chat server:

```
object ChatServer1 extends Actor {
  private var chats: List[String] = Nil

  def act = loop {
    react {
      case s: String => chats ::= s
    }
  }

  this.start // make sure we start the chat server
}
```

Okay, those were the basics. Let's look at an application, the listener pattern.

Implementing a Listener

The listener pattern is a very common design pattern. Let's look at two listener implementations to demonstrate Actors and the power and flexibility of asynchronous messaging.

Listing 6-1 contains the code for this subsection. This code is a traditional implementation that has a subtle bug in it. We'll parse through the code after seeing the whole listing.

Listing 6-1. *Synchronous Listener*

```
trait MyListener {
  def changed(event: Foo, count: Int): Unit
}

class Foo {
  private var listeners: List[MyListener] = Nil
  private var count = 0

  def access() = synchronized {
    notifyListeners
    count += 1
    count
  }

  private def notifyListeners = synchronized {
    listeners.foreach(_.changed(this, count))
  }

  def addListener(who: MyListener): Unit = synchronized {
    listeners ::= who
  }
}

class FooListener(foo: Foo) extends MyListener {
  foo.addListener(this)

  def changed(event: Foo, count: Int): Unit = {
    if (count < 10) event.access()
  }
}
```

We define the listener trait:

```scala
trait MyListener {
  def changed(event: Foo, count: Int): Unit
}
```

Next let's define the class that sends events to those listeners:

```scala
class Foo {
  private var listeners: List[MyListener] = Nil
  private var count = 0

  def access() = synchronized {
    notifyListeners
    count += 1
    count
  }

  private def notifyListeners = synchronized {
    listeners.foreach(_.changed(this, count))
  }

  def addListener(who: MyListener): Unit = synchronized {
    listeners ::= who
  }
}
```

Finally, let's define a concrete class that implements the listener. For some reason, when the listener gets a changed message and the count is too low, the listener will access the object again:

```scala
class FooListener(foo: Foo) extends MyListener {
  foo.addListener(this)

  def changed(event: Foo, count: Int): Unit = {
    if (count < 10) event.access()
  }
}
```

Let's run the code:

```scala
scala> val f = new Foo
```

```scala
f: Foo = Foo@4178d0
```

```
scala> val fl = new FooListener(f)
```

```
fl: FooListener = FooListener@bb1ead
```

```
scala> f.access
```

```
java.lang.StackOverflowError
        at Foo$$anonfun$notifyListeners$1.<init>(Morg.scala:104)
        at Foo.notifyListeners(Morg.scala:104)
        at Foo.access(Morg.scala:98)
        at FooListener.changed(Morg.scala:118)
        at Foo$$anonfun$notifyListeners$1.apply(Morg.scala:104)
        at Foo$$anonfun$notifyListeners$1.apply(Morg.scala:104)
        at scala.List.foreach(List.scala:834)
        at Foo.notifyListeners(Morg.scala:10...
```

D'oh! This is one of the perils of synchronous messaging. If we run this code, we'll get a stack overflow because the listener is mutating the model during the event processing. Even if the increment of count was in the right place in the access() method, listeners that were called subsequent to FooListener would be called with descending rather than ascending count values.

As an Actor

Let's look at the same code written using the Actor paradigm. First, here's the whole code in Listing 6-2, and then we'll see the dissection.

Listing 6-2. *Actor-based Listener*

```
import scala.actors.Actor
import Actor._

case class Add(who: Actor)
case class Changed(what: AFoo, count: Int)
case object Access
```

```
class AFoo extends Actor {
  private var listeners: List[Actor] = Nil
  private var count = 0

  def act = loop {
    react {
      case Add(who) => listeners = who :: listeners
      case Access => access()
    }
  }

  private def access() = {
    notifyListeners
    count += 1
  }

  private def notifyListeners =
  listeners.foreach(a => a ! Changed(this, count))
}

class AFooListener(afoo: AFoo) extends Actor {
  afoo ! Add(this)

  def act = loop {
    react {
      case Changed(f, cnt) => changed(f, cnt)
    }
  }

  def changed(eventFrom: AFoo, count: Int): Unit = {
    if (count < 10) eventFrom ! Access
  }
}
```

First, we import a few things and define our messages:

```
import scala.actors.Actor
import Actor._

case class Add(who: Actor)
case class Changed(what: AFoo, count: Int)
case object Access
```

Next, let's define our AFoo class as an Actor. The big difference is that there are no synchronizations, and everything is private except the event handler, act (explained in the next paragraph).

```
class AFoo extends Actor {
  private var listeners: List[Actor] = Nil
  private var count = 0
```

The act method defines what the Actor will do with messages in its mailbox. We say that the Actor loops over the reaction to a pattern using the pattern matching we saw in Chapter 5. What this means is that the Actor will use the same pattern to test messages over and over again. It is possible to change the messages that the Actor responds to, but in this case, we'll just react to the two messages, Add and Access. The Add message adds who to the List of listeners. The Access message results in a call to the private access method.

```
def act = loop {
  react {
    case Add(who) => listeners = who :: listeners
    case Access => access()
  }
}
```

The access method calls the notifyListeners method and then increments count. The notifyListeners method sends each member of the listeners List a Changed message.

```
private def access() = {
  notifyListeners
  count += 1
}

private def notifyListeners =
  listeners.foreach(a => a ! Changed(this, count))
}
```

Except for using ! instead of . to send or invoke a method, the code looks similar.

Next, let's look at a listener:

```
class AFooListener(afoo: AFoo) extends Actor {
```

The AFooListener's constructor code registers the instance as a listener on the afoo instance by sending an Add message to afoo:

```
afoo ! Add(this)
```

Our Actor event handler receives the Changed message and invokes the private changed method.

```
def act = loop {
  react {
    case Changed(f, cnt) => changed(f, cnt)
  }
}
```

The changed method sends an Access message to eventFrom if the count is less than 10:

```
private def changed(eventFrom: AFoo, count: Int): Unit =
  if (count < 10) eventFrom ! Access
}
```

The listener also looks very similar. However, the behavior is different. The message handling is asynchronous, so we'll never run out of stack space, because the mutating happens when the Access message is processed and does not wait for the listener to process the Changed message. You'll also see that the synchronization is gone from the classes. We've exchanged a little extra syntax and type-safety for a different and in many ways more powerful concurrency mechanism.[7]

Let's run the code:

```
scala> val af = new AFoo
```

```
af: AFoo = AFoo@1aca5e2
```

```
scala> af.start
```

```
res4: scala.actors.Actor = AFoo@1aca5e2
```

```
scala> val afl = new AFooListener(af)
```

```
afl: AFooListener = AFooListener@12ee2a
```

---

7. Actors can receive anything as a message. They are like duck-typed objects in Ruby or Python. Thus, the compiler does not check to see whether the particular message that you are sending to an Actor is one that the Actor can or could process.

```scala
scala> afl.start
```

```scala
res5: scala.actors.Actor = AFooListener@12ee2a
```

```scala
scala> af ! Access
```

No problem—it works.

Actors: More Than Write-Only

So far, we've seen Actors that are pretty much write-only. They know about their state, but unless you're a listener, you have no clue about their state. This is generally less than optimal. It's possible to send a message to an Actor and synchronously wait for a reply:

```scala
ChatServer2 !? GetMessages
```

This will send a GetMessages message to ChatServer2 and wait until ChatServer2 replies. We can pattern match the result:

```scala
val msgs: Option[List[String]] = ChatServer2 !? GetMessages match {
  case Messages(msg) => Some(msg)
  case _  => None
}
```

We can also send the message and wait for a reply. If the reply comes within the timeout period, the method returns Some(response), otherwise the method returns None:

```scala
val msgs2: Option[List[String]] = ChatServer2 !? (500, GetMessages) match {
  case Some(Messages(msg)) => Some(msg)
  case Some(_) => None // got a response we didn't understand
  case None => None // timeout
}
```

In the previous example, we send the GetMessages message to ChatServer2 and wait 500 milliseconds for a response. Let's look at the messages and the ChatServer2 implementation:

```scala
case object GetMessages
case class Messages(msg: List[String])

object ChatServer2 extends Actor {
  private var chats: List[String] = Nil
```

```
def act = loop {
  react {
    case s: String => chats = s :: chats
    case GetMessages => reply(Messages(chats))
  }
}

this.start // make sure we start the chat server
}
```

The `GetMessages` message is processed by `reply(Messages(chats))`. The paradigm is pretty simple. It's much like getters in standard OOP, except it is heavier-weight both in terms of syntax and execution speed. In general, if you keep most of the state in your Actor in immutable data structures and the query messages return all or substantially all of the state as a single request, then the overhead is incurred less frequently than repeatedly calling granular getters on an object:

```
for (i <- 0 until chats.count) yield chats.message(i)
```

Additionally, the difference in the calling syntax triggers something in my brain that says, "This call may time out, so make sure you're testing the return value." This is an important value of the syntactic differences between object method invocation and Actor message sending. The difference says to the developer, "Calculate the costs of invocation and probability of failure differently than for a normal method invocation." Additionally, during code reviews, it's much easier to see where Actors are being accessed.

Beyond the Basics

So far, we've seen the basics of creating Actors, sending messages to Actors, and receiving replies from Actors. In this section, we're going to explore how Actors can change the messages they process depending on their state. This will lead us to a couple of ways to do transactions with Actors. Finally, we'll talk about how exception handling in Actors differs from normal exception processing.

Protocol Handler

We've been writing the `react` part of the Actor as a pattern to match. In Chapter 5, we explored pattern matching. One of the things we learned is that Scala turns patterns into partial functions. Unsurprisingly, the `react` method takes a `PartialFunction` as a parameter. Because `PartialFunctions` are instances, we can do anything with them that we can with other instances. `PartialFunctions` can also be composed, smooshed together. This means that we can dynamically compose the `PartialFunction` that we're going to pass to the react method. This gives us the ability to build an OOP hierarchy that defines how our Actor is going to react to messages.[8] We'll cover the basics in this section and dive in more deeply later in the chapter.

The way we've been writing our react calls, we've hard-coded the partial function, but that's unnecessary. We can calculate the behavior based on the current state of the Actor. We'll implement a chat server that will not allow listeners until there are at least three chats. Let's look at Listing 6-3 and then dissect it.

Listing 6-3. *Chat Server with Dynamic Message Handling*

```
import scala.actors.Actor
import Actor._

case object GetMessages
case class Messages(msg: List[String])
case class Remove(who: Actor)
case class Add(who: Actor)

object ChatServer3 extends Actor {
  private var chats: List[String] = Nil
  private var listeners: List[Actor] = Nil

  def act = loop {
    react(calcReact)
  }

  private def calcReact = {
    val handle: PartialFunction[Any, Unit] = {
      case s: String => chats = s :: chats
        notifyListeners()

      case GetMessages => reply(Messages(chats))
    }
```

---

8. For those at home who are keeping score, Scheme, an early functional language, led to the asynchronous message-passing model and Actors. The Actor model was adopted by Alan Kay when he designed Smalltalk, the mother of all OOP languages. The Actor model was adopted by Joe Armstrong when he designed Erlang. The Scala team adopted Erlang's Actor model into Scala, which is a hybrid OOP/FP language. Using Scala's unique partial-function composing, we are able to build an inheritance mechanism on top of the Actors. Yes, what was, will be again, or "there ain't nothin' new under the sun."

```
    val mgt: PartialFunction[Any, Unit] =
    if (chats.length < 3)
    Map.empty
    else {
      case Add(who) => listeners = who :: listeners
        who ! Messages(chats)

      case Remove(who) => listeners -= who
    }

    handle orElse mgt
  }

  private def notifyListeners() {
    listeners.foreach(a => a ! Messages(chats))
  }

  this.start()
}
```

First we define the messages that the ChatServer3 will accept or send:

```
case object GetMessages
case class Messages(msg: List[String])
case class Remove(who: Actor)
case class Add(who: Actor)
```

And we define the chat server object:

```
object ChatServer3 extends Actor {
  private var chats: List[String] = Nil
  private var listeners: List[Actor] = Nil
```

Instead of defining the parameter to react, we'll call the calcReact method:

```
def act = loop {
  react(calcReact)
}
```

The calcReact method comprises two partial functions. The first, handle, is static. It is the same no matter what is the state of the Actor.

```
  private def calcReact = {
    val handle: PartialFunction[Any, Unit] = {
      case s: String => chats = s :: chats
        notifyListeners()

      case GetMessages => reply(Messages(chats))
    }
```

The second, mgt, is empty if the number of chats is less than three. However, if the number of chats is greater than or equal to three, we allow listeners to register and deregister themselves.

```
    val mgt: PartialFunction[Any, Unit] =
    if (chats.length < 3)
    Map.empty
    else {
      case Add(who) => listeners = who :: listeners
        who ! Messages(chats)

      case Remove(who) => listeners -= who
    }
```

Finally, we compose the two partial functions.

```
    handle orElse mgt
  }
```

We notify the listeners:

```
  private def notifyListeners() {
    listeners.foreach(a => a ! Messages(chats))
  }
```

And we don't forget to start the Actor:

```
  this.start
}
```

This is an example of changing the behavior of the Actor on a message-by-message basis. The mechanism of composing the partial function for react based on the current state can be generalized into a protocol handler that accepts and processes messages based on the current Actor state. Next, let's turn our attention to implementing transactions using Actors.

Actors, Atomic Updates, and Transactions

First, let's talk about ACID. Relational databases like PostgreSQL provide ACID transactions. ACID stands for atomic, consistent, isolated, and durable. Atomic means that if the transaction succeeds, all the rows affected by the transaction are changed at the same instant in the view of other transactions. Consistent means that all of the rows will be updated if the transaction succeeds. Isolated means that until the transaction is committed, no other transactions in the system see any updated rows. Durable means that the transaction is written to media, disk, before the commit is done. In this section, I'm going to build a transaction system that is ACI but not D. There will be no durable writes to disk.

Actors provide a great mechanism for multithreaded processing without explicit synchronization. Using synchronization, we can implement atomic updates by synchronizing the target of our updates and then performing updates on that target. Because Actors cannot be synchronized, we have to figure out another mechanism for performing atomic updates.[9] Because it's possible to pass functions as messages to Actors, we can define messages that contain functions that perform atomic updates.

Performing an Atomic Update

Let's build a simple example for an inventory Actor (see Listing 6-4).

Listing 6-4. *Atomic Updates*

```
import scala.actors.Actor
import Actor._

case object GetInfo
case class Info(i: Map[String, Int])
case class SetInfo(n: String, v: Int)
case class Update(n: String, f: Option[Int] => Int)

object XAct1 extends Actor {
  private var info: Map[String, Int] = Map()
```

---

9. An atomic update is an update that guarantees that the state of the thing being updated will not change between the time the values for calculating the update are retrieved from the thing and the time the update is applied.

```
  def act = loop {
    react {
      case GetInfo => reply(Info(info))
      case SetInfo(n, v) => info += n -> v
      case Update(n, f) => info += n -> f(info.get(n))
    }
  }

  this.start
}
```

First we do some importing:

```
import scala.actors.Actor
import Actor._
```

Next, we define our messages:

```
case object GetInfo
case class Info(i: Map[String, Int])
case class SetInfo(n: String, v: Int)
case class Update(n: String, f: Option[Int] => Int)
```

The Update message is most interesting. It takes the name of the item to update and a function that performs the update. Next, let's define our Actor:

```
object XAct1 extends Actor {
  private var info: Map[String, Int] = Map()

  def act = loop {
    react {
      case GetInfo => reply(Info(info))
      case SetInfo(n, v) => info += n -> v
      case Update(n, f) => info += n -> f(info.get(n))
    }
  }
  this.start
}
```

Note how the Update message is processed. Update is processed just like any other Actor message. That means while the Actor is processing Update, it cannot process any other message. But Update contains code in the form of a function. Update's handler applies the function. The function is processed in the scope of the Actor, but it does not have access to the Actor's state except for the value of the named item. Thus, the message is processed atomically and is thread-safe because the function is applied on the thread that's doing the processing the Update message. Let's see how we would call XAct1:

```
scala> XAct1 ! SetInfo("Apple", 4)
scala> XAct1 ! SetInfo("Orange", 5)
scala> XAct1 !? GetInfo
```

```
res2: Any = Info(Map(Apple -> 4, Orange -> 5))
```

```
scala> XAct1 ! Update("Apple", v => (v getOrElse 0) + 2)[10]
scala> XAct1 !? GetInfo
```

```
res4: Any = Info(Map(Apple -> 6, Orange -> 5))
```

Atomic updates are useful, but they do not tell the whole story. There may be times when we need transactions. We need to be able to have exclusive access to one or more Actor's state for an operation that spans both of the Actors.

Performing Transactions

It turns out that we can use the same techniques of immutable data structures and stateful message processing to build Actors that support transactions (see Listing 6-5).

Listing 6-5. *Transactional Actors*

```
import scala.actors.Actor
import Actor._
import scala.actors.TIMEOUT

case object GetInfo
case class Info(i: Map[String, Int])
case class SetInfo(n: String, v: Int)
case class Update(n: String, f: Option[Int] => Int)
```

---

10. v is Option[Int], so we get its value or default to 0 if v is None.

```scala
case class BeginXAction(id: Int)
case object CommitXAction
case object RollbackXAction

class Acct extends Actor {
  private var info: Map[String, Int] = Map()
  private var service = (normal, false)

  private def normal: PartialFunction[Any, Unit] = {
    case GetInfo => reply(Info(info))
    case SetInfo(n, v) => info += n -> v
    case Update(n, f) => info += n -> f(info.get(n))
    case BeginXAction(id) => begin(id)
  }

  private def begin(xActionId: Int) {
    val oldInfo = info // capture
    val oldService = service
    val tmp: PartialFunction[Any, Unit] = {
      case TIMEOUT => // Rollback
        info = oldInfo
        service = oldService

      case (n, RollbackXAction) if n == xActionId =>
        info = oldInfo
        service = oldService

      case (n, CommitXAction) if n == xActionId => // Commit
        service = oldService

      case (n, v) if n == xActionId &&
        normal.isDefinedAt(v) => normal(v)
    }

    service = (tmp, true)
  }

  def act = loop {
    service match {
      case (pf, false) => react(pf)
      case (pf, true) => reactWithin(500)(pf)
    }
  }
}
```

```scala
    this.start
}

object TestAcct {
  def doTest() = {
    val dpp = new Acct
    dpp ! Update("Savings", v => (v getOrElse 0) + 1000)
    dpp ! Update("Checking", v => (v getOrElse 0) + 100)

    val archer = new Acct
    archer ! Update("Savings", v => (v getOrElse 0) + 2000)
    archer ! Update("Checking", v => (v getOrElse 0) + 50)

    println("Initial balances:")
    println("dpp: "+(dpp !? GetInfo))
    println("archer: "+(archer !? GetInfo))

    var xid = 1

    def transfer(who: Actor, from: String, to: String, amount: Int): Boolean = {
      xid += 1

      who ! BeginXAction(xid)
      who !? (500, (xid, GetInfo)) match {
        case Some(Info(bal)) =>
          if (bal.getOrElse(from, 0) > amount) {
            who ! (xid, Update(from, v => (v getOrElse 0) - amount))
            who ! (xid, Update(to, v => (v getOrElse 0) + amount))
            who ! (xid, CommitXAction)
            true
          } else {
            who ! (xid, RollbackXAction)
            false
          }
        case _ => who ! (xid, RollbackXAction)
          false
      }
    }

    transfer(dpp, "Savings", "Checking", 700)
    println("xfer 1 dpp: "+(dpp !? GetInfo))
    transfer(dpp, "Savings", "Checking", 700)
    println("xfer 2 dpp: "+(dpp !? GetInfo))
```

```scala
def transfer2(src: Actor, sact: String, dest: Actor,
              dact: String, amount: Int): Boolean = {
  xid += 1

  src ! BeginXAction(xid)
  dest ! BeginXAction(xid)
  (src !? (500, (xid, GetInfo)), dest !? (500, (xid, GetInfo))) match {
    case (Some(Info(sbal)), Some(Info(dbal))) =>
      dest ! (xid, Update(dact, v => (v getOrElse 0) + amount))

      if (sbal.getOrElse(sact, 0) > amount) {
        src ! (xid, Update(sact, v => (v getOrElse 0) - amount))
        src ! (xid, CommitXAction)
        dest ! (xid, CommitXAction)
        true
      } else {
        src ! (xid, RollbackXAction)
        dest ! (xid, RollbackXAction)
        false
      }
    case _ =>
      src ! (xid, RollbackXAction)
      dest ! (xid, RollbackXAction)
      false
  }
}

transfer2(dpp, "Checking", archer, "Checking", 700)
println("XFer 700 dpp -> archer:")
println("dpp: "+(dpp !? GetInfo))
println("archer: "+(archer !? GetInfo))

transfer2(dpp, "Checking", archer, "Checking", 700)
println("Again, XFer 700 dpp -> archer:")
println("dpp: "+(dpp !? GetInfo))
println("archer: "+(archer !? GetInfo))

transfer2(dpp, "Checking", archer, "Checking", 10)
println("XFer 10 dpp -> archer:")
println("dpp: "+(dpp !? GetInfo))
println("archer: "+(archer !? GetInfo))
  }
}
```

Let's step through the code. First some imports:

```
import scala.actors.Actor
import Actor._
import scala.actors.TIMEOUT
```

The TIMEOUT message will be useful for staying in the transaction boundary for a certain period of time. Next, let's define some messages:

```
case object GetInfo
case class Info(i: Map[String, Int])
case class SetInfo(n: String, v: Int)
case class Update(n: String, f: Option[Int] => Int)
case class BeginXAction(id: Int)
case object CommitXAction
case object RollbackXAction
```

The XAction messages allow us to define the transactional boundaries. Next, let's define an Acct, account, Actor:

```
class Acct extends Actor {
  private var info: Map[String, Int] = Map()
  private var service = (normal, false)
```

The service variable defines how we're going to service incoming requests. By default, requests will be handled with the normal handler, but if we're in a transaction, the handler can be changed. Next, let's define the normal handler:

```
  private def normal: PartialFunction[Any, Unit] = {
    case GetInfo => reply(Info(info))
    case SetInfo(n, v) => info += n -> v
    case Update(n, f) => info += n -> f(info.get(n))
    case BeginXAction(id) => begin(id)
  }
```

This looks just like our previous example, Listing 6-4, except this time, we have the BeginXAction message. This message calls the begin method with the transaction ID.

```
  private def begin(xActionId: Int) {
```

We now capture the current state of the Actor—both the info and the mechanism for servicing incoming messages:

```
    val oldInfo = info // capture
    val oldService = service
```

Next, we build up a partial function that will service incoming requests. If there's a TIMEOUT, we roll back the transaction by replacing the current state with the state at the beginning of the transaction:

```
val tmp: PartialFunction[Any, Unit] = {
  case TIMEOUT => // Rollback
    info = oldInfo
    service = oldService
```

If we get a `Pair` that contains the current transaction ID and the `RollbackXAction` message, we roll back the transaction:

```
case (n, RollbackXAction) if n == xActionId =>
  info = oldInfo
  service = oldService
```

If we get a `Pair` that contains the current transaction ID and the `CommitXAction` message, we commit the transaction by reverting to the old servicing mechanism and leaving the data the way it was mutated by the current transaction:

```
case (n, CommitXAction) if n == xActionId => // Commit
  service = oldService
```

If we get any other message and it has the correct transaction ID and can be handled by the normal message handler, we pass it on to the normal message handler:

```
case (n, v) if n == xActionId &&
  normal.isDefinedAt(v) => normal(v)
}
```

Finally, we set the servicing mechanism to the new partial function:

```
service = (tmp, true)
}
```

Next, we define our act loop. If we are outside of the transaction boundary, we process the message the normal way with react. However, if we're inside a transaction, we call reactWithin(500). This will process messages the same way as react, except if no message matching the pattern is received in 500 milliseconds, the Actor is sent a TIMEOUT message. This allows us to terminate our transaction automatically if there's no activity on the transaction in a 500 millisecond period. Any messages received outside the transaction will be left in the Actor's mailbox and will be processed after the transaction is complete.

```
def act = loop {
  service match {
    case (pf, false) => react(pf)
    case (pf, true) => reactWithin(500)(pf)
  }
}
```

And **always** remember to start the Actor.

```
this.start
}
```

Testing the Transactional Actor

We've defined a transactional Actor. Let's see how it works. Let's create accounts for two people, dpp and archer, and put funds into the checking and savings accounts.

```
val dpp = new Acct
dpp ! Update("Savings", v => (v getOrElse 0) + 1000)
dpp ! Update("Checking", v => (v getOrElse 0) + 100)

val archer = new Acct
archer ! Update("Savings", v => (v getOrElse 0) + 2000)
archer ! Update("Checking", v => (v getOrElse 0) + 50)

println("Initial balances:")
println("dpp: "+(dpp !? GetInfo))
println("archer: "+(archer !? GetInfo))
```

Let's see what's printed on the console:

```
Initial balances:
dpp: Info(Map(Savings -> 1000, Checking -> 100))
archer: Info(Map(Savings -> 2000, Checking -> 50))
```

Let's define a variable that keeps track of our transaction IDs:

```
var xid = 1
```

Next, let's define a method that will transactionally transfer money between accounts for a single Actor as long as there are sufficient funds:

```
def transfer(who: Actor, from: String, to: String, amount: Int): Unit = {
  xid += 1

  who ! BeginXAction(xid)
```

We begin the transaction and get the current balances:

```
  who !? (500, (xid, GetInfo)) match {
    case Some(Info(bal)) =>
```

If the account has sufficient balances, then we debit one account and credit the other account and commit the transaction.

```
if (bal.getOrElse(from, 0) > amount) {
    who ! (xid, Update(from, v => (v getOrElse 0) - amount))
    who ! (xid, Update(to, v => (v getOrElse 0) + amount))
    who ! (xid, CommitXAction)
} else {
```

If we don't get the balance within 500 milliseconds or there's not sufficient funds, roll back the transaction.

```
    who ! (xid, RollbackXAction)
  }
  case _ => who ! (xid, RollbackXAction)
 }
}
```

Let's test out the transactional transfer and see whether it works by trying to transfer $700 from savings to checking twice. The first transaction should succeed, but the second should fail.

```
transfer(dpp, "Savings", "Checking", 700)
println("xfer 1 dpp: "+(dpp !? GetInfo))
transfer(dpp, "Savings", "Checking", 700)
println("xfer 2 dpp: "+(dpp !? GetInfo))
```

The console says:

```
xfer 1 dpp: Info(Map(Savings -> 300, Checking -> 800))
xfer 2 dpp: Info(Map(Savings -> 300, Checking -> 800))
```

Next, let's define a method that transfers money between two accounts on two separate Actors. Once again, there must be sufficient funds for the transfer, or the transaction will be rolled back.

```
def transfer2(src: Actor, sact: String, dest: Actor,
              dact: String, amount: Int): Unit = {
    xid += 1
```

Begin the transaction for both the Actors.

```
  src ! BeginXAction(xid)
  dest ! BeginXAction(xid)
```

And get the current balance for both the Actors. Note that the second balance is not used, but the result indicates that we're in the transaction for both the Actors.

```
(src !? (500, (xid, GetInfo)), dest !? (500, (xid, GetInfo))) match {
  case (Some(Info(sbal)), Some(Info(dbal))) =>
```

We're going to create the destination account before debiting the source account. This will demonstrate that rolling back the transaction works correctly.

```
        dest ! (xid, Update(dact, v => (v getOrElse 0) + amount))
        if (sbal.getOrElse(sact, 0) > amount) {
          src ! (xid, Update(sact, v => (v getOrElse 0) - amount))
          src ! (xid, CommitXAction)
          dest ! (xid, CommitXAction)
        } else {
          src ! (xid, RollbackXAction)
          dest ! (xid, RollbackXAction)
        }
    case _ =>
      src ! (xid, RollbackXAction)
      dest ! (xid, RollbackXAction)
  }
}
```

We've defined the ability to transactionally transfer money between accounts on two different Actors. Let's see whether it works. Let's transfer $700 from dpp to archer:

```
transfer2(dpp, "Checking", archer, "Checking", 700)
println("XFer 700 dpp -> archer:")
println("dpp: "+(dpp !? GetInfo))
println("archer: "+(archer !? GetInfo))
```

What does the console say?

```
XFer 700 dpp -> archer:
dpp: Info(Map(Savings -> 300, Checking -> 100))
archer: Info(Map(Savings -> 2000, Checking -> 750))
```

Yes, it works correctly. What happens if we try the transfer again?

```
transfer2(dpp, "Checking", archer, "Checking", 700)
println("Again, XFer 700 dpp -> archer:")
println("dpp: "+(dpp !? GetInfo))
println("archer: "+(archer !? GetInfo))
```

The console confirms that the transfer did not take place:

```
Again, XFer 700 dpp -> archer:
dpp: Info(Map(Savings -> 300, Checking -> 100))
archer: Info(Map(Savings -> 2000, Checking -> 750))
```

Now, let's try transferring $10:

```
transfer2(dpp, "Checking", archer, "Checking", 10)
println("XFer 10 dpp -> archer:")
println("dpp: "+(dpp !? GetInfo))
println("archer: "+(archer !? GetInfo))
```

And the console confirms that the transfer was successful:

```
XFer 10 dpp -> archer:
dpp: Info(Map(Savings -> 300, Checking -> 90))
archer: Info(Map(Savings -> 2000, Checking -> 760))
```

In practice, Actors are very flexible. They can be modeled like coarse-grained objects, yet they have built-in concurrency support. The message handling, including the mailbox and flexibility of react, allows you to dynamically control which messages are handled by the Actor given the current state of the Actor. Combined with Scala's built-in support for immutable collections, it's very easy to build transactional support for Actors. Finally, Actor messaging is syntactically lightweight enough to encourage Actor use while at the same time offering the cue to the developer that the cost of passing the message is higher than a method invocation. In the next subsection, we'll see how to compose an Actor out of a series of traits.

Composing Actors

So far in this chapter, we've built Actors as monoliths. A single file contains all the Actor's message handling. However, as Scala is a hybrid OOP/FP language, we're going to combine Scala's OOP and FP sides to create Actors by composing traits. Scala's traits are like Java's interfaces, but traits can contain methods as well as define them. We are going to build two generic traits and compose them together into a specific Actor to provide chat server functionality that we've built in a monolithic fashion earlier in the chapter.

How many listener implementations have you written in your life? Lots, probably. Actors and the listener pattern work well together. Why not build a generic listener and then compose it with a trait that contains business logic into a single Actor? This foreshadows some of the exciting stuff we're going to do in the next chapter, but let's get to writing the code (see Listing 6-6).

Listing 6-6. *Composed Actors*

```scala
import scala.actors.Actor
import Actor._

trait Buildable {
  def handler: PartialFunction[Any, Unit] = Map.empty
}

case class Add(who: Actor)
case class Remove(who: Actor)

trait ListenerMgt extends Buildable {
  private var listeners: List[Actor] = Nil

  override def handler = super.handler orElse {
    case Add(who) =>
      listeners = who :: listeners
      who ! updateMessage
    case Remove(who) => listeners -= who
  }

  protected def updateListeners() {
    val m = updateMessage
    listeners.foreach(a => a ! m)
  }

  protected def updateMessage: Any
}

case object GetInfo

trait GetMgt extends Buildable {
  override def handler = super.handler orElse {
    case GetInfo => reply(updateMessage)
  }
```

```
    protected def updateMessage: Any
}

case class Messages(msgs: List[String])

object Chat extends Actor with ListenerMgt with GetMgt {
  private var msgs: List[String] = Nil
  def act = loop {
    react(handler orElse {
        case s: String => msgs ::= s
          updateListeners()
      })
  }

  protected def updateMessage = Messages(msgs)

  this.start
}

class Listen extends Actor {
  def act = loop {
    react {
      case Messages(m) => println("Got "+m)
    }
  }

  this.start
}
```

That's the whole listing. Let's take it piece by piece. First, we import our Actors:

```
import scala.actors.Actor
import Actor._
```

We define a generic trait called Buildable that has a single handler method. The handler method has the signature that we need to pass to the react method in an Actor, and the implementation is to return a partial function that will match nothing. This is analogous to a blank method in a class that you expect to be overloaded. Your subclass can implement functionality, and when they call super, there is no additional work done.

```
trait Buildable {
  def handler: PartialFunction[Any, Unit] = Map.empty
}
```

Next, we define the messages for a generic listener:

```
case class Add(who: Actor)
case class Remove(who: Actor)
```

We define the `ListenerMgt` trait that extends `Buildable`, has private state and implements the `updateListeners` method, and requires the `updateMessage` method to be implemented:

```
trait ListenerMgt extends Buildable {
  private var listeners: List[Actor] = Nil
```

We implement the `handler` method by composing the superclass's `handler` with this class's message handler:

```
override def handler = super.handler orElse {
  case Add(who) =>
    listeners = who :: listeners
    who ! updateMessage
  case Remove(who) => listeners -= who
}
```

We update all the listeners:

```
protected def updateListeners() {
  val m = updateMessage
  listeners.foreach(a => a ! m)
}
```

Any class that mixes this trait in must implement the `updateMessage` method:

```
  protected def updateMessage: Any
}
```

We've implemented `ListenerMgt`. Now, let's implement a trait, `GetMgt`, which will respond to the `GetInfo` message with the result of the `updateMessage` call:

```
case object GetInfo

trait GetMgt extends Buildable {
  override def handler = super.handler orElse {
    case GetInfo => reply(updateMessage)
  }

  protected def updateMessage: Any
}
```

Finally, let's create a Chat server that composes the ListenerMgt and GetMgt traits into an Actor and then adds Chat-specific functionality:

```
case class Messages(msgs: List[String])

object Chat extends Actor with ListenerMgt with GetMgt {
  private var msgs: List[String] = Nil
  def act = loop {
    react(handler orElse {
        case s: String => msgs = s :: msgs
          updateListeners()
      })
  }

  protected def updateMessage = Messages(msgs)

  this.start
}
```

The composition of Actor with ListenerMgt with GetMgt builds a class that has all of these traits combined. During the composition, ListenerMgt becomes the superclass of GetMgt, so GetMgt's super.handler call will invoke ListenerMgt's handler method. This allows us to chain the calls to handler and compose the PartialFunction that we pass to react. We add in the Chat-specific PartialFunction, and we've got a complete Chat server. Let's write some code to check it out.

```
class Listen extends Actor {
  def act = loop {
    react {
      case Messages(m) => println("Got "+m)
    }
  }

  this.start
}
```

Let's run the code and see what happens:

```
scala> val listen = new Listen
```

```
listen: Listen = Listen@10cc9b4
```

```
scala> Chat ! Add(listen)
```

```
Got List()
```

```
scala> Chat ! "Hello"
```

```
Got List(Hello)
```

```
scala> Chat ! "Dude"
```

```
Got List(Dude, Hello)
```

```
scala> Chat !? GetInfo
```

```
res3: Any = Messages(List(Dude, Hello))
```

This is a simple example of composing an Actor out of generic pieces. The generic pieces can be combined into a single Actor class that provides specific business logic as well as the more generic functionality of listeners and so on.

Summary

In this chapter, we explored Scala Actors. Actors provide an alternative model for concurrency that feels to me a whole lot like coarse-grained OOP. Philipp Haller is a member of Martin Odersky's group and is primarily responsible for Scala's Actor design and implementation. Philipp has written a number of papers on Actors that provide a lot of valuable insight into his design choices as well as Actor implementation.[11] There is plenty more

---

11. Philipp Haller and Martin Odersky, "Event Based Programming without Inversion of Control," http://lampwww.epfl.ch/~odersky/papers/jmlc06.pdf and Philipp Haller and Martin Odersky, "Actors that Unify Threads and Events," http://lamp.epfl.ch/~phaller/doc/haller07coord.pdf.

depth in terms of the use and features of Scala Actors than I covered in this chapter. If Actors seem like a good tool in your software tool chest, please dig deeper, because there is a lot more good stuff to Actors.

Up to now, we've been focusing on what I call the library-consumer coding. We've been writing code that consumes the libraries provided by Scala. Scala has a more complex side based on its type system and traits. In the next chapter, we're going to go where there be dragons and explore the kind of gnarly stuff that library authors use to make sure the programs that library consumers write are type-safe and concise. Please put on your thinking cap and your hip waders, and let's do some hard-core Scala.

CHAPTER 7

■ ■ ■

Traits and Types and Gnarly Stuff for Architects

So far, we've explored Scala from what I consider the "library-consumer" perspective. For the most part, when I'm consuming libraries, I don't worry about complex types, composing many traits into a class, or some of the other powerful features of Scala. "Why?" you may ask. Well, I'm worried about the transformation of input to output, happily mapping Lists, and filtering Seqs. When I'm coding in this mode, I'm not reasoning about my types, but I'm confident that Scala will make sure I don't do anything horribly wrong and that as long as my logic is sound, my code will work. When I'm in this mode, I'm writing code the same way I write Ruby code: I'm looking to get something to work and get some work done.

There are other times when I am designing libraries for other folks to consume. I do this for the Lift Web Framework and for my consulting projects. In this case, I spend a lot more time making sure that the constraints are in place for writing correct code. It takes a lot of time for me to reason about the constraints and then to reduce them to code. When I'm in this mode, I write fewer lines of code, but they are more descriptive. I call this "library producer" mode.

You may be asking, "Why not always code in this mode?" It's because most problems are not solved by coding in this mode. Most of my coding tasks are some variant of, "Here's some user input, and it should be tested this way, and if it's valid then it should update state and send the following events." Reasoning about types is hard and slow work for me. Choosing implicit conversions and designing domain-specific languages (DSLs) takes time, thought, and deliberation. Using types, especially when type inferencing makes them invisible, is simple and doesn't take a lot of thought away from the task at hand. Well-defined types and type interactions will stay out of the library consumer's way but guard against program errors. Similarly, a well-defined DSL will make expressing program logic faster and easier to maintain.

Scala is unique among the languages I've used in that it gives a different set of tools and powers to different team members. Scala's traits, type system, flexible syntax, and implicit conversions give amazingly powerful tools to architects and library designers to build libraries that are simultaneously easy and safe to use. Safety means that tests can focus on the logic of code, not calling conventions. We've seen some examples of the safety of using Option instead of null testing. Being able to reason about the safety by making sure that things have the correct types is very powerful. It also means that the library consumers can focus on their business logic without worrying about declaring lots of fancy types or other distractions. Library consumers don't have to program defensively, because they can trust the correctness of parameters and of return values.

This chapter is a deep dive into the language features that make Scala different from Java. These are tools that I use when I design code bases for other people to consume. These tools let me write code that I can reason is correct, so when I go to write application code, I can be sure that my code is correct if my logic is correct. I can write logic-oriented tests rather than tests that try to fool my code and make sure that I'm guarding against nulls or other parameter and type-related problems.[1]

Show Me Some Bad Java Code

So, I've talked about Java code not being as type-safe as Scala code. You're probably thinking, "But Java is a statically typed language, doesn't it give me all the safety that Scala does?" The answer to that is no. Take a look at the following code and spot the problem:

```
public class Bad {
  public static void main(String[] argv) {
    Object[] a = argv;
    a[0] = new Object();
  }
}
```

This is legal Java code, and here's what happens when we run the code:

```
> java Bad Hello
```

```
Exception in thread "main" java.lang.ArrayStoreException: java.lang.Object
        at Bad.main(Bad.java:4)
```

---

1. Among enthusiasts of other statically typed languages with rich type systems (Standard ML, Haskell, OCaml) the "architect style" is often referred to as "typeful programming," referring exactly to this distinction between "going with the type inference flow" and "using the type system deliberately to encode important invariants."

Java allows us to assign a String[] to Object[]. This is because a String is a subclass of Object, so if the array was read-only, the assignment would make sense. However, the array can be modified. The modification that we've demonstrated shows one of Java's "type-unsafety" features. We'll discuss why this happened and the very complex topic of invariant, covariant, and contravariant types later in this chapter.

Let's start looking at how Scala makes the architect's job easier and makes the coder's job easier.

Library Pimping, Implicit Conversions, and Vampires

We've seen a little bit of stuff so far that looks like magic. The String class seems to have grown methods:

```scala
scala> "Hello".toList
```

```scala
res0: List[Char] = List(H, e, l, l, o)
```

You may be wondering how a Java class that is final could have additional methods on it. Well, Scala has a feature called implicit conversion. If you have an instance of a particular type, and you need another type, and there's an implicit conversion in scope, Scala will call the implicit method to perform the conversion. For example, some date-related methods take Long, and some take java.util.Date. It's useful to have conversions between the two. We create a method that calculates the number of days based on a Long containing a millisecond count:

```scala
scala> def millisToDays(in: Long): Int = (in / (1000L * 3600L * 24L)).toInt
```

We can calculate the number of days by passing a Long to the method:

```scala
scala> millisToDays(5949440999L)
```

```scala
res3: Int = 68
```

However, if we try to pass a Date into the method, we—correctly—get an error:

```scala
scala> import java.util.Date
import java.util.Date
scala> millisToDays(new Date)
```

```
<console>:7: error: type mismatch;
 found    : java.util.Date
 required: Long
        millisToDays(new Date)
                ^
```

But sometimes it's valuable to convert between one type and another. We are used to the conversion in some contexts: Int ➤ Long, Int ➤ Double, and so on. We can define a method that will automatically be called when we need the conversion:

```
scala> implicit def dateToLong(d: Date) = d.getTime
dateToLong: (java.util.Date)Long
```

And this allows us to call millisToDays with a Date instance:

```
scala> millisToDays(new Date)
```

```
res5: Int = 14286
```

You may think that implicit conversions are dangerous and reduce type safety. In some cases that's true. You should be very careful with them, and their use should be an explicit design choice. However, we see that sometimes implicit conversions (e.g., Int ➤ Long) are very valuable, for example, when we have a method that takes a parameter that must be a Long:

```
scala> def m2[T <: Long](in: T): Int = (in / (1000L * 3600L * 24L)).toInt
m2: [T <: Long](T)Int

scala> m2(33)
```

```
<console>:8: error: inferred type arguments [Int] do not conform to method m2's
type parameter bounds [T <: Long]
        m2(33)
        ^
```

So having to type the following could get very old:

```
scala> m2(33.toLong)
```

```
res8: Int = 0
```

This is why implicit conversion is built into the Java compiler and why it's part of the standard Scala Predef.[2]

Library Pimping[3]

The implicit conversion gets us halfway to adding methods to a final class. The second half of the journey is that the Scala compiler will look to a possible implicit conversion from the type you have to a type with the method that you're invoking. The Scala compiler will insert code to call the implicit conversion and then call the method on the resulting instance. For example:

```
"Hello".toList
```

gets converted into

```
Predef.stringWrapper("Hello").toList
```

The ability to add new methods to existing classes has a lot of value for making code more readable and expressive. More importantly, implicit conversions make it possible to define DSLs in Scala.

As a library producer, we can create syntactically pleasing ways of expressing concepts in a type-safe way. Wouldn't it be nice to express a time span as 3 days or 15 seconds? Wouldn't that make code a lot more readable than (3L * 24L * 3600L * 1000L)? Wouldn't it be great to set a timeout or a trigger with 2.hours.later? Let's define a library using implicit conversions. Let's look at the code in Listing 7-1 and then break it down.

---

2. The Predef is the stuff that the compiler imports by default. You can see what implicit conversions are defined in Predef by reading http://lampsvn.epfl.ch/trac/scala/browser/scala/tags/R_2_7_3_final/ src/library/scala/Predef.scala?view=markup.
3. Dr. Martin Odersky, ACM Fellow, Full Professor, coined the term in this blog post: http://www.artima.com/ weblogs/viewpost.jsp?thread=179766.

Listing 7-1. *Timespan DSL*

```
import java.util.Date

object TimeHelpers {
  case class TimeSpanBuilder(val len: Long) {
    def seconds = TimeSpan(TimeHelpers.seconds(len))
    def second = seconds
    def minutes = TimeSpan(TimeHelpers.minutes(len))
    def minute = minutes
    def hours = TimeSpan(TimeHelpers.hours(len))
    def hour = hours
    def days = TimeSpan(TimeHelpers.days(len))
    def day = days
    def weeks = TimeSpan(TimeHelpers.weeks(len))
    def week = weeks
  }

  def seconds(in: Long): Long = in * 1000L
  def minutes(in: Long): Long = seconds(in) * 60L
  def hours(in: Long): Long = minutes(in) * 60L
  def days(in: Long): Long = hours(in) * 24L
  def weeks(in: Long): Long = days(in) * 7L

  implicit def longToTimeSpanBuilder(in: Long): TimeSpanBuilder =
    TimeSpanBuilder(in)

  implicit def intToTimeSpanBuilder(in: Int): TimeSpanBuilder =
    TimeSpanBuilder(in)

  def millis = System.currentTimeMillis

  case class TimeSpan(millis: Long) extends Ordered[TimeSpan] {
    def later = new Date(millis + TimeHelpers.millis)
    def ago = new Date(TimeHelpers.millis - millis)
    def +(in: TimeSpan) = TimeSpan(this.millis + in.millis)
    def -(in: TimeSpan) = TimeSpan(this.millis - in.millis)

    def compare(other: TimeSpan) = millis compare other.millis
  }
```

```
  object TimeSpan {
    implicit def tsToMillis(in: TimeSpan): Long = in.millis
  }


  class DateMath(d: Date) {
    def +(ts: TimeSpan) = new Date(d.getTime + ts.millis)
    def -(ts: TimeSpan) = new Date(d.getTime - ts.millis)
  }


  implicit def dateToDM(d: Date) = new DateMath(d)
}
```

We import `java.util.Date` because we're going to make use of it.

```
import java.util.Date
```

```
object TimeHelpers {
```

We define a class that takes a `Long` as a parameter and has a series of methods that convert the `Long` into a `TimeSpanBuilder` represented by the `length`.

```
  case class TimeSpanBuilder(len: Long) {
    def seconds = TimeSpan(TimeHelpers.seconds(len))
    def second = seconds
    def minutes = TimeSpan(TimeHelpers.minutes(len))
    def minute = minutes
    def hours = TimeSpan(TimeHelpers.hours(len))
    def hour = hours
    def days = TimeSpan(TimeHelpers.days(len))
    def day = days
    def weeks = TimeSpan(TimeHelpers.weeks(len))
    def week = weeks
  }
```

Let's define a bunch of helper methods (called from `TimeSpanBuilder`) that convert to the correct number of milliseconds.

```
  def seconds(in: Long): Long = in * 1000L
  def minutes(in: Long): Long = seconds(in) * 60L
  def hours(in: Long): Long = minutes(in) * 60L
  def days(in: Long): Long = hours(in) * 24L
  def weeks(in: Long): Long = days(in) * 7L
```

Next, we define a bunch of implicit methods that convert from Int or Long into a TimeSpanBuilder. This allows the methods such as minutes or days on TimeSpanBuilder to appear to be part of Int and Long.[4]

```
implicit def longToTimeSpanBuilder(in: Long): TimeSpanBuilder =
                TimeSpanBuilder(in)
```

```
implicit def intToTimeSpanBuilder(in: Int): TimeSpanBuilder = TimeSpanBuilder(in)
```

And we define a helper method that gets the current time in milliseconds:

```
def millis = System.currentTimeMillis
```

We define the TimeSpan class that represents a span of time. We can do math with other TimeSpans or convert this TimeSpan into a Date by calling the later or ago methods. TimeSpan extends the Ordered trait so that we can compare and sort TimeSpans.

```
case class TimeSpan(millis: Long) extends Ordered[TimeSpan] {
  def later = new Date(millis + TimeHelpers.millis)
  def ago = new Date(TimeHelpers.millis - millis)
  def +(in: TimeSpan) = TimeSpan(this.millis + in.millis)
  def -(in: TimeSpan) = TimeSpan(this.millis - in.millis)
```

We compare this TimeSpan to another to satisfy the requirements of the Ordered trait:

```
  def compare(other: TimeSpan) = millis compare other.millis
}
```

Next, we define a companion object that has an implicit method that will convert a TimeSpan into a Long. We'll go into more depth about implicit scoping rules in the next subsection, but briefly, if there is an object with the same name as a class, that object is considered a companion object. If there are any implicit conversions defined in the companion object, they will be consulted if an instance of the class needs to be converted. We define an implicit conversion from TimeSpan to Long in the companion object. This will result in TimeSpan instances being automatically converted to Long if the TimeSpan is assigned to a Long variable or passed as a parameter that requires a Long.

```
object TimeSpan {
  implicit def tsToMillis(in: TimeSpan): Long = in.millis
}
```

---

4. We have to define separate implicit conversions for Int and Long because the Scala compiler will not automatically chain implicit conversions. To Scala, Int and Long are different types, but it will convert Int to Long because of the implicit conversion in Predef.

We can define TimeSpan instances with simple syntax like 3 days. TimeSpans can be converted to Dates with the later and ago methods. But it would be helpful to add addition and subtraction of TimeSpans to Date instances. That's pretty simple using implicit conversions. First, we define a DateMath class that has + and - methods that take a TimeSpan as a parameter.

```scala
class DateMath(d: Date) {
  def +(ts: TimeSpan) = new Date(d.getTime + ts.millis)
  def -(ts: TimeSpan) = new Date(d.getTime - ts.millis)
}
```

And we define the implicit conversion:

```scala
  implicit def dateToDM(d: Date) = new DateMath(d)
}
```

With all the 50 or so lines of code written, let's see how it works.

```scala
scala> import TimeHelpers._
import TimeHelpers._

scala> 1.days
```

```scala
res0: TimeHelpers.TimeSpan = TimeSpan(86400000)
```

```scala
scala> 5.days + 2.hours
```

```scala
res1: TimeHelpers.TimeSpan = TimeSpan(439200000)
```

```scala
scala> (5.days + 2.hours).later
```

```scala
res2: java.util.Date = Mon Feb 16 19:11:29 PST 2009
```

```scala
scala> import java.util.Date
import java.util.Date

scala> val d = new Date("January 2, 2005")
```

```
d: java.util.Date = Sun Jan 02 00:00:00 PST 2005
```

```
scala> d + 8.weeks
```

```
res3: java.util.Date = Sun Feb 27 00:00:00 PST 2005
```

```
scala> val lng: Long = 7.days + 2.hours + 4.minutes
```

```
lng: Long = 612240000
```

So, we've defined a nice DSL for time spans, and it converts itself to Long when necessary. Next, let's talk about implicit scope and vampires.

Inviting Vampires Into Your Code

Implicit conversions are powerful tools and potentially very dangerous. I mean wicked dangerous. Early in my Scala coding career, I put the following implicit into a library:

```
implicit def oToT[T](in: Option[T]): T = in.get
```

This was convenient, very convenient. I no longer had to test Options. I just passed them around, and they were converted from an Option to their underlying type. I mean, really, how often did we get a None anyway? Heh! Boy, did that lead to a lot of bugs. And when I removed the implicit, I had 150 code changes to make. That was 150 latent defects.

I think of implicits like I think of vampires. They are very powerful and very dangerous, and I only invite them into my program's scope when there is a very good reason.[5] Using implicits to convert to a class that has a particular method is a good reason. There's very little likelihood of damage. The Int and Long to TimeSpanBuilder implicits are unlikely to cause a problem, so it's safe to invite them into your code. What is the scope of implicits?

---

5. Part of vampire lore is that a vampire cannot come into your house unless invited (http://en.wikipedia.org/wiki/Vampire#Protection). I think of implicits the same way. They are dangerous and can be kept out of your code if you don't invite them in.

The Scala compiler will consider an implicit in the current scope if

- The implicit is defined in the current class or in a superclass.

- The implicit is defined in a trait or supertrait, or is mixed into the current class or a superclass.

- The implicit is defined on the companion object of the current target class.

- The implicit is available on an object that has been imported into the current scope.

When designing libraries, be careful about defining implicits, and make sure they are in as narrow a scope as is reasonable. When consuming libraries, make sure the implicits defined in the objects are narrow enough and are not going to cause problems like getting stuff from every Option.

Implicit conversions and library pimping is very helpful when building DSLs. Let's turn our attention to other tools that Scala makes available to the library producer. In the last chapter, we explored a little about composing traits together. Let's dive deeper into traits.

Traits: Interfaces on Steroids

We've talked a little about traits. They have all the attributes of Java's interfaces, but they can contain implemented methods. So, Scala's traits provide a contract that a class must fulfill, and they may provide some of that fulfillment. This comes in handy because it means that implementations for shared methods exist in a single place, on the trait, rather than being scattered across your code base.

Let's create a generic OOP listener trait. It can be mixed into any class, and that class will have the methods implemented on it. We have Listing 7-2 first, the walk-though next:

Listing 7-2. *Listener Trait*

```
case class ChangeEvent[OnType](on: OnType)

trait Listener[T] {
  this: T with Listener[T] =>

  type ChangeHandler = {def changed(c: ChangeEvent[T with Listener[T]]): Unit}
  private var listeners: List[ChangeHandler] = Nil

  def addListener(c: ChangeHandler) = synchronized {listeners ::= c}
```

```
  def removeListener(c: ChangeHandler) = synchronized {listeners -= c}

  protected def updateListeners() = synchronized {
    val ch = ChangeEvent(this)
    listeners.foreach(i => i.changed(ch))
  }
}

class Foo extends Listener[Foo] {
  private var _count = 0
  def count = synchronized{_count}
  def inc = synchronized{
    _count += 1
    updateListeners()
  }
}
```

First, let's define a `ChangeEvent` that takes a type parameter of the type of thing that's changed:

```
case class ChangeEvent[OnType](on: OnType)
```

Next, let's define our `Listener` trait that takes the parameter, `T`, of the type that we're mixing the `Listener` into:

```
trait Listener[T] {
```

Next, we define that the type of `this` in the trait is the type of the thing we've mixed `Listener` into. We don't know what `T` is when we define the trait, but we'll know when the trait is mixed into a class. At that time, the type of `T` will be resolved, and we'll know what the type of `this` is.

```
  this: T with Listener[T] =>
```

We define a type, `ChangeHandler`, which is a structural type.[6] It is any class that has a `changed` method that takes as its parameter a `ChangeEvent[T with Listener[T]]`. This means that any instance that has this method signature can register a listener without implementing a particular interface or trait.[7]

```
  type ChangeHandler = {def changed(c: ChangeEvent[T with Listener[T]]): Unit}
```

---

6. We explored structural types in Chapter 4.
7. Structural typing in Scala is achieved via reflection. In practice, there is a 2.5x performance penalty for dispatching a structurally typed method vs. invoking a method on an interface. For very tight loops, this is meaningful. For 99 percent of your code, it's not meaningful.

We define the private variable that holds the listeners:

```
private var listeners: List[ChangeHandler] = Nil
```

We define the addListener and removeListener methods:

```
def addListener(c: ChangeHandler) = synchronized {listeners ::= c}
```

```
def removeListener(c: ChangeHandler) = synchronized {listeners -= c}
```

Finally, we update our listeners:

```
protected def updateListeners() = synchronized {
  val ch = ChangeEvent(this)
  listeners.foreach(i => i.changed(ch))
}
}
```

We've defined the Listener trait. Let's see how easy it is to use. We'll create a Foo class that extends the Listener and add functionality to Foo that demonstrates change events:

```
class Foo extends Listener[Foo] {
```

We define some private state, _count, a read-only count property, and an inc method that increments the count and notifies the listeners:

```
private var _count = 0
def count = synchronized{_count}
def inc = synchronized{
  _count += 1
  updateListeners()
}
}
```

Next, let's test out the Foo class in the REPL:

```
scala> val f = new Foo
```

```
f: Foo = Foo@eabd2f
```

We define an instance that's capable of listening for ChangeEvent[Foo] events:

```
scala> object Bar {
    def changed(c: ChangeEvent[Foo]) {println("changed: "+c.on.count)}
    }
```

```
defined module Bar
```

We add our listener, Bar, to f:

```
scala> f.addListener(Bar)
```

Let's see what happens when we call the inc method:

```
scala> f.inc
```

```
changed: 1
```

```
scala> f.inc
```

```
changed: 2
```

We've just encapsulated a bunch of generic listener functionality in our Listener trait. We have a single place in our code base that defines listener behavior. The code is isolated, so each developer who has to implement a listener doesn't have to start from scratch. It means that if we want to add functionality to our listener, for example logging each change, we can do so in one place rather than in each place that we implement a listener.

Traits and Class Hierarchies

One of the big challenges with developing a class hierarchy when you are constrained by single inheritance is figuring out what things should be base classes and where things should go in the class hierarchy. If we're modeling living things, how do you model things with legs when that can include any animal? Should there be LeggedAnimals and LeglessAnimals? But then, how do you deal with Mammals and Reptiles? Maybe we can make HasLegs an interface, but then I can give a Plant legs. Scala to the rescue.

We've already seen that traits can implement methods. Additionally, traits can have rules about what kind of classes and other traits they can be mixed into. Further, you can declare method parameters that are a consolidation of types, for example:

```
def foo(bar: Baz with Blarg with FruitBat)
```

Only instances of classes that extend Baz, Blarg, and FruitBat may be passed into this method.

Let's go model some living things.

```
abstract class LivingThing
abstract class Plant extends LivingThing
abstract class Fungus extends LivingThing
abstract class Animal extends LivingThing
```

Good so far. A LivingThing must be a plant, fungus, or animal. But, what about legs? Who can have legs?

```
trait HasLegs extends Animal {
  def walk() {println("Walking")}
}
```

The HasLegs trait extends Animal. But Animal is a class, so what does it mean for a trait to extend a class? It means that the compiler will only let you mix HasLegs into something which subclasses from Animal. Thus, we've defined that only animals have legs, but any type of animal can have legs. It's the same for HasWings:

```
trait HasWings extends Animal {
  def flap() {println("Flap Flap")}
}
```

But, only things with wings can fly. This is a different notation. We define the rules of the self type with this: HasWings =>. The compiler will flag an error if this trait is not mixed into a class that also extends HasWings. So, we can use self types to define the rules for what classes a given trait can be mixed into.[8]

```
trait Flies {
  this: HasWings =>
  def fly() {println("I'm flying")}
}
```

And Birds have wings and legs:

```
abstract class Bird extends Animal with HasWings with HasLegs
```

Let's define a couple of different Birds:

```
class Robin extends Bird with Flies
class Ostrich extends Bird
```

---

8. Self types can also be used to discover at compile time what class a trait has been mixed into. See
   http://www.scala-lang.org/node/124.

All mammals have a `bodyTemperature`:

```
abstract class Mammal extends Animal {
  def bodyTemperature: Double
}
```

Some animals know their name, and if they do, we can ask their name:

```
trait KnowsName extends Animal {
  def name: String
}
```

So, a `Dog` is a `Mammal` that has legs and knows its name:

```
class Dog(val name: String) extends Mammal with HasLegs with KnowsName {
  def bodyTemperature: Double = 99.3
}
```

Some animals, cats, and children come to mind who know their own name but will sometimes ignore their name:

```
trait IgnoresName {
  this: KnowsName =>
  def ignoreName(when: String): Boolean

  def currentName(when: String): Option[String] =
    if (ignoreName(when)) None else Some(name)
}
```

Now we can define a `Cat` class that has legs, knows its name, and ignores its name except at dinner time:

```
class Cat(val name: String) extends Mammal with HasLegs with
  KnowsName with IgnoresName {
  def ignoreName(when: String) = when match {
    case "Dinner" => false
    case _ => true
  }
  def bodyTemperature: Double = 99.5
}
```

Some `Animals` can be `Athletes`, and `Runners` are `Athletes` with legs:

```
trait Athlete extends Animal
```

```
trait Runner {
  this: Athlete with HasLegs =>
  def run() {println("I'm running")}
```

```
}
```

A Person is a Mammal with legs and knows its name:

```
class Person(val name: String) extends Mammal with
  HasLegs with KnowsName {
  def bodyTemperature: Double = 98.6
}
```

A Biker is a Person but may only be added to an Athlete:

```
trait Biker extends Person {
  this: Athlete=>
  def ride() {println("I'm riding my bike")}
}
```

And finally, let's define some Genders:

```
trait Gender
trait Male extends Gender
trait Female extends Gender
```

We've defined a complex hierarchy of classes and traits. Let's see what we can do with these classes. First, let's try to create a Dog that's also a Biker:

```
scala> val bikerDog = new Dog("biker") with Athlete with Biker
```

```
<console>:4: error: illegal inheritance; superclass Dog
 is not a subclass of the superclass Person
 of the mixin trait Biker
       val bikerDog = new Dog("biker") with Athlete with Biker
```

Cool, the compiler enforced our rule about Bikers needing to be Persons. Let's create some valid LivingThings. Please note that we can compose together different traits as part of the object creation. So, archer is an instance of a class that is a subclass of Dog that implements Athlete, Runner, and Male. The Scala compiler automatically creates this new, anonymous class for you.

```
scala> val archer = new Dog("archer") with Athlete with Runner with Male
```

```
archer: Dog with Athlete with Runner with Male = $anon$1@18bbc98
```

```
scala> val dpp = new Person("David") with Athlete with Biker with Male
```

```
dpp: Person with Athlete with Biker with Male = $anon$1@7b5617
```

```
scala> val john = new Person("John") with Athlete with Runner with Male
```

```
john: Person with Athlete with Runner with Male = $anon$1@cd927d
```

```
scala> val annette = new Person("Annette") with Athlete with Runner with
        Female
```

```
annette: Person with Athlete with Runner with Female = $anon$1@1ec41c0
```

We've got a bunch of Animals. Let's see what we can do with them:

```
scala> def goBiking(b: Biker) = println(b.name+" is biking")
goBiking: (Biker)Unit
scala> goBiking(dpp)
```

```
David is biking
```

What happens if we try to send Annette on a bike ride?

```
scala> goBiking(annette)
```

```
<console>:7: error: type mismatch;
 found   : Person with Athlete with Runner with Female
 required: Biker
       goBiking(annette)
```

This makes sense. The method requires a Biker, and Annette is not a Biker. However, just as we can compose a class out of traits, we can require that a class implement more than one trait in order to be the parameter to a method:

```
scala> def charityRun(r: Person with Runner) = r.run()
```

```
charityRun: (Person with Runner)Unit
```

The charityRun method can only be called with a parameter that is a subclass of Person and also implements the Runner trait.

```
scala> charityRun(annette)
```

```
I'm running
```

What if we try to call the method with a Runner that is not a Person?

```
scala> charityRun(archer)
```

```
<console>:7: error: type mismatch;
 found    : Dog with Athlete with Runner with Male
 required: Person with Runner
       charityRun(archer)
```

We can define the parameter in terms of traits. The womensRun method may only be called with a parameter that's both a Runner and a Female:

```
scala> def womensRun(r: Runner with Female) = r.run()
```

```
womensRun: (Runner with Female)Unit
```

```
scala> womensRun(annette)
```

```
I'm running
```

```
scala> val madeline = new Cat("Madeline") with Athlete with Runner with Female
```

```
madeline: Cat with Athlete with Runner with Female = $anon$1@11dde0c
```

```
scala> womensRun(madeline)
```

```
I'm running
```

In this way, we've modeled complex relationships. We've modeled things in a way that you cannot model with Java. Scala's compositional rules are very powerful tools for defining very complex class hierarchies and for specifying the rules for composing classes as well as the rules for passing parameters into methods. In this way, we can make sure that the charityRun method can only be called with valid parameters rather than testing for parameter correctness at runtime and throwing an exception if the parameter is not correct. This increased modeling flexibility combined with enhanced type safety gives the architect another tool to help developers write correct code.

Types—It's Beyond Generic

We've seen how Scala allows complex modeling and compile-time type checking that allows us to build complex class hierarchies. What about things that make a developer's life easier? What about things that make a developer, a library consumer, think that Scala is as easy and flexible as a scripting language? In this section, we're going to write a database abstraction layer that allows a developer to define a table mapping simply as follows:

```
class MyTable extends Table[MyTable] {
  val table = "mytable"
  val id = IntColumn("id")
  val name = StringColumn("name")
  val birthday = DateColumn("birthday")
```

```
  type ColumnTypes = (Int, String, Date)
  def columns = id ~ name ~ birthday
}
```

The class will allow type-safe queries such as this:

```
MyTable.findAll(By(MyTable.id, 33))
```

And the compiler will flag an error on a query such as this:

```
MyTable.findAll(By(MyTable.id, "33"))
```

Thus, the library consumer gets the benefits of type safety along with very lightweight syntax for defining the mapping to the table and for defining queries. Scala's type system and type inferencer make this possible.

Table Code

Let's look at the entire listing for the Query Builder (Listing 7-3). After that, we'll slice and dice it to understand how it works from the library-producer standpoint and see how it makes a library consumer's life easier.

Listing 7-3. *Query Builder*

```
import java.util.Date
import java.sql._
import scala.collection.mutable.ListBuffer

trait BasicColumn[TableType <: Table[TableType], T] {
  def default: T
  def name: String
  def getField(rs: ResultSet): T
  def set(st: PreparedStatement, offset: Int, value: T)
}

trait Table[MyType <: Table[MyType]] extends SuperTuple {
  this: MyType =>

  def table: String

  type ColumnTypes <: Product


  def columns: ColumnTypes with FieldProduct[MyType]
```

```scala
trait MyColumn[T] extends BasicColumn[MyType, T] {
  def ~[OT](p: MyColumn[OT]): MyTuple2[MyType, T, OT] = {
    val col = this
    new MyTuple2[MyType, T, OT](col.default, p.default) {
      def fields = List(col, p)
      def fieldProduct: (MyColumn[T], MyColumn[OT]) = (col, p)
    }
  }
}


case class IntColumn(name: String) extends MyColumn[Int] {
  def default = 0
  def set(st: PreparedStatement, offset: Int, value: Int) {
    st.setInt(offset, value)
  }
  def getField(rs: ResultSet): Int = rs.getInt(name)
}


  case class LongColumn(name: String) extends MyColumn[Long] {
    def default = 0
    def set(st: PreparedStatement, offset: Int, value: Long) {
      st.setLong(offset, value)
    }
    def getField(rs: ResultSet): Long = rs.getLong(name)
  }


  case class StringColumn(name: String) extends MyColumn[String] {
    def default = ""
    def set(st: PreparedStatement, offset: Int, value: String) {
      st.setString(offset, value)
    }
    def getField(rs: ResultSet): String = rs.getString(name)
  }
  case class DateColumn(name: String) extends MyColumn[Date] {
    def default = new Date(0)
    def set(st: PreparedStatement, offset: Int, value: Date) {
      st.setDate(offset, new java.sql.Date(value.getTime))
    }
    def getField(rs: ResultSet): Date = rs.getDate(name)
  }
```

```scala
def find[FT <: Product with FieldProduct[MyType]]
 (cols: FT, query: QueryParam[MyType]*): List[FT#ReturnType] = {
  val select = "SELECT "+cols.fields.map(f => table+"."+f.name).mkString(", ")

  val by = query.flatMap{
    case b @ By(_, _) => Some(b)
    case _ => None
  }.toList

  val where = by match {
    case Nil => ""
    case xs => " WHERE "+xs.map(f => table+"."+
                              f.column.name+" = ?").mkString(" AND ")
  }

  val orderBy = query.flatMap{
    case b @ OrderBy(_, _) => Some(b)
    case _ => None
  }.toList match {
    case Nil => ""
    case xs => " ORDER BY "+xs.map(f => table+"."+
                                 f.column.name+
                                 f.order.sql).mkString(", ")
  }

  using(getJDBCConnection) { conn =>
    prepareStatement(conn, select + where + orderBy) { st =>
      by.zipWithIndex.foreach{case (b, idx) => b.bind(st, idx + 1)}
      executeQuery(st) {
        cols.buildResult _
      }
    }
  }
}

protected def getJDBCConnection: Connection

def using[T <: {def close(): Unit}, R](t: T)(f: T => R): R =
try {f(t)} finally {t.close()}
```

```scala
  protected def prepareStatement[T](conn: Connection, sql: String)
  (f: PreparedStatement => T): T =
  using(conn.prepareStatement(sql))(f)

  protected def executeQuery[T](st: PreparedStatement)
  (f: ResultSet => T): List[T] =
  using(st.executeQuery){ rs =>
    val ret = new ListBuffer[T]
    while (rs.next) ret += f(rs)
    ret.toList
  }

}

trait QueryParam[TableType <: Table[TableType]]

case class OrderBy[TableType <: Table[TableType]]
(column: BasicColumn[TableType, _], order: SortOrder) extends
QueryParam[TableType]

sealed trait SortOrder {def sql: String}
case object Ascending extends SortOrder {def sql: String = " "}
case object Descending extends SortOrder {def sql = " DESC "}


case class By[TableType <: Table[TableType], T, PT]
(column: BasicColumn[TableType, T], param: PT)(implicit f: PT => T)
extends QueryParam[TableType] {
  def bind(st: PreparedStatement, offset: Int): Unit = {
    column.set(st, offset, param)
  }
}

trait SuperTuple {
  sealed trait FieldProduct[TableType <: Table[TableType]] {
    def fields: List[BasicColumn[TableType, _]]
    def fieldProduct: Product
    def buildResult(rs: ResultSet): ReturnType
    type ReturnType <: Product
  }
```

```scala
abstract class MyTuple2[TableType <: Table[TableType],
                        A1, A2](a1: A1, a2: A2)
extends Tuple2[A1, A2](a1, a2) with FieldProduct[TableType] {
  def fieldProduct: (BasicColumn[TableType, A1],
                     BasicColumn[TableType, A2])

  type ReturnType = (A1, A2)

  def buildResult(rs: ResultSet): ReturnType =
  (fieldProduct._1.getField(rs),
   fieldProduct._2.getField(rs))

  def ~[OT](p: BasicColumn[TableType, OT]):
  MyTuple3[TableType, A1, A2, OT] ={
    val f = fields
    val fp = fieldProduct

    new MyTuple3[TableType, A1, A2, OT](this._1, this._2, p.default) {
      val fields = f ::: List(p)
      val fieldProduct = (fp._1, fp._2, p)
    }
  }
}

abstract class MyTuple3[TableType <: Table[TableType],
                        A1, A2, A3]
(a1: A1, a2: A2, a3: A3) extends
Tuple3[A1, A2, A3](a1, a2, a3) with FieldProduct[TableType] {
  def buildResult(rs: ResultSet): ReturnType =
  (fieldProduct._1.getField(rs),
   fieldProduct._2.getField(rs),
   fieldProduct._3.getField(rs))

  type ReturnType = (A1, A2, A3)

  def fieldProduct: (BasicColumn[TableType, A1],
                     BasicColumn[TableType, A2],
                     BasicColumn[TableType, A3])
  def ~[OT](p: BasicColumn[TableType, OT]):
```

```scala
    MyTuple4[TableType, A1, A2, A3, OT] = {
      val f = fields
      val fp = fieldProduct
      new MyTuple4[TableType, A1, A2, A3,
                   OT](
        this._1, this._2, this._3, p.default) {
        val fields = f ::: List(p)
        val fieldProduct = (fp._1, fp._2, fp._3, p)
      }
    }
  }

  abstract class MyTuple4[TableType <: Table[TableType],
                          A1, A2, A3, A4]
  (a1: A1, a2: A2, a3: A3, a4: A4) extends
  Tuple4[A1, A2, A3, A4](a1, a2, a3, a4) with FieldProduct[TableType] {
    def fieldProduct: (BasicColumn[TableType, A1],
                       BasicColumn[TableType, A2],
                       BasicColumn[TableType, A3],
                       BasicColumn[TableType, A4])

    type ReturnType = (A1, A2, A3, A4)

    def buildResult(rs: ResultSet): ReturnType =
    (fieldProduct._1.getField(rs),
     fieldProduct._2.getField(rs),
     fieldProduct._3.getField(rs),
     fieldProduct._4.getField(rs))
  }
}

trait ConnectionSupplier {
  protected def getJDBCConnection: Connection = null // do something better
}

class MyTable extends Table[MyTable] with ConnectionSupplier {
  val table = "mytable"
  val id = IntColumn("id")
  val name = StringColumn("name")
  val birthday = DateColumn("birthday")
```

```
  type ColumnTypes = (Int, String, Date)
  def columns = id ~ name ~ birthday
}
```

```
object MyTable extends MyTable
```

The Column

Let's put on our architect hat and get our hands dirty with some of Scala's types. First, let's import some stuff that will be helpful later:

```
import java.util.Date
import java.sql._
import scala.collection.mutable.ListBuffer
```

We're going to define a generic trait that will define the mapping to the column in a particular table. The first parameter is the type of the Table that the column is part of. The second type parameter, T, is the type of the column itself. The column must define a default value of its type, its name, and a method to convert a JDBC ResultSet into the value of the column's type and put the column into a PreparedStatement.

```
trait BasicColumn[TableType <: Table[TableType], T] {
  def default: T
  def name: String
  def getField(rs: ResultSet): T
  def set(st: PreparedStatement, offset: Int, value: T)
}
```

The Table

Next, we define the trait that holds the table itself. The Table trait takes a type parameter that is the type of the class that is implementing the trait. This type, MyType, will also be applied to fields and queries so that we can make sure that the only fields that are specified in queries to a particular table instance are fields defined by that table. We're also extending SuperTuple, which is a builder of Tuples that have extra type information. We'll get to that in a little while.

```
trait Table[MyType <: Table[MyType]] extends SuperTuple {
  this: MyType =>
```

A concrete instance of this trait must define the name of the database table.

```
  def table: String
```

And the instances must also define the type of the columns. This must be a `Product`. `Product` is the supertrait of all the `Tuple` classes. This does not give a lot of type safety standing on its own, because lots and lots of classes subclass from `Product`. However, you'll see how we make sure the type defined here ties to the actual fields, and the compiler will make sure that things are defined correctly.

```
type ColumnTypes <: Product
```

Next, the implementer must specify the columns in the database. The type here is `ColumnTypes with FieldProduct[MyType]`. We just defined `ColumnTypes`, so the type that `columns` returns must check with the types we defined in `ColumnTypes`. Further, the only way to construct a `FieldType` is via the `SuperTuple` building mechanism that we mixed into this trait. So, we know that the `ColumnType` with `FieldProduct[MyType]` will check such that `ColumnTypes` has to be a `Tuple`, and it has to be a `Tuple` with the same arity (number of places) and same type as the columns.

```
def columns: ColumnTypes with FieldProduct[MyType]
```

Concrete Columns

We're going to create a subtrait of `BasicColumn` that has a helper method, ~, that allows chaining of fields in definitions.[9] So, you can write id ~ name ~ birthday as a definition of a Tuple of fields. These Tuples are special as they are subclasses of `FieldProduct[MyType]`.

```
trait MyColumn[T] extends BasicColumn[MyType, T] {
  def ~[OT](p: MyColumn[OT]): MyTuple2[MyType, T, OT] = {
    val col = this
    new MyTuple2[MyType, T, OT](col.default, p.default) {
      def fields = List(col, p)
      def fieldProduct: (MyColumn[T], MyColumn[OT]) = (col, p)
    }
  }
}
```

The `IntColumn` is a column that holds an `Int`, has a default value, and can convert itself to and from JDBC.

```
case class IntColumn(name: String) extends MyColumn[Int] {
  def default = 0
  def set(st: PreparedStatement, offset: Int, value: Int) {
    st.setInt(offset, value)
```

---

9. In Scala, ~ is just a method. It's not a destructor like it is in C++.

```
  }
  def getField(rs: ResultSet): Int = rs.getInt(name)
}
```

And we now define column representations for Long, String, and Date:

```
case class LongColumn(name: String) extends MyColumn[Long] {
  def default = 0
  def set(st: PreparedStatement, offset: Int, value: Long) {
    st.setLong(offset, value)
  }
  def getField(rs: ResultSet): Long = rs.getLong(name)
}

case class StringColumn(name: String) extends MyColumn[String] {
  def default = ""
  def set(st: PreparedStatement, offset: Int, value: String) {
    st.setString(offset, value)
  }
  def getField(rs: ResultSet): String = rs.getString(name)
}

case class DateColumn(name: String) extends MyColumn[Date] {
  def default = new Date(0)
  def set(st: PreparedStatement, offset: Int, value: Date) {
    st.setDate(offset, new java.sql.Date(value.getTime))
  }
  def getField(rs: ResultSet): Date = rs.getDate(name)
}
```

Previously, we've defined the column types. Now, let's see how we define a method that can handle a query. The find method takes two parameters: the columns to return and the query parameters. You might call it as such:

```
findCols(id ~ name, By(age, 33)).
```

Such a call would return a List[(Int, String)]. Let's look at the type declaration. First we define the type parameter FT, which must be a Product with FieldProduct[MyType]. That means it's one of those nifty Tuples that can be constructed by chaining fields together with the ~. The first parameter, cols, must be an FT. That means that the cols parameter is composed of fields that represent columns in the current table. The return type is the ReturnType type on FieldProduct, which will be the column types.

Building a Query

We're going to define the find method, which builds a query and sends it to the database.

```
def find[FT <: Product with FieldProduct[MyType]]
(cols: FT, query: QueryParam[MyType]*): List[FT#ReturnType] = {
```

query: QueryParam[MyType]* is the definition of a variable argument list. So, this method can take zero or more QueryParams. We return a List[FT#ReturnType] with a List of the ReturnType dependent type of FT. This is some fairly gnarly stuff. The find method takes FT as a type parameter. FT is a subclass of FieldProduct. FieldProduct has a dependent type called ReturnType, but that type is not stable; it is variable depending on the FT type parameter. Thus, the # rather than the . says, "Here's a type that's calculated based on the type parameter rather than a type that is stable."

```
val select = "SELECT "+cols.fields.map(f => table+"."+f.name).mkString(", ")
```

Put a List of the By instance into the by variable.

```
val by = query.flatMap{
  case b @ By(_, _) => Some(b)
```

The case b @ By(_, _) code will match any instance of By and assign it to the b variable.

```
  case _ => None
}.toList

val where = by match {
  case Nil => ""
  case xs => " WHERE "+xs.map(f => table+"."+
                            f.column.name+" = ?").mkString(" AND ")
}

val orderBy = query.flatMap{
  case b @ OrderBy(_, _) => Some(b)
  case _ => None
}.toList match {
  case Nil => ""
  case xs => " ORDER BY "+xs.map(f => table+"."+
                            f.column.name+
                            f.order.sql).mkString(", ")
}
```

With a JDBC connection, we prepare a PreparedStatement and bind the query parameters to the ? in the WHERE clause. We execute the PreparedStatement and for each row in the ResultSet build a Tuple to return.

```
  using(getJDBCConnection) { conn =>
    prepareStatement(conn, select + where + orderBy) { st =>
      by.zipWithIndex.foreach{case (b, idx) => b.bind(st, idx + 1)}
      executeQuery(st) {
        cols.buildResult _
      }
    }
  }
}
```

We get a JDBC connection:

```
protected def getJDBCConnection: Connection
```

We define a series of control structures for running queries. We saw control structures like these in Chapter 4.

```
def using[T <: {def close(): Unit}, R](t: T)(f: T => R): R =
try {f(t)} finally {t.close()}

protected def prepareStatement[T](conn: Connection, sql: String)
(f: PreparedStatement => T): T =
using(conn.prepareStatement(sql))(f)

protected def executeQuery[T](st: PreparedStatement)
(f: ResultSet => T): List[T] =
  using(st.executeQuery){ rs =>
    val ret = new ListBuffer[T]
    while (rs.next) ret += f(rs)
    ret.toList

  }
}
```

Making Queries Type-Safe

We've defined our table class. Let's define some QueryParameters. QueryParams are type-safe in that they can only contain fields defined in the Table that we're passing them to. We guarantee this by defining the TableType parameter. In the Table.find method, we only accept QueryParam[MyType], so the compiler will enforce this requirement.

```
trait QueryParam[TableType <: Table[TableType]]
```

Next, we define the OrderBy case class. It takes column and direction parameters. The column's TableType equals the OrderBy's TableType, thus we can only use columns from the table that we're running the query on. SortOrder is a sealed trait. Marking a trait or class sealed means that all classes that implement that trait must be defined in this file, ensuring that subclasses don't sneak into our code. We define two case objects, Ascending and Descending, which implement the trait.

```scala
case class OrderBy[TableType <: Table[TableType]]
  (column: BasicColumn[TableType, _], order: SortOrder) extends
  QueryParam[TableType]


sealed trait SortOrder {def sql: String}
case object Ascending extends SortOrder {def sql: String = " "}
case object Descending extends SortOrder {def sql = " DESC "}
```

Next, we define the By clause of our query. By takes three type parameters:

- TableType, T, PT. T is the type of the column. PT is the type of the parameter to the query.

- column is a BasicColumn[TableType, T].

- param is a PT.

There's also an implicit parameter, f, which converts an instance of PT into an instance of T. Marking the parameter implicit has two effects. First, when we construct an instance of By, the compiler will look for an implicit conversion in the current scope that turns a PT into a T. If one cannot be found, the compiler will flag an error. Second, within the scope of the By, any time you have a PT and you need a T, the compiler will apply the function. The net result of this is that you can pass an Int as a parameter to a query where the column is a Long, and the compiler won't complain.

```scala
case class By[TableType <: Table[TableType], T, PT]
  (column: BasicColumn[TableType, T], param: PT)(implicit f: PT => T)
  extends QueryParam[TableType] {
  def bind(st: PreparedStatement, offset: Int): Unit = {
    column.set(st, offset, param)
  }
}
```

Boilerplate

The next bunch of code is a long slog. We have to define subclasses of Tuples with two to four places that include extra type information that we used in Table. We mix FieldProduct into each of the Tuples so that they contain extra information about the types as well as column information. You may ask, "Why not use a List or some such?" Each element in the List has the same type, where each element in a Tuple has its own information, and because we're tying the types together in Table to ensure that the columns we define have the correct type, we need to know the type of each column.

```
trait SuperTuple {
```

Now we define the FieldProduct trait. It's sealed so that we know that other implementation or subclasses will not sneak into our code.

```
sealed trait FieldProduct[TableType <: Table[TableType]] {
  def fields: List[BasicColumn[TableType, _]]
  def fieldProduct: Product
  def buildResult(rs: ResultSet): ReturnType
  type ReturnType <: Product
}
```

Next we define MyTuple2, which extends Scala's Tuple2 (a two-element Tuple) with FieldProduct, and we define the fieldProduct method as a Tuple2 of the columns in the table. Harking back to Chapter 3, Lists and Tuples are different. Lists contain a variable number of elements, all of the same type. Tuples contain a fixed number of elements, each of which may be a different type. The rest of the code is boilerplate.

```
abstract class MyTuple2[TableType <: Table[TableType],
                        A1, A2](a1: A1, a2: A2)
  extends Tuple2[A1, A2](a1, a2) with FieldProduct[TableType] {
    def fieldProduct: (BasicColumn[TableType, A1],
                       BasicColumn[TableType, A2])

type ReturnType = (A1, A2)
    def buildResult(rs: ResultSet): ReturnType =
    (fieldProduct._1.getField(rs),
     fieldProduct._2.getField(rs))
```

```
    def ~[OT](p: BasicColumn[TableType, OT]):
    MyTuple3[TableType, A1, A2, OT] ={
      val f = fields
      val fp = fieldProduct

      new MyTuple3[TableType, A1, A2, OT](this._1, this._2, p.default) {
        val fields = f ::: List(p)
        val fieldProduct = (fp._1, fp._2, p)
      }
    }
}


abstract class MyTuple3[TableType <: Table[TableType],
                        A1, A2, A3]
(a1: A1, a2: A2, a3: A3) extends
Tuple3[A1, A2, A3](a1, a2, a3) with FieldProduct[TableType] {
  def buildResult(rs: ResultSet): ReturnType =
  (fieldProduct._1.getField(rs),
   fieldProduct._2.getField(rs),
   fieldProduct._3.getField(rs))

  type ReturnType = (A1, A2, A3)

  def fieldProduct: (BasicColumn[TableType, A1],
                     BasicColumn[TableType, A2],
                     BasicColumn[TableType, A3])
  def ~[OT](p: BasicColumn[TableType, OT]):
  MyTuple4[TableType, A1, A2, A3, OT] = {
    val f = fields
    val fp = fieldProduct
    new MyTuple4[TableType, A1, A2, A3,
                 OT](
      this._1, this._2, this._3, p.default) {
      val fields = f ::: List(p)
      val fieldProduct = (fp._1, fp._2, fp._3, p)
    }
  }
}


abstract class MyTuple4[TableType <: Table[TableType],
                        A1, A2, A3, A4]
(a1: A1, a2: A2, a3: A3, a4: A4) extends
```

```
    Tuple4[A1, A2, A3, A4](a1, a2, a3, a4) with FieldProduct[TableType] {
      def fieldProduct: (BasicColumn[TableType, A1],
                          BasicColumn[TableType, A2],
                          BasicColumn[TableType, A3],
                          BasicColumn[TableType, A4])

      type ReturnType = (A1, A2, A3, A4)

      def buildResult(rs: ResultSet): ReturnType =
      (fieldProduct._1.getField(rs),
       fieldProduct._2.getField(rs),
       fieldProduct._3.getField(rs),
       fieldProduct._4.getField(rs))
    }
}
```

Vending JDBC Connections

Are we there yet? Almost. We're finished the hard slogging. Next, we define a trait that vends JDBC connections:

```
trait ConnectionSupplier {
  protected def getJDBCConnection: Connection = null // do something better
}
```

Making a Concrete Class That Implements Table

We define a class that extends Table with ConnectionSupplier. This is our library consumer code that we will write to consume the Library trait. For all the heavy slogging and boiler-plate in SuperTuple, we get something very nice and pleasant, something that's simple and understandable.

```
class MyTable extends Table[MyTable] with ConnectionSupplier {
  val table = "mytable"
  val id = IntColumn("id")
  val name = StringColumn("name")
  val birthday = DateColumn("birthday")

  type ColumnTypes = (Int, String, Date)
  def columns = id ~ name ~ birthday
}

object MyTable extends MyTable
```

We define the `MyTable` class and then the `MyTable` object. We need to do this because the type of the object `MyTable` is not known until the object is fully declared. There is an exception to this requirement when defining classes.[10] So we have to go through two steps to define our `MyTable` object.

Type-Safe Fun

But, oh how we can have some type-safe fun. We can find the `id` and `name` columns matching everyone whose `name` is David and whose `id` is 44. The type inferencer does the right thing and knows that the return type is a `Tuple2[(Int, String)]`.

```
MyTable.find(MyTable.id ~ MyTable.name,
             By(MyTable.name, "David"), By(MyTable.id, 44),
             OrderBy(MyTable.name, Ascending)) match
{
  case (_, name) :: _ => name.length // name is a String
  case _ =>
}
```

And we can get all the columns from our table where the `id` is 33.

```
MyTable.find(MyTable.columns, By(MyTable.id, 33)) match {
  case (_, name, date) :: _ => name.length; date.getTime
  case _ =>
}
```

Pretty neat, huh? We've got the type safety of Scala with very readable library consumer code. But how type-safe is it? Let's define a second table and see what happens when we try to mix things up.

```
class MyTable2 extends Table[MyTable2] with ConnectionSupplier {
  val table = "mytable"
  val id = IntColumn("id")
  val name = StringColumn("name")
  val birthday = DateColumn("birthday")

  type ColumnTypes = (Int, String, Date)
  def columns = id ~ name ~ birthday
}

object MT2 extends MyTable2
```

---

10. See http://www.nabble.com/Re:--scala--Cyclic-reference--p22024739.html.

We've got MT2, which looks just like MyTable. Will the compiler let us build a query partially from MyTable and MT2? No.

```
MyTable.find(MyTable.name ~ MyTable.id, OrderBy(MT2.name, Ascending))
```

```
Query.scala:256: error: type mismatch;
found    : MT2.StringColumn
required: BasicColumn[MyTable, _]
  MyTable.find(MyTable.name ~ MyTable.id, OrderBy(MT2.name, Ascending))
                                                  ^
```

Next, let's see what happens if we try to pass an Int where we expect a String.

```
MyTable.find(MyTable.name ~ MyTable.id, By(MyTable.name, 33))
```

```
Query.scala:258: error: no implicit argument matching parameter type
                        (Int) => String was found.
  MyTable.find(MyTable.name ~ MyTable.id, By(MyTable.name, 33))
                                          ^
```

In this section, we've seen how Scala's type system provides us a very powerful mechanism for defining the rules for passing parameters. We were able to go through a lot of work to create a library that was complex underneath but simple to use. Let's go on to see a little more about how types and class hierarchies work in Scala.

Variance

Variance is an important and challenging concept. It defines the rules by which parameterized types can be passed as parameters. In the beginning of the chapter, we showed how passing a String[] (Java notation) to a method expecting an Object[] can cause problems. Java allows you to pass an array of something to a method expecting an array of something's superclass. This is called covariance. On the surface, this makes a lot of sense. If you can pass a String to a method expecting an Object, why can't you pass an Array[String] (Scala notation) to a method expecting an Array[Object]? Because Array is mutable: it can be written to in addition to being read from, so a method that takes an Array[Object] may modify the Array by inserting something that cannot be inserted into an Array[String].

Defining the type variance for type parameters allows you to control how parameterized types can be passed to methods.

Variance comes in three flavors: invariant, covariant, and contravariant. Type parameters can be individually marked as covariant or contravariant and are by default invariant.

Invariant Parameter Types

In Scala, Array[T] is invariant. This means that you can only pass an Array[String] to foo(a: Array[String]) and that you can only pass an Array[Object] to bar(a: Array[Object]). This ensures that what is read from or written to the array is something of the correct type. So, for anything that's mutable, the type parameter should be invariant. You do this by doing nothing with the type parameter. So, let's define an invariant class:

```
class Holder[T](var data: T)
```

The class holds data of type T. Let's write a method:

```
scala> def add(in: Holder[Int]) {in.data = in.data + 1}
```

```
add: (Holder[Int])Unit
```

```
scala> val h = new Holder(0)
```

```
h: Holder[Int] = Holder@bc0eba
```

```
scala> add(h)
scala> h.data
```

```
res2: Int = 1
```

Because the add method expects an Int to come out of Holder and puts an Int back into the Holder, the type of the Holder must be invariant. That does not mean that invariant containers lose their ability to hold subclasses of their declared type. A Holder[Number] can contain a Double, and an Array[Object] can contain String, Integer, and so on. Let's put a Double into a Holder[Number]:

```
scala> val nh = new Holder[Number](33.3d)
```

```
nh: Holder[java.lang.Number] = Holder@340c9c
```

And we define a method that rounds the number:

```
scala> def round(in: Holder[Number]) {in.data = in.data.intValue}
```

```
round: (Holder[java.lang.Number])Unit
```

We call the round method, and let's see what we get out the other side:

```
scala> round(nh)
```

```
scala> nh.data
```

```
res16: java.lang.Number = 33
```

We put in a Number and got back a Number. What's the underlying class for the Number?

```
scala> nh.data.getClass
```

```
res17: java.lang.Class[_] = class java.lang.Integer
```

Great. Integer is a subclass of Number, so we can put a Integer or a Double into the Holder[Number]. We preserve the ability to use class hierarchies with invariant type parameters. Let's finally see what happens when we try to pass a Holder[Double] into round.

```
scala> val dh = new Holder(33.3d)
```

```
dh: Holder[Double] = Holder@1801e5f
```

```
scala> round(dh)
```

```
<console>:8: error: type mismatch;
 found    : Holder[Double]
 required: Holder[java.lang.Number]
```

So, invariant type parameters protect us when we have mutable data structures like arrays. Let's move on to covariant parameter types.

Covariant Parameter Types

Covariant parameter types are designated with a + before the type parameter. A covariant type is useful for read-only containers. Scala's List is defined as List[+T], which means that it's covariant on type T. List is covariant because if you pass a List[String] to a method that expects a List[Any], then every element of the List satisfies the requirement that is an Any *and* we cannot change the contents of the List.

Let's define an immutable class, Getable. Once an instance of Getable is created, it cannot change, so we can mark its type, T, as covariant.

```
scala> class Getable[+T](val data: T)
```

```
defined class Getable
```

Let's define a method that takes a Getable[Any]:

```
scala> def get(in: Getable[Any]) {println("It's "+in.data)}
```

```
get: (Getable[Any])Unit
```

We define an instance of Getable[String]:

```
scala> val gs = new Getable("String")
```

```
gs: Getable[java.lang.String] = Getable@10a69f0
```

We can call get with gs:

```
scala> get(gs)
```

```
It's String
```

Let's try the same example but passing a Getable[java.lang.Double] into something that expects a Getable[Number]:

```
scala> def getNum(in: Getable[Number]) = in.data.intValue
```

```
getNum: (Getable[java.lang.Number])Int
```

```
scala> def gd = new Getable(new java.lang.Double(33.3))
```

```
gd: Getable[java.lang.Double]
```

```
scala> getNum(gd)
```

```
res7: Int = 33
```

Yes, the covariance works the way we expect it to. We can make read-only classes covariant. I guess that means that contravariance is good for write-only classes.

Contravariant Parameter Types

So, if covariance allows us to pass List[String] to a method that expects List[Any], what good is contravariance? Let's first look at a write-only class, Putable:

```
scala> class Putable[-T] {
        def put(in: T) {println("Putting "+in)}
        }
```

Next, let's define a method that takes a Putable[String]:

```
scala> def writeOnly(in: Putable[String]) {in.put("Hello")}
```

```
writeOnly: (Putable[String])Unit
```

And let's declare an instance of Putable[AnyRef]:

```
scala> val p - new Putable[AnyRef]
```

```
p: Putable[AnyRef] = Putable@75303f
```

And what happens if we try to call writeOnly?

```
scala> writeOnly(p)
```

```
Putting Hello
```

Okay, so we can call a method that expects a Putable[String] with a Putable[AnyRef] because we are guaranteed to call the put method with a String, which is a subclass of AnyRef. Standing alone, this is not particularly valuable, but if we have a class that does something with input that results in output, the value of contravariance becomes obvious. The inputs to a transformation are contravariant. Calling something that expects at least any AnyRef with a String is legal and valid. But the return value can be covariant because we expect to get back a Number, so if we get an Integer, a subclass of Number, we're okay. Let's see how it works. We'll define DS with a contravariant In type and a covariant Out type:

```
scala> trait DS[-In, +Out]{def apply(i: In): Out}
```

```
defined trait DS
```

Let's create an instance that will convert Any into an Int:

```
scala> val t1 = new DS[Any, Int]{def apply(i: Any) = i.toString.toInt}
```

```
t1: java.lang.Object with DS[Any,Int] = $anon$1@14dcfad
```

We define check, a method that takes a DS[String, Any]:

```
scala> def check(in: DS[String, Any]) = in("333")
```

```
check: (DS[String,Any])Any
```

And we call check with t1:

```
scala> check(t1)
```

```
res14: Any = 333
```

Rules of Variance

So, we've successfully defined and used an invariant type. The invariant type was mutable, so it both returned and was called with a particular type. We created a convariant type which was an immutable holder of a value. Finally, we created a transformer that had contravariant input and covariant output. Wait, that sounds like a function. That's right, Scala's FunctionN traits have contravariant parameters and covariant results. This leads us to the simple rules of variance:

- Mutable containers should be invariant.

- Immutable containers should be covariant.

- Inputs to transformations should be contravariant, and outputs from transformations should be covariant.

In very few pages, we've covered a very complex topic. So, thanks for hanging in. Let's go have some fun watching dragons and other monsters kill bunnies.

Poignantly Killing Bunnies: Dwemthy's Stairs

Why the Lucky Stiff is one of the best and most clever programmers in the Ruby community.[11] He wrote *Why's (Poignant) Guide to Ruby*, a most excellent Ruby tutorial.[12] Why introduces some of Ruby's metaprogramming concepts in *Dwemthy's Array*[13] in which a rabbit battles an array of creatures. N8han[14] updated the example to work in Scala.[15] With a tip of the hat to Why, a nod and a wink to N8han, and a huge thanks to Jorge Ortiz for finding this example, I'm going to talk about how `Rabbit * Dwemthy.s.stairs` will cause our hero, our rabbit, to throw a bomb at Dwemthy's stairs, thus casting the first salvo in the battle against the monsters that reside there.

As a library producer, we want to write code that makes it super-simple for library consumers to express their logic. Being able to define weapons like

```
trait Axe { this: Monster =>
  def |^ = Weapon((me, it) => turn(me, it, me.weapon + 45))
}
```

and compose them into `Monsters` like

```
object ScubaArgentine extends Monster with Axe {
  def life = 46
  def strength = 35
  def charisma = 91
  def weapon = 2
}
```

means that our library consumers will focus on the business logic at hand and will be able to write concise, powerful, flexible code that can be read even by those who are not hard-core computer geeks.

The Immutable World

Our example will build the rabbit in the immutable world of Scala and use functions for transformation rather than `method_missing` magic that Why uses in his example. Our object hierarchy contains `Creatures` of which the `Rabbit` is a subclass and `Monster` is a subclass. There are many instances of `Monster`, including `Dragon`. Dwemthy's stairs contains seven `Monsters`. In Why's example, only `Rabbit` could fight any of the `Monsters`, but our `Monsters` will be able to fight each other. We can see what happens when the Dragon uses its tail:

---

11. http://whytheluckystiff.net/
12. http://poignantguide.net/ruby/chapter-1.html
13. http://poignantguide.net/dwemthy/
14. http://technically.us/code
15. http://technically.us/code/x/dwemthy_s-arrayhhhhhlist-in-scally

```
Dragon ---< Dwemthy.s.stairs
```

And we define battles until death:

```
Dragon.---<.tilDeath (Dwemthy.s.stairs)
```

With a poignant wave and a little more flair than usual, let's sashay down the stairs to our Scala implementation.

The Code

Here's the bunny-hoppingly fun code. Please glance through it in one big blob (Listing 7-4), and then we'll parse through it.

Listing 7-4. *Dwemthy's Stairs*

```scala
object Random extends Random

trait Creature[BaseType] {
  this: BaseType with Creature[BaseType] =>
  import Creature._

  type Us = BaseType with Creature[BaseType]

  def life: Int
  def strength: Int
  def charisma: Int
  def weapon: Int

  def setLife(life: Int): Us

  protected def rand(max: Int) = Random.nextInt(max)

  def dead_? = life == 0

  protected case class Weapon(turn: (Us, Them) => (Us, Them)) {
    private var _tilDeath = false
    private def this(f: (Us, Them) => (Us, Them), s: Boolean) = {
      this(f)
      _tilDeath = s
    }
    def tilDeath = new Weapon(turn, true)
```

```scala
def apply(t: Them): (Us, Them) with Rebattle = apply(Creature.this, t)

private[Creature] def apply(seed: Us, t: Them) = {
  val ret = doBattle(seed, t)
  ret match {
    case (nu, nt) if nu.dead_? =>
      println("You're dead: "+seed+" -> "+nu)
      println("Enemy: "+t+" -> "+nt)
    case (nu, nt) if nt.dead_? =>
      println("You won: "+seed+" -> "+nu)
      println("Enemy: "+t+" -> "+nt)
    case _ =>
  }
  new Tuple2[Us, Them](ret._1, ret._2) with Rebattle
}

private def doBattle(u: Us, t: Them): (Us, Them) =
(u.dead_?, t.dead_?) match {
  case (true, _) | (_, true) => (u, t)
  case _ if !_tilDeath => turn(u, t)
  case _ => turn(u,t) match {case (u2,t2) => doBattle(u2, t2)}
}
}

trait Rebattle { this: (Us, Them) =>
  def apply(w: Weapon) = w(_1, _2)
}

protected def round(u: Us, t: Them, damage: Int): (Us, Them) =
t attackedBy u.calcHit(damage) match {
  case e if e.dead_? => (u, e)
  case e => (u attackedBy t.calcHit(e.weapon), e)
}

private def attackedBy(damage: => Int): Us =
calcLife(u => (u.life - damage) match {
    case n if n <= 0 => u.setLife(0)
    case n => u.setLife(n)
  })

private def calcLife[T](f: Us => T): T =
rand(charisma) match {
```

```scala
      case up if up % 9 == 7 =>
        println(this+" magick powers up "+(up / 4))
        f(setLife(life + up / 4))
      case _ => f(this)
    }

  private def calcHit(damage: Int) = {
    val hit = rand(strength + damage)
    println(this+" hits with "+hit+" points of damage!")
    hit
  }

  def >*< = Weapon((u, t) => round(u, t, u.weapon))
}

object Creature {
  type Them = Creature[_]

  implicit def fromSeq(in: Seq[Them]): Them =
    CreatureCons(in.firstOption, in.drop(1))

  case class CreatureCons(head: Option[Them], tail: Seq[Them]) extends
  Creature[CreatureCons] {
    def setLife(n: Int) =
    if (n <= 0) CreatureCons(tail.firstOption, tail.drop(1))
    else CreatureCons(head.map(_.setLife(n)), tail)

    def life = head.map(_.life) getOrElse 0
    def strength = head.map(_.strength) getOrElse 0
    def charisma = head.map(_.charisma) getOrElse 0
    def weapon = head.map(_.weapon) getOrElse 0

    override def toString = "["+ (head.map(_.toString) getOrElse "")+
    (if (tail.isEmpty) "" else "..." + tail.last) + "]"
  }
}

case class Rabbit(life: Int, bombs: Int) extends Creature[Rabbit] {
  val strength = 2
  val charisma = 44
  val weapon = 4
```

```scala
  def setLife(life: Int) = new Rabbit(life, bombs)

  // lettuce will build your strength and extra ruffage
  // will fly in the face of your opponent!!
  def % = Weapon((r, e) => {
      val lettuce = rand(charisma)
      println("[Healthy lettuce gives you "+lettuce+" life points!!]")
      round(r.setLife(r.life + lettuce), e, 0)
    })

  // little boomerang
  def ^ = Weapon((r, e) => round(r, e, 13 ))

  // the hero's sword is unlimited!!
  def / = Weapon((r, e) =>
    round(r, e, rand(4 + ((e.life % 10) * (e.life % 10)))))

  // bombs, but you only have three!!
  def * = Weapon((r, e) =>
    r.bombs match {
      case 0 => println("[UHN!! You're out of bombs!!]")
        round(r, e, 0)
      case n =>
        round(Rabbit(r.life, r.bombs - 1), e, 86)
    })
}

object Rabbit extends Rabbit(10, 3)

trait Monster extends Creature[Monster] {
  def name = "\\w*\\$$".r.findFirstIn(this.getClass.getName).
  flatMap("\\w*".r.findFirstIn) getOrElse "??"

  def setLife(newLife: Int): Monster = new DupMonster(this, newLife)

  override def toString = name+"("+life+")"

  private class DupMonster(old: Monster, val life: Int) extends Monster {
    val strength: Int = old.strength
    val charisma: Int = old.charisma
```

```scala
    val weapon: Int = old.weapon
    override val name: String = old.name
  }
}


trait Tail { this: Monster =>
  def ---< = Weapon((me, it) => round(me, it, rand(me.strength + me.life) +
                                   me.weapon))
}


trait Axe { this: Monster =>
  def |^ = Weapon((me, it) => round(me, it, me.weapon + 45))
}


object ScubaArgentine extends Monster with Axe {
  def life = 46
  def strength = 35
  def charisma = 91
  def weapon = 2
}


object IndustrialRaverMonkey extends Monster {
  def life = 46
  def strength = 35
  def charisma = 91
  def weapon = 2
}


object DwarvenAngel extends Monster with Axe {
  def life = 540
  def strength = 6
  def charisma = 144
  def weapon = 50
}


object AssistantViceTentacleAndOmbudsman extends Monster {
  def life = 320
  def strength = 6
  def charisma = 144
  def weapon = 50
}
```

```
object TeethDeer extends Monster {
  def life = 655
  def strength = 192
  def charisma = 19
  def weapon = 109
}

object IntrepidDecomposedCyclist extends Monster {
  def life = 901
  def strength = 560
  def charisma = 422
  def weapon = 105
}

object Dragon extends Monster with Tail {
  def life = 1340
  def strength = 451
  def charisma = 1020
  def weapon = 939
}

object Dwemthy {
  object s {
    val stairs = List(ScubaArgentine, IndustrialRaverMonkey,
                      DwarvenAngel,
                      AssistantViceTentacleAndOmbudsman,
                      TeethDeer,
                      IntrepidDecomposedCyclist,
                      Dragon)
  }
}
```

Walking Through the Code

First, we create a random number helper because we don't want every battle to come out the same:

```
object Random extends Random
```

We're going to define our type-safe `Creature`. We'll define `Creature[Rabbit]`, `Creature[Monster]`, and so on. These declarations will allow the compiler to enforce what kind of weapons can be mixed into our characters. Further, the self type `BaseType` with `Creature[BaseType]` will ensure that the `Creature` is mixed into its `BaseType`.

```
trait Creature[BaseType] {
  this: BaseType with Creature[BaseType] =>
```

Our `Creature`, be it `Rabbit`, `Monster`, or something else, is going to fight with another `Creature`. We want to use Scala's type system to define what our type is, `Us`, and what another `Creature`'s type is, `Them`, even though every participant in our battles is going to be a subclass of `Creature`. This allows us a lot of flexibility in terms of defining who can use one of our weapons, `Us`, and who we are fighting against, `Them`. We use Scala's dependent types to define the types `Us` and `Them` and use those types in a fair number of places. We import the `Creature` object to get the declaration `Type Them = Creature[_]`, which makes a lot of the method declarations a lot shorter and make more sense.[16]

```
  import Creature._
```

We also defined the `Us` type. This means that `Creature` implementations are type-safe such that a `Dragon` cannot sneak into a `Rabbit`'s method, which takes an `Us` parameter. It allows the compiler to enforce weapon usage as well.

```
  type Us = BaseType with Creature[BaseType]
```

We define the methods that every creature must implement:

```
  def life: Int
  def strength: Int
  def charisma: Int
  def weapon: Int
```

And finally, the `setLife` method that creates a new instance of the specific `Creature` with its `life` updated. Each `Creature` is immutable, so we must create a new instance rather than mutating the `Creature` in place.

```
  def setLife(life: Int): Us
```

We define the random number generator:

```
  protected def rand(max: Int) = Random.nextInt(max)
```

---

16. I originally defined `Type Them = Creature[_]` in the Creature trait, but the result was that the compiler found more than one path to certain `implicit` conversions.

Is the creature dead? Scala allows you to have symbols as well as letters and numbers in method names, but in order to mix symbols and letters and numbers, you have to separate the symbols with the underscore.

```
def dead_? = life == 0
```

An instance of Weapon defines a turn or a whole battle tilDeath between Us and Them. The Weapon takes a function, turn, that transforms instances of Us and Them based on particular rules. For example, our Rabbit has three bombs that he can throw. Each time the Rabbit throws a bomb, we have to update the Rabbit to have fewer bombs. This is the transformation rule for the bomb. We define the transformation rule, and the Weapon instance applies the transformation rule to an instance of our enemy, Them, once or until one of the participants is dead.

```
protected case class Weapon(turn: (Us, Them) => (Us, Them)) {
```

Normally, battles are single turns. This gives you the ability to repeat the battle until one of the participants is dead. There's an alternate constructor that modifies the _tilDeath flag.

```
private var _tilDeath = false
private def this(f: (Us, Them) => (Us, Them), s: Boolean) = {
  this(f)
  _tilDeath = s
}
```

If we want to battle tilDeath, we call this method, which will return a new Weapon instance with the _tilDeath flag set.

```
def tilDeath = new Weapon(turn, true)
```

The apply method is the heart of the class. The public apply method takes a Them parameter and calls the private apply method with the instance of the Creature that created the Weapon and Them. The private method (callable from anything in the Creature scope) takes instances of Us and Them and pits them together in doBattle. If either of the participants dies, it prints a message. Finally, it returns a (Us, Them) with Rebattle, which is the (Us, Them) Tuple contains a Rebattle trait. Rebattle allows you to chain (apply) another Weapon instance type safely such that the result is another (Us, Them) with Rebattle. This means our Rabbit can throw a bomb in the first turn and then use a sword in the next. However, our Rabbit cannot use the Dragon's tail as a weapon.

```
def apply(t: Them): (Us, Them) with Rebattle = apply(Creature.this, t)

private[Creature] def apply(seed: Us, t: Them) = {
  val ret = doBattle(seed, t)
  ret match {
```

```
      case (nu, nt) if nu.dead_? =>
        println("You're dead: "+seed+" -> "+nu)
        println("Enemy: "+t+" -> "+nt)
      case (nu, nt) if nt.dead_? =>
        println("You won: "+seed+" -> "+nu)
        println("Enemy: "+t+" -> "+nt)
      case _ =>
    }
    new Tuple2[Us, Them](ret._1, ret._2) with Rebattle¹⁷
  }
```

doBattle is a recursive method. If either participant is dead, we don't try to battle any more. Otherwise, if we're not repeating, we apply Us and Them to our turn transformation once and return the result. Otherwise, we keep applying the function until someone's dead.

```
  private def doBattle(u: Us, t: Them): (Us, Them) =
  (u.dead_?, t.dead_?) match {
    case (true, _) | (_, true) => (u, t)
    case _ if !_tilDeath => turn(u, t)
    case _ => turn(u,t) match {case (u,t) => doBattle(u, t)}
  }
}
```

The Rebattle trait can only be mixed into a Tuple2[Us, Them]. Its apply method applies the Us and Them instances to the Weapon. The result is yet another (Us, Them) with Rebattle, which can be used for application of yet another weapon.

```
trait Rebattle { this: (Us, Them) =>
  def apply(w: Weapon) = w(_1, _2)
}
```

The next methods are housekeeping used in a turn. Typically, the turn function passed to Weapon will call round to do the actual fighting. First, Them is attacked by Us. If the opponent did not die, Us is attacked by Them.

```
protected def round(u: Us, t: Them, damage: Int): (Us, Them) =
  t attackedBy u.calcHit(damage) match {
    case e if e.dead_? => (u, e)
    case e => (u attackedBy t.calcHit(e.weapon), e)
  }
```

---

17. ret._1 refers to the first element in the Tuple, and ret._2 refers to the second element.

```
  private def attackedBy(damage: => Int): Us =
  calcLife(u => (u.life - damage) match {
      case n if n <= 0 => u.setLife(0)
      case n => u.setLife(n)
    })

  private def calcLife[T](f: Us => T): T =
  rand(charisma) match {
    case up if up % 9 == 7 =>
      println(this+" magick powers up "+(up / 4))
      f(setLife(life + up / 4))
    case _ => f(this)
  }

  private def calcHit(damage: Int) = {
    val hit = rand(strength + damage)
    println(this+" hits with "+hit+" points of damage!")
    hit
  }
```

Every Creature has its claws, >*<, as a Weapon, but we can, and will, give other creatures other Weapons.

```
  def >*< = Weapon((u, t) => round(u, t, u.weapon))
}
```

Why's Dwemthy's Array example demonstrated Ruby's metaprogramming by creating a subclass of Ruby's Array class and using method_missing to forward method calls intended for a particular monster to the first monster in the Array. In Scala, when our hero battles on Dwemthy's Stairs, we use Scala's implicits to convert a Seq[Creature[_]] into a Creature suitable for application of a Weapon. We create a companion object for Creature. It contains the definition on Them, which is any Creature. We define an implicit method that will convert a Seq[Them] into a Them. When the compiler encounters a method that needs a Them, a Creature[_], but has a Seq[Them], it will call Creature.fromSeq to perform the conversion.

```
object Creature {
  type Them = Creature[_]

  implicit def fromSeq(in: Seq[Them]): Them =
  CreatureCons(in.firstOption, in.drop(1))
```

The CreatureCons class is a Creature and holds Creatures. It's got a head, the current Creature, and tail, the rest of the Creatures. The setLife method transforms the Creature to an instance with an updated life field by creating a new instance of CreatureCons with an updated head. If the Creature at the head dies, we promote the first Creature in the tail to the head. The normal Creature methods are passed to the head. Note that we had to manually write each of the methods, rather than using Ruby's metaprogramming to forward the missing methods to the head item.

```scala
case class CreatureCons(head: Option[Them], tail: Seq[Them]) extends
Creature[CreatureCons] {
  def setLife(n: Int) =
  if (n <= 0) CreatureCons(tail.firstOption, tail.drop(1))
  else CreatureCons(head.map(_.setLife(n)), tail)

  def life = head.map(_.life) getOrElse 0
  def strength = head.map(_.strength) getOrElse 0
  def charisma = head.map(_.charisma) getOrElse 0
  def weapon = head.map(_.weapon) getOrElse 0

  override def toString = "["+ (head.map(_.toString) getOrElse "")+
  (if (tail.isEmpty) "" else "..." + tail.last ) + "]"
  }
}
```

We define our hero, Rabbit. It's a Creature[Rabbit] with life, bombs, and fixed charisma, strength, and weapon. setLife creates a new Rabbit instance with updated life. Our Rabbit also has a bunch of weapons: % (lettuce), ^ (boomerang), / (sword), and * (bomb).

```scala
case class Rabbit(life: Int, bombs: Int) extends Creature[Rabbit] {
  val strength = 2
  val charisma = 44
  val weapon = 4

  def setLife(life: Int) = new Rabbit(life, bombs)

  // lettuce will build your strength and extra ruffage
  // will fly in the face of your opponent!!
  def % = Weapon((r, e) => {
      val lettuce = rand(charisma)
      println("[Healthy lettuce gives you "+lettuce+" life points!!]")
      round(r.setLife(r.life + lettuce), e, 0)
    })

  // little boomerang
  def ^ = Weapon((r, e) => round(r, e, 13 ))
```

```
// the hero's sword is unlimited!!
def / = Weapon((r, e) =>
  round(r, e, rand(4 + ((e.life % 10) * (e.life % 10)))))

// bombs, but you only have three!!
def * = Weapon((r, e) =>
  r.bombs match {
    case 0 => println("[UHN!! You're out of bombs!!]")
      round(r, e, 0)
    case n =>
      round(Rabbit(r.life, r.bombs - 1), e, 86)
  })
}
```

We define the default instance of Rabbit with 10 life points and 3 bombs.

```
object Rabbit extends Rabbit(10, 3)
```

Next, we define a Monster trait, which is a Creature[Monster]. It gets its name from its class and some regular expression magic. We create a new Monster instance by creating an instance of DupMonster with updated life and the same everything else.

```
trait Monster extends Creature[Monster] {
  def name = "\\w*\\$$".r.findFirstIn(this.getClass.getName).
  flatMap("\\w*".r.findFirstIn) getOrElse "??"

  def setLife(newLife: Int): Monster = new DupMonster(this, newLife)

  override def toString = name+"("+life+")"
  private class DupMonster(old: Monster, val life: Int) extends Monster {
    val strength: Int = old.strength
    val charisma: Int = old.charisma
    val weapon: Int = old.weapon
    override val name: String = old.name
  }
}
```

Let's define some weapons that a Monster, and only a Monster, can have.

```
trait Tail { this: Monster =>
  def ---< = Weapon((me, it) => round(me, it, rand(me.strength + me.life) +
                                      me.weapon))
}
```

```
trait Axe { this: Monster =>
  def |^ = Weapon((me, it) => round(me, it, me.weapon + 45))
}
```

And we define our Monsters. Some of them have weapon traits mixed in.

```
object ScubaArgentine extends Monster with Axe {
  def life = 46
  def strength = 35
  def charisma = 91
  def weapon = 2
}

object IndustrialRaverMonkey extends Monster {
  def life = 46
  def strength = 35
  def charisma = 91
  def weapon = 2
}

object DwarvenAngel extends Monster with Axe {
  def life = 540
  def strength = 6
  def charisma = 144
  def weapon = 50
}

object AssistantViceTentacleAndOmbudsman extends Monster {
  def life = 320
  def strength = 6
  def charisma = 144
  def weapon = 50
}

object TeethDeer extends Monster {
  def life = 655
  def strength = 192
  def charisma = 19
  def weapon = 109
}
```

```scala
object IntrepidDecomposedCyclist extends Monster {
  def life = 901
  def strength = 560
  def charisma = 422
  def weapon = 105
}

object Dragon extends Monster with Tail {
  def life = 1340
  def strength = 451
  def charisma = 1020
  def weapon = 939
}
```

Finally, we define the Dwemthy's stairs. This is the List of Monsters that our Rabbit (or other Monsters) will battle.

```scala
object Dwemthy {
  object s {
    val stairs = List(ScubaArgentine, IndustrialRaverMonkey,
                      DwarvenAngel,
                      AssistantViceTentacleAndOmbudsman,
                      TeethDeer,
                      IntrepidDecomposedCyclist,
                      Dragon)
  }
}
```

What does our Rabbit look like?

```scala
scala> Rabbit
```

```
res0: Rabbit.type = Rabbit(10,3)
```

And the Dragon?

```scala
scala> Dragon
```

```
res1: Dragon.type = Dragon(1340)
```

What happens when our Rabbit attacks the Dragon?

```scala
scala> Rabbit * Dragon
```

```
Rabbit(10,2) hits with 58 points of damage!
Rabbit(10,2) magick powers up 4
Dragon(1340) hits with 808 points of damage!
You're dead: Rabbit(10,3) -> Rabbit(0,2)
Enemy: Dragon(1340) -> Dragon(1282)
res2: (Rabbit(0,2),Dragon(1282))
```

What about a Dragon fighting a Dragon?

```scala
scala> Dragon >*< Dragon
```

```
Dragon(1340) hits with 1271 points of damage!
Dragon(1340) hits with 572 points of damage!
res3: (Dragon(768),Dragon(69))
```

Not dead this time, let's try again by applying the >*< weapon again:

```scala
scala> res3(Dragon >*<)
```

```
Dragon(768) hits with 53 points of damage!
Dragon(69) hits with 662 points of damage!
res4: (Dragon(106),Dragon(16))
```

These dragons are hardy. Let's use the tail.

```scala
scala> res4(Dragon ---<)
```

```
Dragon(106) hits with 158 points of damage!
You won: Dragon(106) -> Dragon(106)
Enemy: Dragon(16) -> Dragon(0)
res5: (Dragon(106),Dragon(0))
```

Let's go back to the result of the first Dragon vs. Dragon round and try to use the Rabbit's bomb:

```scala
scala> res3(Rabbit *)
```

```
<console>:6: error: type mismatch;
 found    : Rabbit.Weapon
 required: Dragon.Weapon
       res3(Rabbit *)
              ^
```

So, Scala's type safety has saved us from dragons using bombs. That's good. Next, let's see how our hero does tossing bombs at all the monsters on Dwemthy's stairs.

```scala
scala> Rabbit.*.tilDeath(Dwemthy.s.stairs)
```

```
Rabbit(10,2) hits with 20 points of damage!
[ScubaArgentine(46)...Dragon(1340)] hits with 29 points of damage!
You're dead: Rabbit(10,3) -> Rabbit(0,2)
Enemy: [ScubaArgentine(46)...] -> [ScubaArgentine(26)...Dragon(1340)]
res0: (Rabbit(0,2),[ScubaArgentine(26)...Dragon(1340)])
```

Our Rabbit did not do so well. How about a dragon?

```scala
scala> Dragon.---<.tilDeath(Dwemthy.s.stairs)
```

```
[ScubaArgentine(46)...Dragon(1340)] magick powers up 13
Dragon(1340) hits with 1722 points of damage!
[ScubaArgentine(46)...Dragon(1340)] hits with 31 points of damage!
...
Dragon(296) hits with 816 points of damage!
[Dragon(1340)] hits with 84 points of damage!
Dragon(212) hits with 1061 points of damage!
You won: Dragon(1340) -> Dragon(212)
Enemy: [ScubaArgentine(46)...Dragon(1340)] -> []
res6: (Dragon.Us, Creature.Them) with Dragon.Rebattle = (Dragon(212),[])
```

Compared to the Ruby code, the library parts of the Scala code were more complex. We had to do a lot of work to make sure our types were correct. We had to manually rewrite `Creature`'s properties in the `DupMonster` and the `CreatureCons` classes.[18] This is more work than `method_missing`. We also had to do a fair amount of work to support immutability in our `Creatures` and `Weapons`.[19]

On the other hand, the result was much more powerful than the Ruby version. If we had to write tests for our Ruby code to test what the Scala compiler assures us of, we'd need a lot more lines of code. For example, we can be sure that our `Rabbit` could not wield an `Axe`. To get this assurance in Ruby, we'd have to write a test that makes sure that invoking `|^` on a `Rabbit` fails. Our Scala version ensures that only the `Weapons` defined for a given `Creature` can be used by that `Creature`, something that would require a lot of runtime reflection in Ruby.

The end user code is pretty much the same between the Scala and Ruby code. The definition of `Rabbit` and the various `Monsters` is similar lines of code and similar readability to the Ruby code. So, we've seen that as a library producer, our life is more challenging. But it gives the library consumer the same conciseness and flexibility as a scripting language and a materially better set of assurances that the code is correct.

Summary

Wow, that was an awful lot of material to cover in a single chapter. Type systems in general are a very complex topic. Benjamin Pierce spends nearly 500 pages covering the topic in *Types and Programming Languages* (The MIT Press, 2002), a very good read for an in-depth exploration of types and how they can be used to write better programs.[20] We also covered a lot of the features that make Scala a powerful language for writing programs. We saw how Scala's implicit conversions lead to very simple and concise DSLs. We saw how Scala's traits can be composed into very powerful classes. You can even do dependency injection without external libraries using Scala's traits.[21] We saw how complex concepts such as covariance and contravariance lead to safe and powerful ways to use type parameters.

18. We could have avoided some of that by using the JVM's proxy-generation facilities. See http://java.sun.com/j2se/1.3/docs/guide/reflection/proxy.html.
19. The use of Array and Tuples here strongly motivates the development of "HList for Scala," which would reduce the size and complexity of the "library code" a lot; see http://www.artima.com/forums/flat.jsp?forum=283&thread=237780
20. *Types and Programming Languages* is intended for computer science grad students who are thinking about designing new programming languages.
21. See http://jonasboner.com/2008/10/06/real-world-scala-dependency-injection-di.html.

Finally, we saw how some extra thought and work as the library producer leads to easy-to-use and type-safe libraries that allow the library consumers to write code that's as concise and easy to read as scripting language code but that's got the compiler making sure that dragons don't use bombs that are meant for use by rabbits.

In the next chapter, we're going to roll many of Scala's concepts together by building parsers using Scala's parser combinator library. We're going to be library consumers and experience how easy it is to use a well-written Scala library.

CHAPTER 8

■■■

Parsers—Because BNF Is Not Just for Academics Anymore

We've covered a lot of ground so far, but most of the examples have been one or two lines of code. Sure, the control structures are helpful, and of course most of our programming projects pit dragons and bunnies in battle, but one of the biggest challenges we face is dealing with real-world data. If we're lucky, the real-world data will be well formed in XML. But sometimes we're not so lucky. Sometimes we're handed a spec for a wire format or a text file format and told to "deal with it." Good news: Scala is very good at helping you deal with it.

Scala comes with a parser combinator library that makes writing parsers simple. Furthermore, because your parser is written in Scala, there's a single compilation step, and you get all the benefits of Scala's type safety. In this chapter, we're going to explore combinators and Scala's parser combinatory library.

Higher-Order Functions and Combinators

You may be wondering why something so mundane as parsing input comes this late in the book. Why have we gone through Chapter 7 just to deal with parsing? Scala's parser combinator library gives us a view of a powerful DSL, and it has its roots in a lot of computer science and mathematics. Let's look at higher-order functions (functions that take functions as parameters), then at how higher-order functions can be combined to yield powerful functionality.

Higher-Order Functions

We've been using higher-order functions all book long. These are functions, or methods, that take functions as parameters. List.map is a higher-order function:

```scala
scala> List(1, 2, 3).map(_ + 1)
```

```
res0: List[Int] = List(2, 3, 4)
```

We've also seen how we can compose functions:

```scala
scala> def plus1(in: Int) = in + 1
```

```
plus1: (Int)Int
```

```scala
scala> def twice(in: Int) = in * 2
```

```
twice: (Int)Int
```

```scala
scala> val addDouble = plus1 _ andThen twice
```

```
addDouble: (Int) => Int = <function>
```

```scala
scala> List(1,2,3).map(addDouble)
```

```
res2: List[Int] = List(4, 6, 8)
```

In this example, we've composed a function, addDouble, out of two other functions, plus1 and twice. We can compose very complex functions. We can even compose functions dynamically based on user input. We saw an example of this in the "Building New Functions" section in Chapter 4.

Combinators

"What's a parser combinator?" you ask.[1] A combinator is a function that takes only other functions as parameters and returns only functions. Combinators allow you to combine small functions into big functions. In the case of the parser combinator library, you can combine small functions that match individual characters or small groups of characters into bigger functions that can parse complex documents.

So, you have input that is a Seq[Char] (sequence of characters), and you want to parse the stream, which will either contain t, r, u, e or f, a, l, s, e—true or false. So, we would express such a program as

```
def parse = (elem('t') ~ elem('r') ~ elem('u') ~ elem('e')) |
            (elem('f') ~ elem('a') ~ elem('l') ~ elem('s') ~ elem('e'))
```

where the elem method returns a subclass of Function[Seq[Char], ParseResult[Char]] that also has ~ and | methods. The first call to elem returns a function that will attempt to match the first character in an input stream to the letter "t." If the first letter of the input stream matches, then the function returns Parsers.Success; otherwise it returns a Parsers.NoSuccess.

The ~ method is called "and then," so we can read the first part as t and then r and then u and then e. So, elem('t') ~ elem('r') returns another one of these special Function[Seq[Char], ParseResult[List[Char]]] things. So we combine the functions together with the ~ method into one bigger function. We keep doing this with each successive ~ method invocation. The following code:

```
elem('t') ~ elem('r') ~ elem('u') ~ elem('e')
```

builds a single function that will consult the characters t, r, u, e and return a Parsers.Success[List[Char]] or a Parsers.NoSuccess if the input does not contain true.

The | operator also takes two of these combined function thingies and combines them into a single function thingy that will test the first clause, true, and if that succeeds, its value is returned, but if it does not succeed, then the second clause, false, is tried. Let's call that function thingy a Parser. So, we can combine these Parser instances with each other into other Parser instances using operators like "and then," "or else," and so on. We can combine little Parsers into big Parsers using logic and thus construct complex grammars out of little building blocks.

Let's use a little bit of Scala's implicit functionality to make the definition of our grammar easier. Scala's parser combinator library has implicit conversions from Char into Parser[Char], so we can write

```
def p2 = ('t' ~ 'r' ~ 'u' ~ 'e') |
         ('f' ~ 'a' ~ 'l' ~ 's' ~ 'e')
```

---

1. As in the rest of this book, here I'm dealing with the practicalities of combinators. There is a lot of theory and math behind combinators. This Wikipedia article touches on them: http://en.wikipedia.org/wiki/Combinator.

Yes, that definitely looks better. But, there's still a question of what these Parsers return when we pass a Seq[Char] into them. Or put another way, we want to get a Boolean true or false when we pass our input into them. So, let's define the return type of our expression:

```
def p3: Parser[Boolean] = ('t' ~ 'r' ~ 'u' ~ 'e') |
                          ('f' ~ 'a' ~ 'l' ~ 's' ~ 'e')
```

That's what we want, but the compiler complains that it doesn't know how to convert the combined Parser into a Boolean. So, let's add a little bit of code to tell the Parser how to convert its result into a Boolean.

```
def p3: Parser[Boolean] = ('t' ~ 'r' ~ 'u' ~ 'e' ^^^ true) |
                          ('f' ~ 'a' ~ 'l' ~ 's' ~ 'e' ^^^ false)
```

That works. The ^^^ method on Parser says, "If we match the input, return this constant." We've built a function that will match true or false and return the appropriate Boolean value if either pattern of characters is matched.

But we can also use the characters that are part of the pattern to create the value returned when the input is applied to the function using the ^^ method. We'll define positiveDigit and digit Parsers:[2]

```
def positiveDigit = elem('1') | '2' | '3' | '4' | '5' | '6' | '7' | '8' | '9'


def digit = positiveDigit | '0'
```

In positiveDigit, we needed to specify elem('1') as the first part of the expression because '1' | '2' is a legal expression, so the implicit conversion of '1' to elem('1') does not take place. Note that we combined the positiveDigit Parser with elem('0') into a Parser that accepts all digits. Let's make this into a Parser that converts the digits into a Long:

```
def long1: Parser[Long] = positiveDigit ~ rep(digit) ^^ {
  case (first: Char) ~ (rest: List[Char]) => (first :: rest).mkString.toLong
}
```

We create a Parser that matches a positiveDigit and then zero or more digits using rep(digit). If application of the predicate (positiveDigit ~ rep(digit)) succeeds, then we convert to a Long by applying the conversion function: case (first: Char) ~ (rest: List[Char]) => (first :: rest).mkString.toLong. The ^^ method on Parser causes the conversion function to be applied if the predicate succeeds. In this example, I was explicit about the types, but the type inferencer will get it right.

---

2. The type inferencer will infer the correct return type, Parser[Char].

Let's tighten up the example a little by only accepting rest if it's fewer than 18 digits so we don't overflow the Long:

```
lazy val long2: Parser[Long] = positiveDigit ~ rep(digit) ^? {
  case first ~ rest if rest.length < 18 => (first :: rest).mkString.toLong
}
```

In this case, we've used the ^? method to connect the predicate to the conversion. In order for the Parser to succeed, we need to satisfy the predicate, and the partial function passed to ^? must be defined for the result of the predicate. In this case, the partial function will be satisfied if the length of rest is fewer than 18 characters.

We've also changed from a method to a lazy val. This is because the method does not do the parsing; rather, the method combines smaller Parsers into a single Parser. This building of the Parser need only happen once, and the resulting Parser can be used over and over, even simultaneously on multiple threads. With the basics under our belt, let's put our parser mojo to use.

The Calculator Parser

In this section, we're going to using the parser combinator to build a four-function calculator. Yep, it's time to swat flies with a Buick. You'll see how easy it is to describe what we want to build, create a Parser for it, and then make sure the Parser returns the correct things. But first, let's define a utility trait that will allow us to more easily run the Parsers from the Scala REPL. The RunParser trait can be mixed into any Parser and adds a run method.

```
import scala.util.parsing.combinator._

trait RunParser {
  this: RegexParsers =>

  type RootType

  def root: Parser[RootType]

  def run(in: String): ParseResult[RootType] = parseAll(root, in)
}
```

The RunParser trait can be mixed into a class that extends RegexParsers. By mixing RunParser into your Parser, you can type MyParser.run("Thing to test") and see the result. It's a convenience trait.

We'll define the skeleton of our four-function calculator. Let's first describe how our calculator works. A sum expression is a product expression followed by zero or more + or − symbols followed by a product expression. A product expression is a factor followed by zero or more * or / symbols followed by another factor. This means that the precedence of production expressions is higher than the precedence of sum expressions. Finally, we define a factor as a number or parentheses around a sum expression. In BNF,[3] we'd write

```
<sumExpr>   ::= <prodExpr> [("+" <prodExpr>) | ("-" <prodExpr>)]
<prodExpr>  ::= <factor> [("*" <factor>) | ("/" <factor>)]
<factor>    ::= <float> | ("(" <sumExpr> ")")
```

We've described our parsing rules in English and BNF. Now let's see how that translates to Scala.

```
object CalcSkel extends JavaTokenParsers with RunParser {
  lazy val sumExpr = multExpr ~ rep("+" ~ multExpr | "-" ~ multExpr)

  lazy val multExpr = factor ~ rep("*" ~ factor | "/" ~ factor)

  lazy val factor: Parser[Any] = floatingPointNumber | "(" ~ sumExpr ~ ")"

  type RootType = Any

  def root = sumExpr
}
```

We've extended `JavaTokenParsers`, which gives us access to a bunch of stuff that will parse tokens as defined by the Java Language Specification.[4] We're taking advantage of `floatingPointNumber` and automatic white space consumption between elements. Cool. Let's see how this works in the REPL.

```
scala> CalcSkel.run("1")
```

```
res0: [1.2] parsed: ((1~List())~List())
```

```
scala> CalcSkel.run("1 + 1")
```

---

3. BNF stands for Backus-Naur Form, a common way to describe grammars. See http:// en.wikipedia.org/wiki/Backus-Naur_form.
4. http://java.sun.com/docs/books/jls/third_edition/html/j3TOC.html

```
res1: [1.6] parsed: ((1~List())~List((+~(1~List())))))
```

```
scala> CalcSkel.run("1 + 1 / 17")
```

```
res2: [1.11] parsed: ((1~List())~List((+~(1~List((/~17))))))
```

```
scala> CalcSkel.run("1 + 1 / archer")
```

```
res3: CalcSkel.ParseResult[CalcSkel.RootType] =
[1.9] failure: `(' expected but ` ' found
1 + 1 / archer
        ^
```

This is pretty encouraging. Our English and BNF descriptions of what we wanted to parse correspond very closely to our Scala code. Furthermore, our parse correctly parses valid input and rejects input with errors in it. The results, however, are pretty tough to read.

Next, let's turn the results into something that performs the calculations. Our Parser doesn't change, but we add a function to convert the parsed items into a Double. First comes Listing 8-1, and then we'll comb through the code.

Listing 8-1. *Calculator Parser*

```
import scala.util.parsing.combinator._

object Calc extends JavaTokenParsers with RunParser {

  lazy val sumExpr = prodExpr ~
  rep("+" ~> prodExpr ^^ (d => (x: Double) => x + d) |
      "-" ~> prodExpr ^^ (d => (x: Double) => x - d)) ^^ {
    case seed ~ fs => fs.foldLeft(seed)((a, f) => f(a))
  }
```

```
    lazy val prodExpr = factor ~
  rep("*" ~> factor ^^ (d => (x: Double) => x * d) |
      "/" ~> factor ^^ (d => (x: Double) => x / d)) ^^ {
    case seed ~ fs => fs.foldLeft(seed)((a, f) => f(a))
  }

    lazy val factor: Parser[Double] =
  floatingPointNumber ^^ (_.toDouble) | "(" ~> sumExpr <~ ")"

    type RootType = Double

    def root = sumExpr
}
```

First we import the appropriate classes and then get down to business:

```
import scala.util.parsing.combinator._
```

```
object Calc extends JavaTokenParsers with RunParser {

    lazy val sumExpr = prodExpr ~
  rep("+" ~> prodExpr ^^ (d => (x: Double) => x + d) |
      "-" ~> prodExpr ^^ (d => (x: Double) => x - d)) ^^ {
    case seed ~ fs => fs.foldLeft(seed)((a, f) => f(a))
  }
```

The rep method results in a List of whatever is parsed by the parameter of rep. When we match the + ~> prodExpr, we convert this into a function that adds the two numbers. Please note the ~> method. This method matches both items but only passes the stuff on the right to the converter function. There's a corresponding <~ operator. Back to the code. We've got a prodExpr, which is a Parser[Double] and then a Parser[List[Double => Double]], and we need to convert this into a Parser[Double]. The line

```
case seed ~ fs => fs.foldLeft(seed)((a, f) => f(a))
```

extracts the seed and the list of functions (add or subtract) and uses foldLeft to perform the calculation.

We do the same for multiplication and division:

```
    lazy val prodExpr = factor ~
  rep("*" ~> factor ^^ (d => (x: Double) => x * d) |
      "/" ~> factor ^^ (d => (x: Double) => x / d)) ^^ {
    case seed ~ fs => fs.foldLeft(seed)((a, f) => f(a))
  }
```

Next, we define `factor`, which is either a number or parentheses around a `sumExpr`. Because `sumExpr`, `prodExpr`, and `factor` reference each other and, thus, are recursive, we must define the type of at least one of the three `val`s so the type inferencer can do its work.

```
lazy val factor: Parser[Double] =
floatingPointNumber ^^ (_.toDouble) | "(" ~> sumExpr <~ ")"
```

We convert `floatingPointNumber` into a `Double` by passing a function that converts a `String` to a `Double`. Next, we use `~>` and `<~` to discard the parentheses around `sumExpr`.

Calc mixes in `RunParser`, so we have to define the abstract `RootType` type and the `root` method.

```
type RootType = Double

def root = sumExpr
}
```

That's it. We've defined the conversions from the `Strings` and `List` to `Doubles`. Let's see how well it works.

```
scala> Calc.run("1")
```

```
res0: Calc.ParseResult[Calc.RootType] = [1.2] parsed: 1.0
```

```
scala> Calc.run("1 + 1")
```

```
res1: Calc.ParseResult[Calc.RootType] = [1.6] parsed: 2.0
```

```
scala> Calc.run("1 + 1 / 17")
```

```
res2: Calc.ParseResult[Calc.RootType] = [1.11] parsed: 1.0588235294117647
```

```
scala> Calc.run("(1 + 1) / 17")
```

```
res3: Calc.ParseResult[Calc.RootType] = [1.13] parsed: 0.11764705882352941
```

In this section, we've converted from BNF description of the grammar to a running application using Scala's parser combinator library. The example, a four-function calculator, was very simple. In the next section, we're going to tackle something more complex. We're going to parse JSON.

JSON Parsing

JSON, or JavaScript Object Notation, is a common and lightweight mechanism for exchanging data over the Internet. JSON is a subset of JavaScript and can be parsed by the fast, stable, efficient JavaScript parsers that are built into browsers. JSON is as readable as XML, more compact than XML and corresponds to the types built into most dynamic languages: strings, numbers, Booleans, arrays, and dictionaries or hash maps.

In this section, we're going to follow the ECMAScript spec to build our `Parser`: we're going to copy and paste the spec into our Scala code and literally code our `Parser` to the spec as we go. The only new concept in this `Parser` is the regular-expression `Parser`. The `RegexParsers` trait has an implicit conversion from a regular expression to a `Parser[String]`. If the input matches the regular expression, the matching string will be returned by the `Parser`. We use this in the definition of spaces: `"""\s*""".r`.[5] The triple quotes contain a `String` that does not support any form of escaping, so \s is the literal \s, rather than escaping s, and the regular expression \s stands for space. The `.r` at the end of the `String` converts the `String` into a regular expression.

The code in Listing 8-2 creates a JSON `Parser`.

Listing 8-2. *ECMAScript Spec -> JSON Parser*

```
import scala.util.parsing.combinator._
object JSON extends RegexParsers with RunParser {
  // translation from ECMAScript spec
  // http://www.ecma-international.org/publications/files/ECMA-ST/Ecma-262.pdf

  /*
  Whitespace
  */
  lazy val spaces: Parser[String] = """\s*""".r
```

---

5. See the Java RegEx Pattern documentation: `http://java.sun.com/javase/6/docs/api/java/util/regex/Pattern.html`.

```
/*
Source characters (any valid unicode character)
*/
lazy val sourceCharacter: Parser[Char] = elem("Source Character", c => true)


/*
HexDigit :: one of
0 1 2 3 4 5 6 7 8 9 a b c d e f A B C D E F
*/
lazy val hexDigit: Parser[Char] =
elem("Hex Digit", c => ((c >= '0' && c <= '9') ||
                        (c >= 'a' && c <= 'f') ||
                        (c >= 'A' && c <= 'F')))


/*
7.8 Literals
Syntax
Literal ::
NullLiteral
BooleanLiteral
NumericLiteral
StringLiteral
*/
lazy val literal: Parser[Any] =
nullLiteral |
booleanLiteral |
numericLiteral |
stringLiteral


/*
7.8.1 Null Literals
Syntax
NullLiteral ::
null
*/
lazy val nullLiteral: Parser[Any] = spaces ~ "null" ~ spaces ^^^ None


/*
7.8.2 Boolean Literals
Syntax
BooleanLiteral ::
true
```

```
 false
 */
lazy val booleanLiteral: Parser[Boolean] = spaces ~>
("true" ^^^ true | "false" ^^^ false) <~ spaces


/*
 7.8.3 Numeric Literals
 Syntax
 NumericLiteral ::
 DecimalLiteral
 HexIntegerLiteral
 */
lazy val numericLiteral: Parser[Double] = spaces ~>
(hexIntegerLiteral | decimalLiteral) <~ spaces


/*
 DecimalLiteral ::
 DecimalIntegerLiteral . DecimalDigits(opt) ExponentPart(opt)
 . DecimalDigits ExponentPart(opt)
 DecimalIntegerLiteral ExponentPart(opt)
 */
lazy val decimalLiteral: Parser[Double] =
(decimalIntegerLiteral ~ '.' ~ opt(decimalDigits) ~ opt(exponentPart)) ^^
{case lit ~ _ ~ frac ~ optExp =>
    val d: Double = frac.map(f =>
      (lit.toString + "." + f.mkString).toDouble) getOrElse  lit.toDouble
    optExp.map(_(d)) getOrElse d
} |
'.' ~> decimalDigits ~ opt(exponentPart) ^^ {
  case dd ~ optExp =>
    val d = ("." + dd.mkString).toDouble
    optExp.map(_(d)) getOrElse d
} |
decimalIntegerLiteral ~ opt(exponentPart) ^^ {
  case dd ~ optExp =>
    optExp.map(_(dd)) getOrElse dd
}
```

```
/*
  DecimalIntegerLiteral ::
  0
  NonZeroDigit DecimalDigits(opt)
  */
lazy val decimalIntegerLiteral: Parser[Long] = '0' ^^^ 0L |
nonZeroDigit ~ opt(decimalDigits) ^^ {
  case first ~ rest => (first :: (rest getOrElse Nil)).mkString.toLong
}


/*
  DecimalDigits ::
  DecimalDigit
  DecimalDigits DecimalDigit
  */
lazy val decimalDigits: Parser[List[Char]] = rep1(decimalDigit)

/*
  DecimalDigit :: one of
  0 1 2 3 4 5 6 7 8 9
  */
lazy val decimalDigit = elem("Decimal Digit", c => c >= '0' && c <= '9')

/*
  NonZeroDigit :: one of
  1 2 3 4 5 6 7 8 9
  */
lazy val nonZeroDigit = elem("Non-zero Digit", c => c >= '1' && c <= '9')


/*
  ExponentPart ::
  ExponentIndicator SignedInteger
  */
lazy val exponentPart: Parser[Double => Double] =
exponentIndicator ~> signedInteger ^^ {
  si => n => n.doubleValue * Math.pow(10.0, si.doubleValue)
}
```

```scala
/*
ExponentIndicator :: one of
e E
*/
lazy val exponentIndicator = elem("exp ind", c => c == 'e' || c == 'E')


/*
SignedInteger ::
DecimalDigits
+ DecimalDigits
- DecimalDigits
*/
lazy val signedInteger: Parser[Long] =
decimalDigits ^^ (_.mkString.toLong) |
'+' ~> decimalDigits ^^ (_.mkString.toLong) |
'-' ~> decimalDigits ^^ (_.mkString.toLong * -1L)


/*
HexIntegerLiteral ::
0x HexDigit
0X HexDigit
HexIntegerLiteral HexDigit
*/
lazy val hexIntegerLiteral: Parser[Double] =
(elem('0') ~ (elem('x') | 'X')) ~> rep1(hexDigit) ^^
(s => java.lang.Long.parseLong(s.mkString, 16).toDouble)


/*
7.8.4 String Literals
A string literal is zero or more characters enclosed in single or double quotes.
Each character may be represented by an escape sequence.
Syntax
StringLiteral ::
" DoubleStringCharacters(opt) "
' SingleStringCharacters(opt) '
*/
lazy val stringLiteral: Parser[String] =
'"' ~> opt(doubleStringCharacters) <~ '"'  ^^ (_ getOrElse "") |
'\'' ~> opt(singleStringCharacters) <~ '\'' ^^ (_ getOrElse "")
```

```
/*
  DoubleStringCharacters ::
  DoubleStringCharacter DoubleStringCharacters(opt)
  */
lazy val doubleStringCharacters: Parser[String] =
rep1(doubleStringCharacter) ^^ (_.mkString)


/*
  SingleStringCharacters ::
  SingleStringCharacter SingleStringCharacters(opt)
  */
lazy val singleStringCharacters: Parser[String] =
rep1(singleStringCharacter) ^^ (_.mkString)


/*   DoubleStringCharacter ::
  SourceCharacter but not double-quote " or backslash \ or LineTerminator
  \ EscapeSequence
  */
lazy val doubleStringCharacter: Parser[Char] =
('\\' ~> escapeSequence) |
((not('"') ~ not('\\') ~ not(lineTerminator)) ~> sourceCharacter)

/*
  LineTerminator ::
  <LF>
  <CR>
  <LS>
  <PS>
  */
lazy val lineTerminator = elem("Line Terminator",
                            c => (c == '\r' ||
                                  c == '\n' ||
                                  c == '\u2028' ||
                                  c == '\u2029'))

/*
  SingleStringCharacter ::
  SourceCharacter but not single-quote ' or backslash \ or LineTerminator
  \ EscapeSequence
  */
```

```
lazy val singleStringCharacter: Parser[Char] =
('\\' ~> escapeSequence) |
((not('\'') ~ not('\\') ~ not(lineTerminator)) ~> sourceCharacter)


/*
 EscapeSequence ::
 CharacterEscapeSequence
 HexEscapeSequence
 UnicodeEscapeSequence
 */
lazy val escapeSequence: Parser[Char] =
characterEscapeSequence | hexEscapeSequence | unicodeEscapeSequence


/*
 CharacterEscapeSequence ::
 SingleEscapeCharacter
 NonEscapeCharacter
 */
lazy val characterEscapeSequence: Parser[Char] =
singleEscapeCharacter | nonEscapeCharacter


/*
 SingleEscapeCharacter :: one of
 ' " \ b f n r t
 */
lazy val singleEscapeCharacter: Parser[Char] =
'\'' ^^^ '\'' |
'"' ^^^ '"' |
'\\' ^^^ '\\' |
'b' ^^^ '\b' |
'f' ^^^ '\f' |
'n' ^^^ '\n' |
'r' ^^^ '\r' |
't' ^^^ '\t'


/*
 NonEscapeCharacter ::
 SourceCharacter but not EscapeCharacter or LineTerminator
 */
lazy val nonEscapeCharacter: Parser[Char] =
(not(escapeCharacter) ~ not(lineTerminator) ~> sourceCharacter)
```

```
/*
  EscapeCharacter ::
  SingleEscapeCharacter
  DecimalDigit
  x
  u
  */
lazy val escapeCharacter: Parser[Unit] =
(singleEscapeCharacter | decimalDigit | 'x' | 'u') ^^^ ()
```

```
/*
  HexEscapeSequence ::
  x HexDigit HexDigit
  */
lazy val hexEscapeSequence: Parser[Char] =
'x' ~> hexDigit ~ hexDigit ^^
{case d1 ~ d2 => Integer.parseInt(d1.toString + d2, 16).toChar}
```

```
/*
  UnicodeEscapeSequence ::
  u HexDigit HexDigit HexDigit HexDigit
  */
lazy val unicodeEscapeSequence =
'u' ~> hexDigit ~ hexDigit ~ hexDigit ~ hexDigit ^^
{case d1 ~ d2 ~ d3 ~ d4 =>
    Integer.parseInt(d1.toString + d2 + d3 + d4, 16).toChar}
```

```
/*
  ArrayLiteral :
  [ Elision(opt) ]
  [ ElementList ]
  [ ElementList , Elision(opt) ]
  */
lazy val arrayLiteral: Parser[List[Any]] =
spaces ~ '[' ~ spaces ~> elementList <~
spaces ~ opt(elision) ~ spaces ~ ']' ~ spaces
```

```
/*
  ElementList :
  Elision(opt) AssignmentExpression
  ElementList , Elision(opt) AssignmentExpression
  */
```

```
lazy val elementList: Parser[List[Any]] =
repsep(spaces ~> jsonObject, elision)


/*
 Elision :
 ,
 Elision ,
 */
lazy val elision: Parser[Unit] =
rep1(spaces ~ ',' ~ spaces) ^^^ ()


/*
 ObjectLiteral :
 { }
 { PropertyNameAndValueList }
 */
lazy val objectLiteral: Parser[Map[String, Any]] =
spaces ~ '{' ~ spaces ~ '}' ~ spaces ^^^ Map[String, Any]() |
spaces ~ '{' ~ spaces ~> propertyNameAndValueList <~
spaces ~'}' ~ spaces ^^ (vl => Map(vl :_*))


/*
 PropertyNameAndValueList :
 PropertyName : AssignmentExpression
 PropertyNameAndValueList , PropertyName : AssignmentExpression
 */
lazy val propertyNameAndValueList:Parser[List[(String, Any)]] =
rep1sep((spaces ~> propertyName) ~
        (spaces ~ ':' ~ spaces ~> jsonObject) ^^ {
   case n ~ v => (n, v)},
        spaces ~ ',' ~ spaces)


/*
 PropertyName :
 Identifier
 StringLiteral
 NumericLiteral
 */
lazy val propertyName: Parser[String] = stringLiteral |
numericLiteral ^^ (_.longValue.toString) | identifier
```

```scala
/*
 IdentifierName ::
 IdentifierStart
 IdentifierName IdentifierPart
 */
lazy val identifier: Parser[String] =
identifierStart |
identifier ~ identifierPart ^^ {
  case a ~ b => a+b
}

/*
 IdentifierStart ::
 UnicodeLetter
 $

 _
 */
lazy val identifierStart: Parser[String] =
'$' ^^^ "$" | '_' ^^^ "_" | unicodeLetter ^^ (_.toString)

/*
 IdentifierPart ::
 IdentifierStart
 UnicodeDigit
 */
lazy val identifierPart: Parser[String] =
identifierStart | unicodeDigit ^^ (_.toString)

lazy val unicodeLetter = elem("Letter", Character.isLetter)

lazy val unicodeDigit = elem("Letter", Character.isDigit)

lazy val jsonObject: Parser[Any] = objectLiteral | arrayLiteral | literal

type RootType = Any

def root = jsonObject
}
```

So, that's it. Let's see how the `Parser` does with various JSON input:

```scala
scala> JSON.run("1")
```

```
res0: JSON.ParseResult[JSON.RootType] = [1.2] parsed: 1.0
```

```scala
scala> JSON.run("'Elwood Eats Mice'")
```

```
res1: JSON.ParseResult[JSON.RootType] = [1.19] parsed: Elwood Eats Mice
```

```scala
scala> JSON.run("'Elwood \u0021 Eats Mice'")
```

```
res2: JSON.ParseResult[JSON.RootType] = [1.21] parsed: Elwood ! Eats Mice
```

```scala
scala> JSON.run("[1,2,3,]")
```

```
res3: JSON.ParseResult[JSON.RootType] = [1.9] parsed: List(1.0, 2.0, 3.0)
```

```scala
scala> JSON.run("{a:true, 'hello':33}")
```

```
res4: parsed: Map(a -> true, hello -> 33.0)
```

Great. We've converted the ECMAScript spec into a running `Parser`. Let's see what we can layer on top of the JSON `Parser`. Let's build some code that will parse Twitter APIs.

Twitter JSON Parsing

JSON is great for storing and transmitting dynamically typed information, but Scala is a statically typed language. It would be great to be able to convert the dynamic stuff parsed from JSON data into statically typed Scala. As an example, we're going to use some of the

Twitter APIs that return Twitter's public timeline.[6] We'll request the data in JSON format, parse it, and then run the parsed data through a conversion to create Scala instances that represent the Twitter data.

Utilities

In order to use Scala's for comprehension to safely and easily extract data from the result of the JSON parsing, we're going to write a helper trait, SafeMap, which does type-safe testing and casting. SafeMap has an is method that takes an implicit parameter, man, which is a Manifest representing the type T. The Scala compiler correctly builds the Manifest and passes it to the method.[7] We use the Manifest to get the class for T and do testing. First we have the code in Listing 8-3 and then a dissection.

Listing 8-3. *Type-Safe Map Utility*

```
trait SafeMap {
  import scala.reflect._
  class SafeCast(in: Any) {
    def is[T](implicit man: Manifest[T]): Option[T] = {
      // special case for Boolean
      val cls = if (man.toString == "boolean") classOf[java.lang.Boolean]
      else man.erasure

      in match {
        case null => None
        case t: AnyRef if cls.isAssignableFrom(t.getClass) =>
          Some(t.asInstanceOf[T])
        case _ => None
      }
    }
  }
}
```

---

6. http://apiwiki.twitter.com/REST+API+Documentation. Alex Payne, co-author with Dean Wampler of the fine book *Programming Scala* (O'Reilly, forthcoming), maintains Twitter's APIs.
7. Manifest is an experimental feature introduced in Scala 2.7.2, but it's so very useful that I'm including it in the book.

```
class SafeMapC[A, B](m: Map[A, B]) {
  def sGet[T](key: A)(implicit man: Manifest[T]): Option[T] =
  m.get(key).flatMap(v => new SafeCast(v).is(man))
}
implicit def mToSM[A, B](in: Map[A, B]) = new SafeMapC(in)
implicit def iToIs(v: Any) = new SafeCast(v)
}
```

When the Java Virtual Machine was introduced in 1996, the Java language did not include generics. In Java 1.0, an `ArrayList` contained only `Object`. You had to manually cast each element of `ArrayList` into the class that you wanted. Java 1.5 introduced generics so that at compile time you could specify `ArrayList<String>`. This avoided the manual cast because the compiler did the casting for you. However, the JVM was not updated to keep track of the generics associated with `ArrayList<?>`, so under the covers, an `ArrayList<String>` is just an `ArrayList`, not an `ArrayList<String>`. The type, `<String>`, is erased, which means it is known at compile time but not at runtime. This design was perpetuated through to Scala.

Scala introduced a feature in 2.7.2 called `Manifests`. They were an experimental, undocumented feature, but they are very, very useful. They allow a method implicitly to take a `Manifest` as a parameter for each type parameter passed to the method. The `Manifest` contains information including the type that is to be erased when the bytecode is rendered. Thus, the `Manifest` allows us to reify the erased type.[8]

We will use this feature in our `SafeMap` trait to do syntactically pleasing, type-safe casting. First, we define a `SafeMap` trait that we can mix into any class or object and make use of type-safe access to `Maps`.

```
trait SafeMap {
```

We import the `scala.reflect` package to the `Manifest`:

```
import scala.reflect._
```

We define the `SafeCast` class. It has a single method, `is`, which takes an implicit `Manifest` as a parameter and tests to see whether the class of `in` is assignable from the class contained by the `Manifest` and accessed using the `erasure` method.

```
class SafeCast(in: Any) {
  def is[T](implicit man: Manifest[T]): Option[T] = {
    // special case for Boolean
    val cls = if (man.toString == "boolean") classOf[java.lang.Boolean]
    else man.erasure
```

---

8. See http://scala-blogs.org/2008/10/manifests-reified-types.html.

We do the actual testing of the `in` variable:

```
in match {
  case null => None
  case t: AnyRef if cls.isAssignableFrom(t.getClass) =>
    Some(t.asInstanceOf[T])
  case _ => None
    }
  }
}
```

SafeMapC is a class that contains a method that gets the key and uses SafeCast to ensure that the key is of the class we want to cast it to. sGet will test that the key is in the Map and returns the value associated with the key if the value is of type T, otherwise None.

```
class SafeMapC[A, B](m: Map[A, B]) {
  def sGet[T](key: A)(implicit man: Manifest[T]): Option[T] =
  m.get(key).flatMap(v => new SafeCast(v).is(man))
}
implicit def mToSM[A, B](in: Map[A, B]) = new SafeMapC(in)
implicit def iToIs(v: Any) = new SafeCast(v)
}
```

Parsing the JSON

First, let's look Listing 8-4, and then we'll work through it.

Listing 8-4. *Twitter Parser*

```
trait TwitterElem

/*
<status>
created_at
id
text
source
truncated
in_reply_to_status_id
in_reply_to_user_id
favorited
*/
```

```
case class TwitterStatus(id: Long,
                         createdAt: String,
                         text: String,
                         source: String,
                         truncated: Boolean,
                         inReplyToStatus: Option[Long],
                         inReplyToUser: Option[Long],
                         favorited: Boolean,
                         user: TwitterUser) extends TwitterElem

object TwitterStatus extends SafeMap {
  def apply(in: Any): Option[TwitterStatus] =
  for {m <- in.is[Map[String, Any]]
      id <- m.sGet[String]("id").map(_.toLong)
      createdAt <- m.sGet[String]("created_at")
      text <- m.sGet[String]("text")
      source <- m.sGet[String]("source")
      truncated <- m.sGet[Boolean]("truncated")
      inRepSt = m.sGet[Double]("in_reply_to_status_id").map(_.toLong)
      inRepUsr = m.sGet[Double]("in_reply_to_user_id").map(_.toLong)
      fav = m.sGet[Boolean]("favorited") getOrElse false
      userObj <- m.sGet[Map[String, Any]]("user")
      user <- TwitterUser(userObj)
  } yield new TwitterStatus(id, createdAt, text, source,
                            truncated,
                            inRepSt, inRepUsr, fav, user)

  def fromList(in: Any): List[TwitterStatus] = {
    for {list <- in.is[List[Any]].toList
        item <- list
        st <- apply(item)
    } yield st
  }

}

/*
<user>
 id
 name
 screen_name
 description
```

```
  location
  profile_image_url
  url
  protected
  followers_count
  */
case class TwitterUser(id: Long,
                       name: String,
                       screenName: String,
                       description: Option[String],
                       location: Option[String],
                       image: Option[String],
                       url: Option[String],
                       protectd: Boolean,
                       followerCount: Option[Int]) extends TwitterElem


object TwitterUser extends SafeMap {
  def apply(in: Any): Option[TwitterUser] =
  for {m <- in.is[Map[String, Any]]
       id <- m.sGet[String]("id").map(_.toLong)
       name <- m.sGet[String]("name")
       scrName <- m.sGet[String]("screen_name")
       desc = m.sGet[String]("description")
       loc = m.sGet[String]("location")
       image = m.sGet[String]("profile_image_url")
       url = m.sGet[String]("url")
       prot = m.sGet[Boolean]("protected") getOrElse false
       fc = m.sGet[Double]("followers_count").map(_.toInt)
  } yield new TwitterUser(id, name, scrName,
                          desc, loc, image, url, prot,
                          fc)
}
```

We define a basic trait that all of Twitter-related classes extend:

```
trait TwitterElem
```

Next, let's define a class that represents a status. The structure of the class is based on the definition of the Status in the API document.

```
/*
<status>
created_at
id
```

```
    text
    source
    truncated
    in_reply_to_status_id
    in_reply_to_user_id
    favorited
    */
case class TwitterStatus(id: Long,
                         createdAt: String,
                         text: String,
                         source: String,
                         truncated: Boolean,
                         inReplyToStatus: Option[Long],
                         inReplyToUser: Option[Long],
                         favorited: Boolean,
                         user: TwitterUser) extends TwitterElem
```

In order to convert from the JSON data, we need to extract each field and build up all the parameters necessary to construct a TwitterStatus. Using is and sGet from SafeMap along with the for comprehension, we extract the data from the JSON data and create a type-safe TwitterStatus instance.

```
object TwitterStatus extends SafeMap {
  def apply(in: Any): Option[TwitterStatus] =
  for {m <- in.is[Map[String, Any]]
       id <- m.sGet[String]("id").map(_.toLong)
       createdAt <- m.sGet[String]("created_at")
       text <- m.sGet[String]("text")
       source <- m.sGet[String]("source")
       truncated <- m.sGet[Boolean]("truncated")
       inRepSt = m.sGet[Double]("in_reply_to_status_id").map(_.toLong)
       inRepUsr = m.sGet[Double]("in_reply_to_user_id").map(_.toLong)
       fav = m.sGet[Boolean]("favorited") getOrElse false
       userObj <- m.sGet[Map[String, Any]]("user")
       user <- TwitterUser(userObj)
  } yield new TwitterStatus(id, createdAt, text, source,
                            truncated,
                            inRepSt, inRepUsr, fav, user)
```

The fromList method extracts a series of TwitterStatus instances from a List of JSON data.

```
def fromList(in: Any): List[TwitterStatus] = {
  for {list <- in.is[List[Any]].toList
       item <- list
       st <- apply(item)
  } yield st
}
}
```

TwitterStatus includes a TwitterUser instance. We define the TwitterUser class the same way we defined TwitterStatus.

```
/*
<user>
id
name
screen_name
description
location
profile_image_url
url
protected
followers_count
*/
case class TwitterUser(id: Long,
                       name: String,
                       screenName: String,
                       description: Option[String],
                       location: Option[String],
                       image: Option[String],
                       url: Option[String],
                       protectd: Boolean,
                       followerCount: Option[Int]) extends TwitterElem

object TwitterUser extends SafeMap {
  def apply(in: Any): Option[TwitterUser] =
  for {m <- in.is[Map[String, Any]]
       id <- m.sGet[String]("id").map(_.toLong)
```

```
      name <- m.sGet[String]("name")
      scrName <- m.sGet[String]("screen_name")
      desc = m.sGet[String]("description")
      loc = m.sGet[String]("location")
      image = m.sGet[String]("profile_image_url")
      url = m.sGet[String]("url")
      prot = m.sGet[Boolean]("protected") getOrElse false
      fc = m.sGet[Double]("followers_count").map(_.toInt)
  } yield new TwitterUser(id, name, scrName,
                          desc, loc, image, url, prot,
                          fc)
}
```

We've got our classes all defined. Let's use the REPL to see how well it works.

```
scala> import scala.io._
import scala.io._

scala> val timeline = "http://twitter.com/statuses/public_timeline.json"
```

```
timeline: java.lang.String = http://twitter.com/statuses/public_timeline.json
```

```
scala> val src = Source.fromURL(timeline)
```

```
src: scala.io.Source = non-empty iterator
```

```
scala> val json = JSON.run(src.mkString)
```

```
json: JSON.ParseResult[JSON.RootType] = [1.11894] parsed: List(…)
```

```
scala> json.map(TwitterStatus.fromList _)
```

```
res0: JSON.ParseResult[List[TwitterStatus]] = List(TwitterStatus(1242017450,…))
```

Very cool. We've layered our Twitter-specific code on top of the JSON `Parser` in a way that allows us to parse Twitter-related data. The `json.map(TwitterStatus.fromList _)` piece reinforces the value of functional programming. We were able to convert a `ParseResult` that returned JSON data into a `ParseResult` that returns Twitter data just by `mapping` the JSON data into Twitter data.

Summary

Scala's parser combinator library demonstrates the flexibility of Scala's syntax, the usefulness of implicit conversions, and the power of functional composition. The parser combinator is an excellent example of a domain-specific language. The domain is parsing text, and the syntax is nearly one-for-one with BNF. We were able to create the JSON `Parser` by taking the ECMAScript spec and translate it directly into Scala code. This library also gives you some idea of the kind of domain-specific languages you can create using Scala. There's nothing specific in the Scala compiler for the parser combinator library—it's just that, a library.

On a practical level, using a single language—Scala—for defining your `Parser` rather than using a tool like ANTLR[9] means that you and your team use a single language for describing your system. This means that your brain thinks Scala. This means that you edit code in a single language and take advantage of the type safety of the language.

This concludes our tour of Scala the language. In the next chapter, we'll explore how you can integrate Scala into your projects, better build teams and divide work using Scala, and take advantage of the power of Scala without losing the infrastructure that you've built around Java.

---

9. `http://www.antlr.org/`

■ ■ ■

CHAPTER 9

Scaling Your Team

Thanks for hanging in and reading all this way. We've covered a lot of ground so far. We've discussed the Scala language and developed a whole bunch of idioms for building applications using Scala. We've explored how Scala can be used by different team members in different ways. We've seen how Scala allows you to compose fine-grained pieces of code together into complex systems that work well together.

But no technology is an island. No matter how good Scala is in the abstract, it's only valuable if it can help your organization produce better and more maintainable code, faster. The good news is that Scala compiles down to JVM bytecode and works great with existing Java libraries. If you're working at a Java shop, the cost of using Scala on some projects is minimal. You can test Scala with your existing Java test tools. You store compiled Scala code in JAR and WAR files, so it looks and feels to the rest of your organization like what they're used to, Java bytecode. The operational characteristic of Scala code on web servers is indistinguishable from the operational characteristics of Java code.

In this chapter, we're going to explore the practicalities of integrating Scala into your project and perhaps your organization. We'll look at testing Scala code, potential changes to team structure, best practices to look for during code reviews, and selling Scala into your organization. Let's start by looking at testing and Scala.

Testing: Behavior-Driven Development

So far, we've talked a lot about the type of testing that Scala code does not need. You do not need to write tests that catch type errors or test that method names exist. You can use `Option` to avoid `null` pointer problems. You use Scala's type system and strong typing to ensure that your code is well formed and valid. That does not mean that your logic is correct; therefore you need to write tests to ensure that the logic of your program is correct. I find that Behavior-Driven Development (BDD) provides the best way to write tests because business people can read and understand BDD, and BDD tests tend to be higher-level and focus on the logic, not the mechanics, of code.

Scala can be tested using existing Java frameworks including JUnit. However, there are better ways to test Scala code, and these better ways play nicely with JUnit and other Java testing frameworks. That means you get a better way to write Scala tests, but they run the same old ways. It's the best of both worlds. In this section, I'm going to give a brief overview of two Scala test frameworks: Specs and ScalaTest.

Specs

Specs[1] is a Behavior-Driven Design framework.[2] Tests are expressed in a domain-specific language that is very descriptive and readable. For example, here's a Specs definition for testing some of Lift's utility classes:

```
class BoxSpecTest extends Runner(BoxSpec) with JUnit with Console
object BoxSpec extends Specification {
  "A Box" can {
    "be created from a Option. It is Empty if the option is None" in {
      Box(None) mustBe Empty
    }
    "be created from a Option. It is Full(x) if the option is Some(x)" in {
      Box(Some(1)) must_== Full(1)
    }
```

Specs provides a lot of different matchers that allow you to test `Strings` by testing them against a regular expression:

```
"'hello world' matches 'h.* w.*'" in {
    "hello world" must beMatching("h.* w.*")
  }
```

Specs provides XML testing against an XPath-style expressions.

```
<a><b><c><d></d></c></b></a> must \\("c").\("d")
```

Specs integrates with JUnit so that you can use your existing testing infrastructure to run Specs tests. The line

```
class BoxSpecTest extends Runner(BoxSpec) with JUnit with Console
```

is all that's required to integrate with JUnit. The `BoxSpecsTest` can be run with your JUnit runner of choice. Specs also integrates with jMock 2.

---

1. http://code.google.com/p/specs/
2. http://behaviour-driven.org/

Scala is a functional language, and many of your tests can stress functions without having the set-up complex state. ScalaCheck does just this.[3] While ScalaCheck is not part of Specs, Specs wraps ScalaCheck. It's super-simple to use ScalaCheck inside Specs test. It generates random input based on rules and tests your method against the random input. For example, this will test 500 e-mail addresses against the pattern:

```
mailAddresses must pass { address =>
  address must beMatching(companyPattern)
}
```

Specs test can be read by and often written by business users of your code. This is important because the more transparent the tests, the more likely your application will perform the way that business people expect it to, and when that happens, you get fewer tickets filed and more time to write new, cool code … or drink a beer.

Scala Test

Scala's software ecosystem is rich, and there's more than one excellent testing framework. ScalaTest[4] is written and maintained by Artima[5] founder and *Programming in Scala* co-author Bill Venners. Bill has taken a slightly more Java-flavored approach in ScalaTest but also offers the BDD goodness that Specs has. Bill says that his goal for ScalaTest is that "It really tries to … integrate with the past while at the same time letting you adopt new styles that Scala enables better than Java did. People are comfortable doing things the way they have been doing them, and I want to make the transition as gentle as possible." For example, a simple ScalaTest test looks like:

```
test("addition") {
  val sum = 1 + 1
  assert(sum === 2)
  assert(sum + 2 === 4)
}
```

This looks to me like a more pleasant version of the kind of tests that I'd write in JUnit. In fact, ScalaTest has excellent integration with JUnit, so you can use JUnit as your test runner. ScalaTest has TestNG integration as well. ScalaTest wraps ScalaCheck just as Specs does, and you can write BDD-style tests using ScalaTest as well:

```
describe("A Stack") {
  it("should pop values in last-in-first-out order") {
    val stack = new Stack[Int]
```

---

3. http://code.google.com/p/scalacheck/
4. http://www.artima.com/scalatest/
5. http://artima.com/

```
    stack.push(1)
    stack.push(2)
    stack.pop() should equal (2)
    stack.pop() should equal (1)
}
```

ScalaTest and Specs both offer integration with Ant and Maven, so you can integrate your tests into your existing Java build environment. With both tools, you can describe tests for your business logic in simple, readable, powerful ways and run those tests using your existing build and test infrastructure. In this way, Scala integrates very well into your organization.

Build Tools

Scala works with most popular Java-related build tools including Maven, Ant, and Buildr. This means that integrating Scala into an existing Java-oriented workflow is simple and painless. In this section, I'm going to do a quick survey of the tools available for building, testing, and packaging Scala apps, and that includes apps that contain Scala, Java, JRuby, and so on. Basically, these tools convert source code to bytecode and stuff that bytecode into JAR and WAR files. The order I've chosen is most verbose to least verbose.

Maven

My personal favorite build and dependency-management tool of all time is Maven (I duck as people throw things at me.[6]) Maven is far more than a build tool: it's a complete dependency-management system and will even ensure that you don't mix items in a project where there are license conflicts (e.g., GPL 2 and Apache 2.0).

Maven arranges things as dependencies and goals. Maven will figure out what dependencies are necessary to resolve in order to achieve a goal. Maven may need to download a JAR file in order to resolve a dependency. Maven will go to different repositories, including well-known repositories of open source code, in order to download dependencies. Maven also determines what code to run in order to resolve a dependency in order to reach a goal. For example, if the goal is `jetty:run` (run the web application inside a Jetty container), Maven will download the JARs that your code depends on, compile your source code, package your code into a WAR directory layout, download the Jetty runtime, and then invoke Jetty. With Maven, you only worry about your own code and defining its dependencies, and Maven takes care of the rest.

---

6.   Paul Snively: As well you should! :-)

Maven is well integrated into the Java ecosystem. There are test goals for JUnit, TestNG, and so on. There are Maven plug-ins to most of the IDEs. Every Apache JVM-related open source project publishes its JARs to the central Maven repository, as do most other open source projects.

There's excellent Maven support for Scala courtesy of David Bernard and Josh Suereth. You can learn more about it at `http://scala-tools.org/mvnsites/maven-scala-plugin/`. The Lift Web Framework uses Maven, and I use Maven in all my projects and love it. Others disagree because Maven is opaque in how it resolves dependencies; Maven "downloads the entire Internet" (all your dependencies and those dependencies' dependencies, and so on) the first time you build; Maven is challenging when debugging failures; and Maven's XML verbosity is overly verbose. The last complaint is one I heartily agree with. Here's a sample Maven file:

```xml
<?xml version="1.0" encoding="UTF-8"?>
<project xmlns="http://maven.apache.org/POM/4.0.0"
 xmlns:xsi="http://www.w3.org/2001/XMLSchema-instance">
  <modelVersion>4.0.0</modelVersion>
  <groupId>info.spitballs</groupId>
  <artifactId>spitballs</artifactId>
  <version>0.1.0-SNAPSHOT</version>
  <packaging>jar</packaging>
  <name>spitballs</name>
  <inceptionYear>2009</inceptionYear>
  <properties>
    <scala.version>2.7.3</scala.version>
  </properties>

 <repositories>
    <repository>
      <id>scala-tools.org</id>
      <name>Scala-Tools Maven2 Repository</name>
      <url>http://scala-tools.org/repo-releases</url>
    </repository>
  </repositories>

 <pluginRepositories>
    <pluginRepository>
      <id>scala-tools.org</id>
      <name>Scala-Tools Maven2 Repository</name>
      <url>http://scala-tools.org/repo-releases</url>
    </pluginRepository>
  </pluginRepositories>
```

```
<dependencies>
  <dependency>
    <groupId>org.scala-lang</groupId>
    <artifactId>scala-library</artifactId>
    <version>${scala.version}</version>
  </dependency>

  <dependency>
      <groupId>junit</groupId>
      <artifactId>junit</artifactId>
      <version>3.8.1</version>
      <scope>test</scope>
  </dependency>
  <dependency>
      <groupId>org.specs</groupId>
      <artifactId>specs</artifactId>
      <version>1.4.3</version>
      <scope>test</scope>
  </dependency>
  <dependency>
      <groupId>junit</groupId>
      <artifactId>junit</artifactId>
      <version>4.4</version>
      <scope>test</scope>
  </dependency>
</dependencies>

<build>
  <sourceDirectory>src/main/scala</sourceDirectory>
  <testSourceDirectory>src/test/scala</testSourceDirectory>

  <plugins>
    <plugin>
      <groupId>org.scala-tools</groupId>
      <artifactId>maven-scala-plugin</artifactId>
      <executions>
        <execution>
          <goals>
            <goal>compile</goal>
            <goal>testCompile</goal>
          </goals>
        </execution>
```

```xml
        </executions>
        <configuration>
          <scalaVersion>${scala.version}</scalaVersion>
        </configuration>
      </plugin>
    </plugins>
  </build>
  <reporting>
    <plugins>
      <plugin>
        <groupId>org.scala-tools</groupId>
        <artifactId>maven-scala-plugin</artifactId>
        <configuration>
          <scalaVersion>${scala.version}</scalaVersion>
        </configuration>
      </plugin>
    </plugins>
  </reporting>
</project>
```

The good news is that Maven is very powerful, and as my project has more dependencies, Maven will take care of downloading them and getting them right. This also means that I don't have to have a bunch of JAR files in my source repository. The bad news is that the Maven pom.xml is a big hairy mess. Good thing there are other build tools.

Ant

Ant is to Java build tools as make is to Unix build tools. It's good enough to get most jobs done and bad enough for everyone to complain about it. Scala itself uses Ant as its build system, and the Scala Ant plug-in has been very stable for a very long time. Here's an Ant build script for a generic Scala project:

```xml
<project name="Basic Scala Project" default="build" basedir="../">
  <property name="base.dir" value="${basedir}" />
  <property name="sources.dir" value="${base.dir}/src" />
  <property name="build.dir" value="${base.dir}/build//classes.tmp" />

  <property environment="env"/>
  <property name="scala.home" value="${env.SCALA_HOME}" />

  <target name="init">
```

```xml
    <property name="scala-library.jar"
      value="${scala.home}/lib/scala-library.jar" />

    <path id="build.classpath">
      <pathelement location="${scala-library.jar}" />
      <pathelement location="${build.dir}"   />
    </path>

    <taskdef resource="scala/tools/ant/antlib.xml">
      <classpath>
        <pathelement location="${scala.home}/lib/scala-compiler.jar" />
        <pathelement location="${scala-library.jar}" />
      </classpath>
    </taskdef>
  </target>

  <target name="build" depends="init">
    <mkdir dir="${build.dir}"   />
    <scalac srcdir="${sources.dir}"
            destdir="${build.dir}"
            classpathref="build.classpath"
            force="changed">
      <include name="**/*.scala" />
    </scalac>
  </target>

  <target name="run" depends="build">
    <java classname="test.Test"
  classpathref="build.classpath">
    </java>
  </target>
</project>
```

Ant scripts are marginally shorter than Maven scripts, but they do not do any dependency management. Ant scripts are about the compilation and packaging tasks, and that's it.[7] But there's a Scala task for Ant, and Ant works well with Scala.

---

7. But that's what http://ant.apache.org/ivy is for.

Buildr

Now, if you want the power of Maven with a very concise and amazingly readable syntax, you want Buildr.[8] Buildr is a JVM-targeted build tool written in Ruby. I asked Alex Boisvert, a Buildr committer, to convert the previous Maven Project Object Model (POM) file into Buildr, and he came back with the following for `build.yml`:

```
scala.specs: 1.4.3
junit: 4.4
```

and the following for `Buildfile`:

```
require "buildr/scala"

repositories.remote << "http://www.ibiblio.org/maven2/"
repositories.remote << "http://scala-tools.org/repo-releases"

desc "Spitball Secure Event-based Messaging"
define "spitballs" do
  project.version = "0.1.0-SNAPSHOT"
  project.group = "info.spitballs"
  package(:jar)
end
```

So, if you want concise, readable build files, Buildr is a great tool. It works with Java, Groovy, Scala, and most other things JVM-related, and it's a top-level Apache project, so it's got a track record and a community around it.

Other Build Tools

There are a couple of other build tools gestating in the Scala world. Simple Build Tool (sbt, `http://code.google.com/p/simple-build-tool/`) is a Scala-based build tool that focuses on dependency management. With traits, implicits, and so on, Scala provides far more dependency-management challenges than does Java. sbt seeks to navigate Scala's dependency challenges with better support for incremental compilation. Brian Clapper is also working on a Scala build tool that has the syntactic DSLishness of Buildr without the dependence on Ruby. You can read more about Brian's build tool at `http://brizzled.clapper.org/id/87`.

---

8. `http://buildr.apache.org/`

Team Structure

With the infrastructure pieces of test and build tools, the next step for Scala adoption is getting the people in your organization to start coding in Scala. People are the most important part of the equation. If the individuals on your team have repeated good experiences with Scala, they'll have every reason and incentive to work harder with Scala. If individuals have a bad initial experience, they will resist Scala, and you'll never see the benefits of Scala translated into tangible code. In this section, I'll make some recommendations for introducing Scala to your team.

Bringing New Team Members on Board

Introducing a new team member into a Scala project and helping that team member be successful in his first few weeks is critical. As you plan to bring team members on board, I recommend looking at each member's strengths and weaknesses. Create a series of tasks that each team member can succeed with. Each task should take one to three days to complete and be subject to feedback. For example:

- You might ask a team member to augment existing Specs or ScalaTest-based tests. This gives familiarity with Scala's syntax and some exposure to Scala's flexibility.

- You might give a developer the task to manually serialize and deserialize objects to and from XML. This will give the developer an exposure to XML and immutability.

- You might give the developer the task of adding concrete methods to one or two traits or interfaces that are commonly used.

- You might ask them to write simple servlets or do other things demonstrating interoperability with Java.

I strongly recommend pairing a new-to-Scala team member with someone who has a little bit of experience. This allows for sharing of knowledge. If you are bringing more than one developer onto your project at once, you might also want to have a 30-minute meeting toward the end of the day every day or three times a week. The goal of the meeting is to have a single developer share with the other developers "one cool thing about Scala and one sucky thing about Scala." This format gives the developer a chance to brag about something cool and share this knowledge with the team. It also gives each developer a chance to complain about things.

Perhaps the complaint will be met with a solution from another team member, or perhaps the complaint will be met with collective nodding and grumbling. The complaining will happen one way or another, and giving it a shared outlet channels the complaints into something potentially more productive. For example, when Twitter started using Scala, they created the Graceless Failures blog (`http://www.gracelessfailures.com/`). This serves as a way to share Scala experiences, good and bad, with the community.

No matter what the specifics of adding team members are, I strongly recommend that Scala adoption be positioned to the whole team as a way to write code more successfully. Acknowledge the problems of Scala's youth, which include weaker tools, less documentation, and so on. But help your team members stay focused on what they can achieve with Scala in spite of the challenges of learning a new language and using a new tools chain. As they have small successes and the values of concise code, immutability, powerful type systems, type inferencing, and so on show up as revised coding idioms, they will move into a self-reinforcing cycle of learning more, getting better, and getting better results. When they walk into a meeting and say, "I don't know how I could ever go back to Java," then you know they're hooked and that you've succeeded in bringing them on board.

Organizing Teams Around Scala

I've consulted for a lot of companies over the years. I often see a sad thing happen: the very best coders become architects. It's a pay raise and often a death sentence for those who love to get their hands dirty with code. The architects get to attend meetings, write on white boards, do a few UML diagrams, and do code reviews. While some architects like this kind of work, others pine for the days of code slinging.

There is good news for those architects who like to code: Scala offers you a chance to get your hands dirty, because you can express a lot of complex coding rules using Scala's type system. You can be the architect, go to meetings, and use Scala rather than UML to express high-level concepts and complex relationships; and best of all, you don't have to worry about round trips because all the code is Scala. So, let's see how different team members fit into different parts of a project with Scala.

A senior developer with a good sense of the business domain and the coding conventions may do well to design domain-specific languages for use by other team members. DSLs deliver value because they allow the program to more closely match the language that business people use to describe solutions in a given domain. As we've seen with Scala's parser combinator library as well as Specs, Scala makes it easy to create code that corresponds to the language a human would use to describe the answer to a problem. Putting senior developers on projects to design DSLs allows them to model the language of solutions beyond OOP's "is a" and "has a" to relations and actions that object can take on each other.

Junior developers and folks more comfortable with scripting languages (Ruby, Python, Groovy) are well suited to be library consumers. They can assemble applications out of the DSLs created by the senior developers based on the rules and structures defined by the architects. These developers should have a coding experience that is not dissimilar from that of writing Ruby or Python code. At the same time, the junior developers who have grown up with Java have the comfort of Scala's static type system.

Business people should be able to view the code written using the DSLs as well as the BDD-style tests and understand how the system works. It should be a goal to have business people involved from time to time in code reviews. This provides a two-way feedback system. If your business people understand the code, and they should if the DSLs are well crafted, they will be able to give direct feedback as to the program reflecting the business rules.

Best Practices

It took me a long time, more than 18 months, until I felt like I was good at Scala. Most programming languages come easily to me, but Scala was not just a programming language; it was a new way of thinking and reasoning about programming. Perhaps if I had taken Lisp courses in college or had formal training in ML-derived languages, Scala's learning curve would not have been so bad for me. That did not deter me from trying to write Scala code, nor did it deter me from working on the Lift Web Framework. Also, there were far fewer books and materials to help me get up to speed with Scala when I started back in November 2006.[9]

The first step in writing Scala is not being afraid of the fact that Scala's going to warp your brain. The next step in writing Scala is accepting that your code is going to look like Java, Ruby, Python, whatever code for a while. It will take you time and effort and more time to code Scala using the idioms in this book. It will take you time to design code that fits into Scala paradigms and to discover and devise paradigms of your own. It will take your team members time as well. In this section, I'm going to talk about coding activities and questions and styles that you can apply to your code as well as suggest to team members when you're doing code reviews on this code. So, write that Java-style code in Scala and then apply the concepts below and see how your code changes and how your thought patterns change.

Options Instead of Null Testing

The first thing to do is ban `null` from any of your code. You should never return `null` from a method, ever, ever, ever. If you are calling Java libraries that may return `null` or throw an exception because of input problems, convert these to `Options`. We did this for parsing `Strings` to `Ints`. The pattern is basic: no `nulls`.

When you write code, ban `null` from your code. In the case of uninitialized instance variables, either assign a default value that is not `null` or, if there's a code path where the

---

9. I view this book as a "gateway drug" to Scala. I tried to orient it to beginners. *Programming in Scala* by Martin Odersky, Lex Spoon, and Bill Venners (Artima, 2008) is an excellent next step for learning Scala.

variable could be used prior to initialization, use `Option`, and the default value becomes `None`. If there's no logical value that can be returned from a method given legal input, the return type should be `Option`. The `get` method should never be called on an `Option`. Instead, `Option`s should be unpacked using `map`/`flatMap`, the `for` comprehension, or pattern matching.

The first benefit using `Option` is the obvious avoidance of `null` pointer exceptions. The second benefit is a little more subtle. The use of `Option` and the transformative nature of `mapping` `Option`s leads to a different style of approaching your code. The style is more transformative, more functional. The impact of repeatedly using immutable data structures will move your brain toward the functional side.

Focus on Immutability

In Java, mutability is the default. Variables are mutable unless they're marked `final`. Java-Beans have getters and setters. Data structures in Java are instantiated, set, and passed along to other methods. Try changing the paradigm in your Scala code.

The first thing to do is use immutable collections classes by default. If you choose to use a mutable collections class, make a comment in your code as to why you chose mutability. There are times when mutable collections make sense. For example, in a method where you are building a `List`, using `ListBuffer` is more efficient, but don't return the `ListBuffer`, return the `List`. This is like using a `StringBuilder` in Java but ultimately returning a `String`. So, use immutable collections by default, and use mutable data structures with a justification.

Use `val`s by default, and only use `var`s if there is a good reason that is justified by a comment. In your methods, use `val` unless there's going to be a significant performance hit. Using `val` in methods often leads to thinking recursively. Let's look at a mutable implementation of a method that consumes all the lines from a `BufferedReader`:

```
def read1(in: java.io.BufferedReader): List[String] = {
  var ret: List[String] = Nil
  var line = in.readLine
  while (line != null) {
    ret ::= line
    line = in.readLine
  }
  ret.reverse
}
```

The above code is readable but uses a couple of vars. Let's rewrite the code without vars and see how we can use tail recursion to give us a `while` loop:

```
def read2(in: java.io.BufferedReader): List[String] = {
  def doRead(acc: List[String]): List[String] = in.readLine match {
    case null => acc
```

```
    case s => doRead(s :: acc)
  }
  doRead(Nil).reverse
}
```

Look ma, no vars. We defined the doRead method, which reads a line of input. If the line is null, we return the accumulated List. If the line is non-null, we call doRead with the accumulated List. Because doRead is in the scope of read2, it has access to all of read2's variables. doRead calls itself on the last line, which is a tail call. The Scala compiler will optimize the tail call into a while loop, and there will only be one stack frame created no matter how many lines are read. The last line of read2 calls doRead with Nil as the seed value for the accumulator.

Using vals in your code makes you think about alternative, immutable, functional code. This small example demonstrates that removing vars leads to refactoring. The refactoring leads to new coding patterns. The new coding patterns lead to a shift in your approach to coding. This shift in approach will yield transformative code that has fewer defects and is easier to maintain.

Keep Methods Short

Keep methods short. See whether you can code methods in a single line. If not a single line, see whether you can code them in a single statement. If you keep methods short, then the logic in each method is more obvious when you or someone else looks at the code. Let's see how the previous code can be made into single statements:

```
private def readLines(in: java.io.BufferedReader,
                      acc: List[String]): List[String] =
in.readLine match {
  case null => acc
  case s => readLines(in, s :: acc)
}

def read3(in: java.io.BufferedReader): List[String] =
  readLines(in, Nil).reverse
```

When I code Scala, I try not to have a curly brace around my method body. If I can't write my code this way, I have to justify to myself why my method should exceed a single statement. Keeping methods short allows you to encapsulate a single piece of logic in a method and have methods that build upon each other. It also allows you to easily understand the logic in the method.

Refactor Mercilessly

In the beginning, you can write your Scala code as you would your Java code. It's a great place to start. Then, start applying the above rules. Let's go back to our validByAge example from Chapter 3 (see Listing 3-3). We'll start with the imperative code:

```scala
def validByAge(in: List[Person]): List[String] = {
  var valid: List[Person] = Nil
  for (p <- in) {
    if (p.valid) valid = p :: valid
  }

  def localSortFunction(a: Person, b: Person) = a.age < b.age

  val people = valid.sort(localSortFunction _)

  var ret: List[String] = Nil

  for (p <- people) {
    ret = ret ::: List(p.first)
  }

  return ret
}
```

Turn your vars into vals.

```scala
def validByAge(in: List[Person]): List[String] = {
  val valid: ListBuffer[Person] = new ListBuffer // displaced mutability
  for (p <- in) {
    if (p.valid) valid += p
  }

  def localSortFunction(a: Person, b: Person) = a.age < b.age

  val people = valid.toList.sort(localSortFunction _)

  val ret: ListBuffer[String] = new ListBuffer
```

```
  for (p <- people) {
    ret += p.first
  }

  ret.toList
}
```

Turn your mutable data structures into immutable data structures.

```
def validByAge(in: List[Person]): List[String] = {
  val valid = for (p <- in if p.valid) yield p

  def localSortFunction(a: Person, b: Person) = a.age < b.age

  val people = valid.sort(localSortFunction _)

  for (p <- people) yield p.first
}
```

Make your method into a single statement:

```
def validByAge(in: List[Person]): List[String] =
  in.filter(_.valid).
  sort(_.age < _.age).
  map(_.first)
```

While you can argue that this is too terse, we can refactor another way:

```
def filterValid(in: List[Person]) = in.filter(p => p.valid)

def sortPeopleByAge(in: List[Person]) = in.sort(_.age < _.age)

def validByAge(in: List[Person]): List[String] =
  (filterValid _ andThen sortPeopleByAge _)(in).map(_.name)
```

Either of the refactoring choices you make, the business logic of your code is a lot more visible. The refactoring also moves you toward thinking about the transformations in your code rather than the looping constructs in your code.

Compose Functions and Compose Classes

In the previous example, we composed filterValid and sortPeopleByAge into a single function. This function is the same as this:

```
(in: List[Person]) => sortPeopleByAge(filterValid(in))
```

However, the composition of the two functions results in code that reads like what it does. We started by turning our methods into single statements. This makes testing easier and makes the code more readable. Next we compose a new function by chaining the two functions together. Functional composition is a later stage Scala-ism, but it results naturally from making methods into single statements.

In Chapter 7, we explored how Scala's traits can be composed into powerful, flexible classes that are more type-safe than Java classes. As you evolve your Scala coding skills and begin to refactor classes rather than methods, start looking for common methods across your interfaces and traits. Move methods from concrete classes into traits. Soon, you'll likely find that many of your classes have little in them other than the logic that is specific to that class and the `vals` that are needed to evaluate that logic. Once you reach this level in your coding, you will likely find that your traits are polymorphic, that your traits represent logic that can be applied to a contained type, and then you can feel secure that your mind has completely warped into thinking Scala.

Once you're thinking Scala or thinking that you're thinking Scala, you might want to go hard-core on selling Scala into your organization. The next section provides some talking points for selling Scala. It gives you the benefits of my experience selling new technologies in organizations. Please keep in mind that "because it's cool" is not a justification for an organization to adopt a new technology. The new technology must solve a problem. However, it's pretty safe to say that most organizations want to make their developers happier and more productive, and Scala provides a great way to achieve those goals.

Selling Scala in Your Organization

So, you're convinced that Scala is the right language for writing code. You've done a few Skunk Works projects and gotten a few team members on board with Scala. Now it's time to sell Scala to management. This is perhaps the trickiest sell. There will likely be people in your organization who oppose change and are fearful of new things. It happens everywhere. In this section, I'm going to talk about techniques you might try and arguments you might use to get Scala into your organization.

The Super-Soft Sell

One interesting technique that I've heard about for selling an organization on Scala is to start asking people to write tests using Specs rather than JUnit or TestNG. Because this is not "production code," there's less organizational resistance to this idea. Further, because tests are not production code, the operations guys don't have to worry about tests in Scala. There's no credible argument that somehow Scala-based tests would fail to execute correctly.

So, propose that you and a couple of team members write BDD tests in Scala. The tests will run just fine alongside your existing Java tests with the existing test harnesses. But you'll give other developers a chance to use Scala, and you'll give the business people and management folks a chance to see the readability differences between the Java-based tests and the Scala-based tests.

The Back-Office Project

If you've got a small, not-mission-critical, back-office project in your organization, then it may also be a good fit for Scala. Such projects often have a short life span and are viewed as disposable. Thus, if you succeed with Scala, it's great. If you fail, the business will not fail. If you succeed and then leave the company, the worst case is that the whole thing gets thrown away and rewritten in Java or something else. Pitching Scala for the back-end project should be a pretty simple sell, and ultimately it gives you the opportunity to show your coworkers and management the benefits of Scala while easing their concerns about how Scala runs and integrates with Java code.

The Big Sell

I've been a user of leading-edge technology for my whole career. In 1977, when I was 14, I sold the Federal Emergency Management Agency on using Apple][computers for displaying dynamic content for the visual part of emergency broadcasts and was awarded a contract to implement the software. I started using NextStep (now Mac OS X) in 1990 and launched Mesa, the first real-time spreadsheet, in 1992 on NextStep. It's only been in the last few years that developers have discovered the AppKit for OS X and iPhone development. I was an early user of WebLogic and ran the first Java-only high-volume site on the Internet. I was the one who led the charge for using Java. I have been an early adopter of a lot of technologies that are now part of the mainstream.[10]

It is possible that someone who wants to block the adoption of something new will escalate the issue to the CEO or even the board level. I had an interesting dinner with a board member one time because a team member escalated up to the board the decision to move to .NET and managed code. One board member had written some Commodore 64 code back in the day but was a business and deal guy. More than half the meal was spent explaining garbage collection, with the board member insisting that reference counting was really the only sure way to do managed memory.

But I digress. The important thing for you is to be prepared to answer any question about Scala. Please also answer every question honestly. You gain a lot of credibility by saying, "Java developers will miss a lot of the refactoring tools that they are used to. On the

---

10. To be fair, I've had my share of bad calls, too. I was a proponent of OS/2, OpenDoc, and BeOS. Please, stop laughing.

other hand, Scala's software composition idioms make obsolete some of the refactoring idioms." The statement is accurate and verifiable, so when the CEO or board member asks his trusted advisor to look at Scala, the trusted advisor will likely validate that statement. On the other hand, if you say, "Scala has complete IDE support, so it will work with our existing tool chain," it's likely that you will lose credibility because as of this writing, Scala IDE support is not on par with Java IDE support.

Some people will raise the specter of the "operational characteristics" of Scala code. Because Scala code compiles down to JVM bytecode, the operational characteristics of Scala code are no different than Java code, and stack traces in Scala or mixed Scala and Java code look just like stack traces in Java code.

Addressing the Potential Risks of Scala

Over the last 18 months, as I've sold a lot of Scala, I've received a lot of questions. Some are rational:

- Q: If you build this project in Scala and/or Lift, who else can maintain it? A: The Scala and Lift communities have thousands of members, are growing, and contain a number of people actively seeking Scala- and Lift-related jobs and consulting.

- Q: What does Lift give us? A: A much faster time to market with collaborative applications than anything else out there.

- Q: Why not use Rails, which has great developer productivity? A: Rails is great from person-to-computer applications, but when you're building a chat app or something that's person-to-person collaborative, Lift's Comet[11] support is much more effective than that of Rails. Plus, if you have to scale your app to hundreds of users simultaneously using your app, you can do it on a single box with Lift, because the JVM gives great operational benefits.

And there are some less rational questions:

- Q: Why use new technology when we can outsource the coding to India and pay someone 5 percent of what we're paying you? A: Because I'm more than 20 times better than the coders you buy for 5 percent of my hourly rate, plus there's a lot less management of my development efforts.

- Q: Why not write it in Java to get the operational benefits of Java? A: Prototyping is hard. Until you know what you want, you need to be agile. Java is not agile. Ruby/ Rails and Scala/Lift are agile. Choose one of those to do prototyping, and then port to Java if there's a reason to.

---

11. http://en.wikipedia.org/wiki/Comet_(programming)

- Q: Will Scala be incompatible with our existing Java code? A: No. Read my lips … no. The same guy who wrote the program (javac) that converts Java to JVM bytecode wrote the program that converts Scala to JVM bytecode. There's no one on this planet who could make a more compatible language than Martin Odersky.

My Direct Experience (YMMV)

My experience with building Buy a Feature and other Innovation Games for Enthiosys has yielded a lot of useful data. Buy a Feature went through prototyping, revisions, and all the normal growth that software goes through. It works. (Yeah, it still needs more, but that's the nature of software versions.) Other developers, US-based and India-based, have joined the project. Bringing the new developers on board was not materially different than when I hired a bunch of Java developers and asked them to write C# code. There are new tools, new idioms, new libraries, but the learning curve was fairly smooth. It took between 5 and 40 hours of pairing time to get new developers up to speed. That's not a bad investment.

On the operational side, we also had an occasion to have 2,000 simultaneous (as in at the same time, pounding on their keyboards) users of Buy a Feature and we were able to, thanks to Jetty Continuations, service all 2,000 users with 2,000 open connections to our server and an average of 700 requests per second on a dual-core Opteron with a load average of around 0.24.

One of the customers of Buy a Feature wanted it integrated into their larger, Java-powered web portal along with two other systems. I did the integration. The customer asked, "Where's the Scala part?" I answered, "It's in this JAR file." He said, "But I looked at the bytecode and it's just Java." I answered, "It's Scala, but it compiles down to Java bytecode, and it runs in a Java debugger, and you can't tell the difference." He said, "You're right."

So to this customer's JVM, the Scala and Lift code looks, smells, and tastes just like Java code. If I renamed the `scala-library.jar` file to `apache-closures.jar`, nobody would know the difference at all.

Okay, but with each set of people I talk to, I hear a similar variation about the "operational risks" of using Scala. Let's step back for a minute. There are development and team risks for using Scala.

Selecting Team Members

Some Java programmers can't wrap their heads around the triple concepts of (1) type inference, (2) passing functions/higher-order functions and (3) immutability as the default way of writing code. Most Ruby programmers I've met don't have those limitations. So, find a Ruby programmer who knows some Java libraries, or find a Java programmer who's done some moonlighting with Rails or Python or JavaScript, and you've got a developer who can pick up Scala in a week and be very productive with Scala in two months.

Even with the limitation of weak IDE support, head-to-head people can write Scala code two to ten times faster than they can write Java code, and maintaining Scala code is much easier because of Scala's strong type system and code conciseness.

Yeah, But How Compatible?

You can make the assertion that at the operational level, Scala code and Java code are indistinguishable. I wrote a Scala program and compiled it with -g:vars (put all the symbols in the class file), started the program under jdb (the Java Debugger) and set a break point. This is what I got:

```
Step completed: "thread=main", foo.ScalaDB$$anonfun$main$1.apply(), line=6 bci=0
6 args.zipWithIndex.foreach(v => println(v))
main[1] dump v
```

```
v = {
_2: instance of java.lang.Integer(id=463)
_1: "Hello"
}
```

```
main[1] where
```

```
[1] foo.ScalaDB$$anonfun$main$1.apply (ScalaDB.scala:6)
[2] foo.ScalaDB$$anonfun$main$1.apply (ScalaDB.scala:6)
[3] scala.Iterator$class.foreach (Iterator.scala:387)
[4] scala.runtime.BoxedArray$$anon$2.foreach (BoxedArray.scala:45)
[5] scala.Iterable$class.foreach (Iterable.scala:256)
[6] scala.runtime.BoxedArray.foreach (BoxedArray.scala:24)
[7] foo.ScalaDB$.main (ScalaDB.scala:6)
[8] foo.ScalaDB.main (null)
```

```
main[1] print v
```

```
v = "(Hello,0)"
```

My code worked without any fancy footwork inside of the standard Java Debugger. The text of the line that I was on and the variables in the local scope were all there, just as if it was a Java program. The stack traces work the same way. The symbols work the same way. Everything works the same way. Scala code looks and smells and tastes to the JVM just like Java code. Now let's explore why.

A Tad Bit of History

A long time ago, when Java was Oak and it was being designed as a way to distribute untrusted code into set-top boxes (and later browsers), the rules defining how a program executed and what were the means of the instruction set (bytecodes) was super-important. Additionally, the semantics of the program had to be such that the Virtual Machine running the code could verify that (1) the code was well behaved and (2) the source code and the object code had the same meaning. For example, the casting operation in Java compiles down to a bytecode that checks that the class can actually be cast to the right thing and the verifier ensures that there's no code path that could put an unchecked value into a variable.

Put another way, there's no way to write verifiable bytecode that can put a reference to a non-`String` into a variable that's defined as a `String`. It's not just at the compiler level but at the actual Virtual Machine level that object typing is enforced.

In Java 1.0 days, there was nearly a 1:1 correspondence between Java language code and Java bytecode. Put another way, there was only one thing you could write in Java bytecode that you could not write in Java source code (it has to do with calling super in a constructor). There was one source code file per class file.

Java 1.1 introduced inner classes, which broke the 1:1 relationship between Java code and bytecode. One of the things that inner classes introduced was access to private instance variables by the inner class. This was done without violating the JVM's enforcement of the privacy of private variables by creating accessor methods that were compiler-enforced (but not JVM-enforced) ways for the anonymous classes to access private variables. But the horse was out of the barn at this point anyway, because 1.1 brought us reflection, and `private` was no longer private.

An interesting thing about the JVM: from 1.0 through 1.6, there has not been a new instruction added to the JVM. Wow. Think about it. Java came out when the 486 was around. How many instructions have been added to Intel machines since 1995? The Microsoft CLR has been around since 2000 and has gone through three revisions, and new instructions have been added at every revision, and source code compiled under an older revision does not work with newer revisions. On the other hand, I have Java 1.1–compiled code that works just fine under Java 1.6. Pretty amazing.

Even to this day, Java Generics are implemented using the same JVM bytecodes that were used in 1996. This is why you get the "type erasure" warnings. The compiler knows the type, but the JVM does not, so a `List<String>` looks to the JVM like a `List`, even though the compiler will not let you pass a `List<String>` to something that expects a `List<URL>`. On the server side, where we trust the code, this is not an issue. If we were writing code for an untrusted world, we'd care a lot more about the semantics of the source code being enforced by the execution environment.

So, there have been no new JVM instructions since Java was released. The JVM is perhaps the best-specified piece of software this side of ADA-based military projects. There are specs and slow-moving JSRs for everything. Turns out, this works to our benefit.

Present-Day Compatibility

The JVM has a clearly defined interface to debugging. The information that a class file needs to provide to the JVM for line numbers, variable names, and so on, is very clearly specified. Because the JVM has a limited instruction set and the type of each item on the stack and of each instance variable in a class is known and verified when the class loads, the debugging information works for anything that compiles down to Java bytecode and has semantics of named local variables and named instance variables. Scala shares these semantics with Java, and that's why the Scala compiler can compile bytecode that has the appropriate debugging information so that it "just works" with jdb. And, just to be clear, jdb uses the standard, well-documented interface into the JVM to do debugging, and every other IDE for the JVM uses this same interface. That means that an IDE that compiles Scala can also hook into the JVM and debug Scala.

Scala's operational characteristics are the same as Java's. The Scala compiler generates bytecode that is nearly identical to the Java compiler. In fact, that you can decompile Scala code and wind up with readable Java code, with the exception of certain constructor operations. To the JVM, Scala code and Java code are indistinguishable. The only difference is that there's a single extra library file to support Scala.

Popping the Stack to the CEO or Board

Now, in most software projects, you don't have CEOs and board members and everybody's grandmother asking what libraries you're using. In fact, in every project I've stepped into, there have been at least two libraries that the senior developers did not add but somehow got introduced into the mix. (I believe in library audits to make sure there's no license violations in the library mix.) So, in the normal course of business, libraries are added to projects all the time. Any moderately complex project depends on dozens of libraries. I can tell you to a 100 percent degree of certainty that there are libraries in that mix that will not pass the "Is the company that supports them going to be around in five years?" test. Period. Sure, memcached will be around in five years, and most of the memcached clients will not.

Making the choice to use Scala should be a deliberate, deliberated, well-reasoned choice. It has to do with developer productivity, both to build the initial product and to maintain the product through a two-to-five-year life cycle. It has to do with maintaining existing QA and operations infrastructure (for existing JVM shops) or moving to the most scalable, flexible, predictable, well-tested, and well-supported web infrastructure around: the JVM.

Recruiting team members who can do Scala may be a challenge. Standardizing on a development environment may be a challenge as the Scala IDE support is immature. (But there's always emacs, vi, jEdit and TextMate, which work just fine.) Standardizing on a coding style is a challenge. These are all people challenges and all localized to recruiting and development and management thereof. The only rational parts of the debate are the trade-off between recruiting and organizing the team and the benefits to be gained from Scala.

Bottom line: to anyone other than the folks with hands in the code and the folks who have to recruit and manage them, "For all you know, it's just another Java library."

Why Is Scala Different?

If Scala looks like Java to the JVM, why shouldn't a company stick with Java? Put another way, if there's nothing that can be written in Scala that can't be written in Java, why use Scala? These are important questions, and they are the kind of strategic questions that you will need to answer when selling Scala into your organization.

What Scala gives you is aids in concurrent programming:

- Syntactic flexibility

- Excellent default libraries for doing concurrent programming (immutable data structures and Actors)

- Pattern matching

Scala's syntactic flexibility means that you can express concurrency-related calls in a way that allows you to have a different syntax for concurrent operations. The syntax was borrowed from Erlang:

```
gameBoard ! Chat(who, "Hey guys, this is a chat message")
```

So when I'm coding in Scala, I know that the previous method invocation is going to send an asynchronous message to my gameBoard. It's got the benefits of Hungarian Notation[12] without the verbosity or ugliness. This call syntax also means that the new programmer isn't going to put a call like this inside a loop. How many times have we all seen the junior developer put a remote method invocation (RMI) call inside a loop and wonder why performance sucks?

---

12. http://en.wikipedia.org/wiki/Hungarian_notation

Scala supports immutability by default. This means that I can pass an immutable data structure to other threads, and they can use that data without synchronization. There's no need to worry about concurrent access to data because the data is not going to change out from under you. There are eight synchronized code blocks in the 15,000-line Buy a Feature code base, and we have not had a single concurrency-related defect.

Scala's Actor library (which is implemented entirely as a library and has no compiler support) sits on top of Doug Lea's Fork-Join library. Actors allow for event-based programming. It turns out that this model works very, very well for games and for asynchronous browser-based applications. Yes, a fair number of Python game applications are based on the Twisted event library. It turns out that the event-based semantics are very similar for both Actors and Twisted, so it's no surprise that they are both choices for multiplayer games. (There's a French company building a massive multiplayer online game [MMO] in Scala.) Actors are threadless, stackless event handlers. They only consume stack/thread resources when there's a message for the Actor to process. This is very handy as you can have millions of Actors hanging out waiting to do something, and they only consume system resources when there's something to do. Additionally, it's possible to write a custom scheduler so that you can have all one million Actors processing messages, but they only consume a bounded number of threads.

Finally, Scala's pattern matching provides a powerful way to compose event handlers (even dynamically).

Anything You Can Do, I Can Do Better (in Scala)

So, there's nothing I can do in Scala that I can't do in Java, with enough time. There's nothing I can do in Java that I can't do in C. However, Scala lends itself to much more developer- and machine-efficient patterns. In fact, Scala gives me the coding efficiency and flexibility that I had with Ruby along with the type safety and performance characteristics of Java and the JVM.

Buy a Feature contains 15,000 Scala lines of code (LoC) and represents about one manyear of effort. Measured in this vector, there's nothing surprising. Buy a Feature compiles down to 2,300 classes and has roughly the functionality of a 2,300-class Java program (think ClearSpace). So, if I were to tell you that two people wrote 2,300 Java classes in a year or two, you'd tell me I was nuts. Yes, simple Scala statements explode into many classes. But the fact is that the complexity embodied in the simple statement represents the complexity associated with many Java classes. Scala is to Java as C++ is to assembly language. In Scala, I can concisely express far more business logic, that is also far more type-safe, in a single line than in Java. This means that the developer productivity is much higher in Scala than in Java.

Giving Scala a Lift

The Lift Web Framework has Comet support. That means that state change on the server side is immediately pushed to the browser. Lift's Comet support makes chat applications, multiuser games, and other browser-based applications trivial to write. Here's the entire code required to write a multi-user chat application in Lift:

```
case class Messages(msgs: List[String])

object ChatServer extends Actor with ListenerManager {
  private var msgs: List[String] = Nil

  protected def createUpdate = Messages(msgs)

  override def highPriority = {
    case s: String if s.length > 0 =>
      msgs ::= s
      updateListeners()
  }
  this.start
}

class Chat extends CometActor with CometListenee {
  private var msgs: List[String] = Nil

  def render =
  <div>
    <ul>{msgs.reverse.map(m => <li>{m}</li>)}</ul>
    {ajaxText("", s => {ChatServer ! s; Noop})}
  </div>

  protected def registerWith = ChatServer

  override def lowPriority = {
    case Messages(m) => msgs = m ; reRender(false)
  }
}
```

There's nothing magic about Lift's Comet support, but it would be much harder to do in Java.

How Lift's Comet Support Works

Lift has CometActors, which represent server-side state in a section of browser real estate. The real estate is demarcated by a <span> with a GUID. All Lift pages are rendered using Scala's built-in XML support. After the render phase, but before the page is streamed to the browser, Lift looks through the page to see whether the page contains HTML that points to any CometActors. If yes, Lift rewrites the XML and inserts JavaScript to do Comet-style long polling. After the page is loaded, the browser opens an XMLHTTPRequest to the server with the GUIDs of all the Comet components on the page along with the version number of each of the Comet components.

The server receives the request and creates an Actor for each GUID, and each Actor registers itself as a listener with the appropriate Comet component. The registration includes the version number of the component as contained by the browser. If the servlet is running in Jetty or a Servlet 3.0 container, Lift automatically invokes the container's "continuation" mechanism so that the pending request is consuming no threads. It is consuming an NIO socket, and it's also consuming one Actor per Comet component on the page.

When the Comet component receives the listener registration, it compares the version number with the current version number. If they differ, the Comet component immediately sends the Actor a message containing the diffs between the version that the Actor/browser has and the current version of the Comet component. If the version number is current, the Comet component does nothing. If the Comet component receives a message and updates itself, it notifies the listener of the diff between the old version and the new version of the component.

During the "no changes" phase, the only system resources being consumed are memory and an NIO connection. No threads or stacks are involved.

When the Actor receives an update from the Comet component or after 110 seconds, the Actor creates a response to the Ajax request. It then invokes the continuation and sends the response to the browser (either JavaScript containing commands to perform the diffs or a Noop). The browser executes the JavaScript, waits 100 milliseconds, and restarts the process.

I could have implemented all of this in Java. In fact, there is a Comet library that sits on top of Jetty and Dojo that has the same scaling characteristics. However, the amount of code to implement this scheme in Scala contains roughly the same number of characters as the above description. I'm sure that would not be the case in Java.

Summary

Designing and building complex computer software is a very serious thing. Our livelihoods, and increasingly our whole society, depend on the stability and flexibility of our interconnected computer systems. Our cars and our banks and our grocery stores and our hospitals and our police departments all work better because they are interconnected by computer systems. Those systems run on the software that we write.

In this book, I've taken a very lighthearted approach to introducing you to the Scala programming language. I've approached the daunting task of learning a new language and possibly a new set of programming patterns in a fun way. I hope that you have enjoyed the journey and are already thinking about new ways to reason about designing software and writing code. I want to end this journey by talking a bit about architecture.

Architecture is very important in overall system performance and team performance. Scala has a lot of the tools that allow for much better architectural decisions. It's kind of a *Zen and the Art of Motorcycle Maintenance* thing—you use the patterns that your language and its libraries make easiest. Scala makes it easier for coders to implement architecturally solid designs than does Java or Ruby.

Thank you!

Index

You Need the Companion eBook

Your purchase of this book entitles you to buy the companion PDF-version eBook for only $10. Take the weightless companion with you anywhere.

We believe this Apress title will prove so indispensable that you'll want to carry it with you everywhere, which is why we are offering the companion eBook (in PDF format) for $10 to customers who purchase this book now. Convenient and fully searchable, the PDF version of any content-rich, page-heavy Apress book makes a valuable addition to your programming library. You can easily find and copy code—or perform examples by quickly toggling between instructions and the application. Even simultaneously tackling a donut, diet soda, and complex code becomes simplified with hands-free eBooks!

Once you purchase your book, getting the $10 companion eBook is simple:

❶ Visit **www.apress.com/promo/tendollars/**.

❷ Complete a basic registration form to receive a randomly generated question about this title.

❸ Answer the question correctly in 60 seconds, and you will receive a promotional code to redeem for the $10.00 eBook.

THE EXPERT'S VOICE™

2855 TELEGRAPH AVENUE | SUITE 600 | BERKELEY, CA 94705

Offer valid through 11/09.